BETWEEN LEVINAS
AND HEIDEGGER

SUNY series in Contemporary Continental Philosophy

Dennis J. Schmidt, editor

BETWEEN LEVINAS

AND HEIDEGGER

Edited by

JOHN E. DRABINSKI

and

ERIC S. NELSON

STATE UNIVERSITY OF NEW YORK PRESS

Published by
STATE UNIVERSITY OF NEW YORK PRESS, ALBANY

© 2014 State University of New York

All rights reserved

Printed in the United States of America

For information, contact
State University of New York Press, Albany, NY
www.sunypress.edu

Production, Laurie D. Searl
Marketing, Anne M. Valentine

Library of Congress Cataloging-in-Publication Data

Between Levinas and Heidegger / edited by John E. Drabinski and Eric S. Nelson.
    pages cm. — (SUNY series in contemporary continental philosophy)
    Includes bibliographical references and index.
    ISBN 978-1-4384-5257-9 (hc : alk. paper) 978-1-4384-5258-6 (pb : alk. paper)
    1. Lévinas, Emmanuel. 2. Heidegger, Martin, 1889–1976. 3. Ontology.
4. Ethics. I. Drabinski, John E., 1968– II. Nelson, Eric Sean.

B2430.L484B48 2014
194—dc23   2013033746

10 9 8 7 6 5 4 3 2 1

CONTENTS

INTRODUCTION

John E. Drabinski and Eric S. Nelson

It is only then that the relation to exteriority would no longer catch its breath. The metaphysics of the face therefore *encloses* the thought of Being, presupposing the difference between Being and the existent at the same time as it stifles it.

—Derrida, "Violence and Metaphysics"

REVISITING THE QUESTION OF LEVINAS AND HEIDEGGER

Who is Heidegger to Levinas? Who is Levinas to Heidegger? What would it mean to think *between* ontology and ethics, *between* the history of Being and the beyond Being? What sorts of issues emerge at these crossroads, and what do those issues have to say about the beginnings and ends of philosophy?

The chapters collected here engage these sorts of questions in pursuit of another kind of relation between Levinas and Heidegger. To be sure, much has been written of this relationship, especially from the perspective of Levinasians concerned with the historical and philosophical roots of ethics as first philosophy. Levinas's texts offer numerous examples of critique, and perhaps as a result, commentary has often—maybe too often—adopted Levinas's polemical tone. Levinas's reading of Heidegger is never especially subtle or restrained. And Heidegger scholars—Heidegger of course did not write on Levinas—have not been especially enthusiastic or especially interested in Levinas's claim to have subverted and overcome fundamental ontology. At first glance, the Levinas-Heidegger relation appears stalled and, at best, wholly one-sided. But what would it mean to pursue this relation beyond the limits of textual evidence or mere polemic? Another kind of relation; what is the *philosophical* meaning and even possible promise of this relation?

1

BETWEEN LEVINAS AND HEIDEGGER

The present volume is organized around four thematic groupings. As evident in the reflections in this collection, and in the existing literature on the Heidegger-Levinas relationship, the crux of Levinas's critique of Heidegger is the distinction between ethics and ontology and different understandings of being, immanence, and transcendence. The opening section "Immanence and Transcendence" poses these questions in the contexts of the intersection and ambivalence of ethics and politics, religion and secularization, and history and what transcends history. This crux of ethics and ontology is immanent to both the Levinasian and Heideggerian projects, as neither can avoid the other term. While Heidegger is largely preoccupied with the question of Being, his "Letter on Humanism" reminds us in bold and unforgettable terms how ontology encroaches upon, then fundamentally alters, the meaning of ethics and even constitutes a more originary ethics, an ethos of dwelling.[4] Levinas's conception of ethics as first philosophy has the provocative rhetoric of "beyond Being," but it does not escape ontological claims. The second section "Temporalities" adds additional terms to the standard cleavage between Levinas and Heidegger, such as violence, secularization, and history, asking whether and how these problems might draw together and re-form our thinking.

The French feminist Michèle Le Doeuff has shown how idiom and imagery reveal important clues about the philosophy that uses them such that theoretical content is not independent of its presentation in words and images. Ann Murphy pursues this strategy in the context of Levinas's critique of Heidegger. Murphy traces how the idiom and imagery of violence function ambivalently and mark a tension in his writings, working with and against Levinas's ethical claims of breaking with the power and violence that he contends are inherent in Heidegger's ontology, and what this ambivalent complicity entails for the relationship between ontology and ethics. As ontology and ethics are tied up in relations of collusion and difference, and images of power and violence remain at work in Levinas's portrayal of ethical relations, Levinas's ethics does not escape the power and violence it exposes and questions. Nevertheless, ethics can imperfectly confront while submitting itself to power in politics. To this extent, power is transformed into justice and is "as close as possible to nonviolence," in response to being confronted by the Other.

Philip J. Maloney examines issues of religion and secularization and immanence and transcendence in Heidegger and Levinas in light of Levinas's reception of the later Heidegger in his writings of the 1970s, in which the problem of ontotheology plays a crucial role and reveals their shared horizon and profound disagreement. For Levinas, Heidegger did not pursue the dismantling of ontotheology radically enough to question the primacy of being and the neglect of transcendence in the history of Western philosophy. Whereas Heidegger abandons his earlier interest in transcendence, as it is inescapably entangled in ontotheological metaphysics, Maloney unfolds how Levinas contests ontotheology precisely through transcendence and a reinterpretation of the "religious." In response to the paradox that modernity is irredeemably secular, and the secular questionable and insufficient, Heidegger and Levinas articulate two alternative models of secularizing transcendence: poetry and prayer.

In the context of Levinas's critique of history as violence and totality, and facticity as brutality and indifference, Eric S. Nelson explores Heidegger's early differentiation of history as object of inquiry and as lived enactment, and his endeavor in the late 1930s to rethink history from an inherently futural—and not merely subjectively or objectively grounded—event (*Ereignis*) of the not-yet (*noch-nicht*) and the other beginning (*der andere Anfang*). Events and works of history are neither simply factual nor socially constructed but exhibit a hermeneutical event of disclosure—via understanding, interpretation, and appropriation—in relation to the facticity and possibilities of the enactment and practices of historical being. Nelson articulates the significance of Heidegger's thinking of history while recognizing the ethical and social-political failures and limits exposed by Levinas.

What, then, about time? In our second section, "Temporalities," Didier Franck, Emilia Angelova, and Simon Critchley locate important theoretical sites between Levinas and Heidegger in the structuring and dismantling function of time, which lie at the heart of both Levinas's and Heidegger's work. Whether in terms of the temporal stretch of the existential structure of care in *Being and Time* or the later works' preoccupation with the history of Being, Heidegger's work sets the problematic of Being in the element of time. Levinas as well will insist on temporal language as the language of separation and the for-the-Other, especially in *Otherwise than Being*, where diachrony marks so much of the discussion.

Didier Franck and Emilia Angelova begin their chapters with the motif of death and shift quickly to problems of signification and time. Franck's chapter, "The Sincerity of the Saying," is a short and intense meditation on the structure of *Saying*, that central motif of the opening sections of Levinas's *Otherwise than Being*. Framed by the problem of truth—in particular, the truth of the subject as hostage—Franck establishes important links between subjectivity, testimony, and the infinite in order to isolate a crucial break of Levinas from Heidegger: what is the price of finitude? Whereas for Heidegger finitude culminates in *my* death; for Levinas, Franck argues, finitude initiates my awareness of a surplus of responsibility, which alters our conceptions of truth as finitude and the finitude of truth. For Angelova, the problem of finitude is also a problem of the structure and nexus of significance. In setting the problem of meaning and finitude within the horizon of time, Angelova argues, Levinas's critique of Heidegger remains limited by the address to the latter's earlier work. The withdrawal of being and the logic of the trace in Heidegger's late work offer a different conception of time and finitude, one in which the kairological temporality of Being's excess, found in the early Freiburg lectures, is replaced by an account of "language as that spacing of the thought on which Being is founded." This motif from the later work brings Heidegger into an unexpected proximity with Levinas, especially around the notions of trace, separation, and disinterestedness.

Simon Critchley's chapter offers a close reading of two passages from Heidegger's *Being and Time*, both of which are linked to the transformative function of death in that work. "Dasein is thrown projection" and "Dasein exists factically" begin Critchley's long meditation, which is dedicated to the elaboration of how the experience of finitude builds a sense of enigma into the heart of a subjectivity subjected to time. This sense of enigma provokes both Heidegger's famous claim that death is the possibility of impossibility *and* Levinas's reverse claim that death is the impossibility of possibility. Critchley's careful reconstruction of Heidegger's account of death and the companion notions of authenticity and inauthenticity suggests important connection to Levinas's various accounts of how time fractures and separates subjectivity from the alterity constitutive of its (authentic?) sense.

The third section, entitled "Subjectivities," is of course woven quite closely to both prerogatives. The function of *Dasein* and the interval or even sign of Being comprises one of the strongest threads—whatever the alterations, transformations, and overturnings—through Heidegger's early to late work. Levinas's work turns increasingly toward the enigma of subjectivity in the period following the publication of *Totality and Infinity*, culminating in the descriptions of obsession, recurrence, and persecution in the "Substitution" chapter of *Otherwise than Being*. Indeed, the philosophical problem of subjectivity today is barely conceivable without the destabilizing accounts of Heidegger and Levinas.

Responding to Levinas's critique of Heidegger has opened up the reconsideration of Heidegger's thinking; is it too not a reflection of sociality and alterity and perhaps more radically and appropriately than Levinas's asymmetrical ethics of the other that remains complicit with monadological thinking? Reconsidering the relation of ethics to philosophy, ontology, and ethics, in the divergence between Heidegger and Levinas, Françoise Dastur contrasts in her contribution Heidegger's prioritizing of the sociality of being-with, and solitude as its deficient mode, with Levinas's emphasis on the solitude, separation, and asymmetry between self and other. She argues that for Levinas being and world are part of the I, its intentionality and self-identification, and thus fundamentally lack alterity as the other can only be outside of and otherwise than this. Alterity in a sense then begins with me, the identity of the ego cogito, which remains the point of departure for Levinas's analysis of how the I recuperates its world and remains itself, responsible, even in being fundamentally questioned by and responding to the absolute alterity of the other person. Since the I remains central in being questioned by the invocation of the other, as it is always about my responsibility rather than the other's, there is not so much dialogue between I and other as there is apology; that is, the other is the occasion of my apology for myself. If temporal and social relationality are the condition of alterity, difference, and individuation, the identity of self and other to some extent remain what they are outside of the relational dynamic that would make a difference. Dastur concludes by returning to the freedom of affirmation that she uncovers in Heidegger.

Robert Bernasconi's contribution to this volume offers a close and provocative reading of Levinas's notion of sacrifice, in particular the phrase "ethics of sacrifice." Though the term appears only briefly in Levinas's essay "Dying for . . . ," Bernasconi makes the case that a significant point of (alleged) departure between Levinas and Heidegger is located in the relationship between sacrifice and death. Levinas claims that the problematic of authenticity, inseparable as it is from Heidegger's account of death in *Being and Time*, renders sacrifice impossible. This would *seem* to mark Levinas's departure from Heidegger precisely because it poses the ethical against Dasein and fundamental ontology. Yet, Bernasconi argues—by way of Derrida, but just as much by way of Levinas's own reading of Heidegger—that Levinas's conception of sacrifice, and the gravity of the ethical contained therein, is close to that of Heidegger, except at the precise moment at which the question of justification is left behind. In letting go of the question of justification, Levinas's "ethics of sacrifice" becomes a deformalized, concrete sense of sacrifice without reason or egoism, which gives measure to his distance from Heidegger on one and the same matter for thinking.

The intimacy of Levinas's claims to Heidegger's work takes a different turn in François Raffoul's essay "The Question of Responsibility between Levinas and Heidegger." In this essay, Raffoul traces out the reversal of Descartes in Levinas's work, underscoring not only the radical critique in Levinas of Cartesian "egology," but also how important features of that egology remain intact in the reversal. Raffoul characterizes this as how Levinas's revolutionary notion of the ethical "owes perhaps more than it would like to admit to the egological tradition that it seeks to reverse, *precisely insofar as it determines itself in symmetrical opposition to it and as its reversal.*" This symmetrical opposition provides an opening for reasserting the force of ontology against the Levinasian subject and sense of the ethical. Heidegger's work thereby reemerges as a powerful critique of the ethical subject, as well as, perhaps more urgently, drawing our attention to the continuing need for the development of ontological senses of responsibility.

The fourth and final section extends the question of otherness beyond the transcendences found in Heidegger's and Levinas's work. The animal interrupts the interhuman sense of place. Peter E. Gordon's chapter "Displaced" takes up the phenomenological mode of inquiry in relation to this very interruption in asking about the limits of Heidegger's and Levinas's accounts of the foreign and the strange. For both, Gordon argues, place and home function as central motifs and indeed set many of the parameters of inquiry. Yet, any phenomenological account of our place in home, our home in place, must also account for the uncanny. The uncanny is also part of Heidegger's and Levinas's accounts of place, of course; there is always interruption, the strange, and the unexpected in transcendence.

In his chapter, Krzysztof Ziarek identifies two points of proximity in Heidegger and Levinas. First, there is what Ziarek calls the "dignity" restored by attention to a posthumanist humanism. Second, there is the force of alterity, which is borne by the face in Levinas and for Heidegger in the notion of *Seyn* as a freedom without power. This latter item from Heidegger's late work is nicely distinguished by Ziarek from what Levinas describes as Being's impersonality and propensity toward violence. Yet, whatever this proximity between Heidegger and Levinas, Ziarek raises the question of whose sense of the ethical is best suited to the problems of twenty-first-century life. In particular, Ziarek's attention to the "power-free event" in Heidegger's work, the thinking of ethics in the *Da*, allows us to begin thinking how the dignity of the human, this shared proximity with Levinas, might open upon the animal and the nonanimal as sites of ethical life.

The final chapter in this collection concerns the problem of language and home. For both Heidegger and Levinas, language stands in a peculiar and unstable relation to our sense of home. On the one hand, language makes home possible. We find ourselves in language and the possibility of address from and to the Other—whether the alterity of Being or the alterity of the other person—derives at least in part from that sense of being-at-home in words. On the other hand, language is always disrupted by this address from what is *elsewhere* of the home. John E. Drabinski's contribution "Elsewhere of Home" begins with an examination of this movement between home and elsewhere in Heidegger and Levinas, with special attention to how language provokes this incessant movement. Yet, Drabinski argues, Heidegger and Levinas are seen to share an unexpected presupposition: the monolingualism of address and its disruption. What would it mean to consider the address from within language by those for whom the home of language is already an elsewhere? And, further, how is the movement of home and elsewhere transformed by the *creolizing*, rather than *disrupting* or *fracturing*, of language—which begins with what we might call, in a Levinasian turn of phrase, the *preoriginality* of this elsewhere in language? Drabinski draws on the very potent, yet underappreciated resources of the *creolité* movement to indicate an other other in the other of home, language, and the now global sense of any elsewhere.

EPIGRAPH

In the epigraph to the present reflections, Derrida remarked on the double movement of Being and the existent, noting the tension between Levinas and Heidegger as the oscillation between ontological difference and the claims of the existent over Being. In that remark, Derrida captures something at stake in this collection: is the difference between Levinas and Heidegger, between ethics and ontology, and so between kinds of fractured subjectivities a decidable difference? Or do the profundity and gravity of *both* Levinasian and Heideggerian thinking render such differences undecidable? And what would it mean to call this difference or between "undecidable"? Are their discourses simply incommensurable, with no paths of communication much less argumentation, or do they both intensify the stakes of communication and the philosophical game? For both, after all, the destiny of the West ends in the first half of the twentieth century—which is to say, the destiny reaches its end in technologically enabled mass death and suffering. Whether we conceive that end as totality as totalitarianism or technology as the epoch of calculative thinking, the stakes of identifying or not identifying sites of resistance to history's great violence and trajectory toward *even more* violence and standardization are clear. It is a matter of how we are to live after such death and disaster and the specter of an "end" that is only more of the same. What interrupts this terrifying history and its shadow? An ethics of the face and the priority of the Other or an ethos of dwelling in the openness of Being? To be sure, there is no easy or readily desirable answer. There is perhaps only the cross-saturation of ontological difference and the stifling presence of the Other person. In that perhaps undecidable, certainly saturated, space is precarious and urgent thinking.

NOTES

1. E. Levinas, *The Theory of Intuition in Husserl's Phenomenology*, 2nd ed., trans. A. Orianne (Evanston: Northwestern University Press, 1995), 153–58.

2. E. Levinas, *Existence and Existents*, trans. A. Lingis (Dordrecht: Martinus Nijhoff, 1988), 19.

3. E. Levinas, "Signature," trans. S. Hand (Baltimore: Johns Hopkins University Press, 1997), 293.

4. M. Heidegger, "Letter on Humanism," *Basic Writings*, ed. D. F. Krell (New York: HarperCollins, 1993), 256–58.

PART I

IMMANENCE AND TRANSCENDENCE

CHAPTER ONE

CRITIQUE, POWER, AND ONTOLOGICAL VIOLENCE

The Problem of "First" Philosophy

Ann Murphy

The human only lends itself to a relation that is not a power.

—Emmanuel Levinas, "Is Ontology Fundamental?"

This chapter queries the rhetoric and imagery of violence as it traffics in Emmanuel Levinas' critique of Martin Heidegger. The French feminist Michèle Le Doeuff claims that the imagery embedded in philosophical texts—while typically conceived as derivative, incidental, or extrinsic to the theory itself—is actually radically implicated in the theoretical content. In *The Philosophical Imaginary*, Le Doeuff argues that despite claims to the contrary, philosophy commonly relies on pictures and images to communicate its message.[1] Perhaps more importantly, the traffic in these images reveals something about the philosophy in which it appears. Le Doeuff's diagnosis of this clandestine traffic in imagery leads her to entertain an important hypothesis regarding the motivations at play in the circulation of philosophical imagery. She suggests that the images bear deep ambivalence in relation to the text, working both for it and against it: "*For*, because they sustain something that the system cannot itself justify, but which is nevertheless needed for its proper working. *Against*, for the same reason—or almost: their meaning is incompatible with the system's possibilities" (*PI*, 3). Crucially, imagery emerges at those moments when a tension persists between what a text seeks to justify and what it cannot. Hence images are said to signal moments of trouble, where a theory itself is relying on imagery that it cannot itself justify, but which it employs nonetheless in its own attempts at self-justification. Images signal instances of tension, trouble, and even incoherence. "Imagery copes with problems posed by the philosophical enterprise itself" (*PI*, 5). Images may even mark attempts at evasion. Drawing upon these comments concerning the philosophical imaginary, this chapter queries the circulation of the imagery of violence in Levinas's critique of Heidegger, with an eye toward what it may reveal about the relationship between ontology and ethics, their simultaneity and incommensurability.

In *Totality and Infinity*, Levinas's criticism of Heidegger centers on the claim that ontology itself, when conceived as the thought of Being, accomplishes a kind of violence.[2] This accusation is crucially grounded in the assertion that "ontology as first philosophy is a philosophy of power" (*TI*, 46/37). Such a rendering of ontology is intended in a pejorative sense; as first philosophy, ontology is complicit in the renunciation of the Other and the imperialism of the same. From the outset, the Levinasian critique of Heidegger is justified by this attribution of violence to ontology. Yet ontology itself is not precisely the problem; rather it is a problem of primacy. The violence of ontology is linked to its conception as *first philosophy*, to which Levinas will respond with a subversion of this hierarchy, affording ethics the priority instead. The power that Levinas affords ontology is linked not to the question of Being itself, but to the primacy of Being on Heidegger's account. As such, the question does not simply concern two domains—the ontological and the ethical—and the manner in which these domains are circumscribed; the essential problem that motivates Levinas is a problem of priority, not ontology per se, but "ontological imperialism."

To reduce the theoretical encounter between Levinas and Heidegger to a debate about priority or primacy, however, would be to risk concealing the vexed tone that marks both thinkers' engagement with the very notion of first philosophy, or philosophy proper. A worry persists here: if the confrontation between Levinas and Heidegger is frequently construed as a question of priority, the fundamental suspicion of "first philosophy" that imbues both of their respective philosophies gets obscured. As both Levinas and Heidegger concern themselves with the unveiling or revelation of a question or problem that has been obscured by philosophy as it is typically conceived, they do undoubtedly champion certain domains of inquiry, namely the question of Being in Heidegger and the ethical relation in Levinas. Even as Heidegger insists that Western metaphysics has obscured the question of Being, and Levinas in turn insists that fundamental ontology vitiates the ethical relation, both philosophies are marked by a critical spirit and a suspicion of any "first" philosophy, or philosophy proper for that matter. For this reason, any debate concerning the primacy of ethics or ontology must never devolve into a reductive championing of one or the other; not only would this obscure this critical dimension of both the Heideggerian and Levinasian projects, but it would have the further effect of masking the nuances in the relationship between ethics and ontology in either thinker. More meaningful than a debate concerning the validity of any claim to first philosophy is an investigation of the structure that marks the relation between ethics and ontology, a structure that in some ways undermines the pretense of first philosophy itself.

In the context of the encounter between Levinas and Heidegger, the fragility of any claim to first philosophy is tied to phenomenology and to the critical inheritance of the phenomenological movement. To claim that experience is meaningful, and beyond that to insist that philosophy remains bound to those experience in which it finds its genesis, is to interrogate the very notion of philosophy proper. Indeed, phenomenology as philosophy— more so than other domains of philosophical inquiry—is necessarily impure, necessarily improper. This is of some consequence in examining Levinas's Heideggerian inheritance, for phenomenology is not something with which Levinas precisely breaks. Indeed, in his descriptions of the ethical relation, he is forced to bend the evidence of phenomenology against itself. Even as he contests the subjectivism of the phenomenological subject, Levinas never abandons phenomenology altogether. Indeed, phenomenology demands an attentiveness to the concrete that is sacrosanct for Levinas.

Hence to claim that Levinas's confrontation with Heidegger can be reduced to a question of priority between fundamental ontology and ethics is to obscure at least one truth of this encounter: at stake is not a battle for primacy or priority so much as different attempts to destabilize the very notion of first philosophy to begin with. I suggest that in Levinas's critique of Heidegger, these tensions come through in the rhetorical invocation of images of violence that symptomatize the co-constitutive nature of ontology and ethics. In this sense, what follows is not a defense of Heidegger in light of Levinas's criticism, but an investigation of Levinas's philosophy of power that takes as its starting point his response to Heidegger's phenomenology. As such, this chapter remains agnostic with regard to many questions concerning the validity and accuracy of Levinas's critique of Heidegger and focuses instead on the way in which the deployment of certain rhetorical strategies, and well as images, in Levinas's critique, productively troubles the notion of first philosophy itself. Crucially, this is not to suggest that Levinas did not intend to claim that ethics must assume priority. Of course he did. But the mood of Levinas's writings also signals that this priority is more or less permanently menaced. Just as Levinas read the phenomenological tradition against itself, so too may one read Levinas against himself, and read his insistence on ethics as first philosophy not as a dogmatic assertion of rigid hierarchy, but rather as a claim that forces recognition of the impossibility of entirely parsing these two domains of inquiry.

It is here that Le Doeuff's insight into the ambivalent status of the imaginary—as it works both for and against theory—is brought to bear on the Levinasian critique of the violence of ontology. In *The Philosophical Imaginary*, Le Doeuff suggested that tropes, images, and metaphors frequently serve to mask moments of tension and incoherence within a certain theory, where the reader is being asked to think an impossible simultaneity. For this reason, the sheer ubiquity of images of violence in Levinas's critique of Heidegger merits critical attention and solicits what Le Doeuff called an "iconographic investigation." The images of power and violence that pervade Levinas's descriptions of the ethical relation serve to problematize the strict elevation of the ontological over the ethical. Indeed, it might be argued that the very notion of ethics as "first" philosophy—indeed the very notion of a first philosophy at all—is problematized by the presence of these rhetorical and imaginary structures, structures that seem to betray the fact that ontology and ethics are not so easily parsed. As such, an investigation of the place of violence in the Levinasian philosophical imaginary may inspire a productive querying of the distinction between the ethical and the ontological and, still further, a critical engagement with the broader notions of "first" philosophy and philosophy "proper." Even as the ethical never relinquishes its claim to priority in Levinas's corpus, its elevation in this regard is one that is permanently frustrated, in part due to the fact that Levinas neither would nor could entirely break with phenomenology, and so as a consequence could not break with the concrete in favor of the abstract.

Many of Levinas's descriptions of the ethical relation demonstrate a tendency to render ethics as allergic to power in some sense. This tendency is born out in a number of places in Levinas's body of work, but it is most apparent in his engagement with Heidegger. One challenge of this chapter is to reconcile this allergy to power with the fact that the discourse of ethics is replete with images of power, persuasion, and violence. Here one might think especially of those images that emerge in the later *Otherwise than Being*,[3] of a subject who is held hostage, and accused by an other for whom one is infinitely responsible. Responsibility for the suffering and the welfare of others is described as a kind of persecution and accusation, an "irreparable wounding." Indeed, among the most renowned descriptions of sensibility from *Otherwise than Being* is a scene rife with violence: "Vulnerability, exposure to outrage, to wounding, passivity more passive than all patience, passivity of the accusative form, trauma of accusation suffered by a hostage to the point of persecution, implicating the identity of the hostage who substitutes himself for others: all this is the self, a defecting or defeat of the ego's identity" (OB, 15/31). Much of *Otherwise than Being* is dedicated to the exploration of a passivity in the face of the Other that Levinas describes as "a vulnerability and a paining exhausting themselves like a hemorrhage" (OB, 72/116). Subjectivity itself is rendered as the pure undergoing of a body suffering for another (OB, 79/127). Again and again, Levinas relies upon images of vulnerability and exposure to power, many of them tarrying with violence, to render the ethical relation.

One must critically query the force of these descriptions. If ethics is allergic to power—if ontology is the very domain of violence and war—then what is at stake in the reemergence of the rhetoric and imagery of power and violence in many of Levinas's most incisive descriptions of the ethical relation? Crucially, this is not to question the legitimacy of this rhetoric and this imaginary. Nor is it to insist that the provocation or force of the ethical summons is of the same kind as the ontological power from which Levinas goes to such lengths to distance himself. Still none of this renders illegitimate an iconographic investigation of violence as it pertains to Levinas's texts. What are we to make of Levinas's own deployment of the motif of violence in his description of ethics, particularly as it rests alongside his relegation of power to the domain of ontology? In fact, the Levinasian corpus is rife with instances of violence that are not so neatly relegated to the domain of ontology. Indeed, the motif of violence is quite expansive and refuses this confinement, a fact that problematizes any neat polarization of ethics, eschatology, and peace over and against ontology, war, and violence. (TI, 21/5) Further complicating any diagnosis of the motif of violence in Levinas is the ubiquity of those tropes in which violence is embedded—persecution, destitution, accusation, and martyrdom—albeit in ways that are often veiled. While Levinas hardly shies away from the motif of power, the sheer ubiquity of those contexts in which he employs this term can be dizzying.

If power is conceived as akin to comprehension and so to totalization and imperialism, what is at stake in the rhetoric of power and violence that continues to pervade Levinas's description of the ethical relation? One might argue that given the complexities of the relationship between ethics and politics in Levinas's work, power as a political entity and the summons to ethics must be different in kind. The worry would be that a conflation of political and ethical power is not only unjustified in reference to Levinas's writing, but that it would also run the risk of gravely distorting this relation- ship, having the effect of breaching the chasm between ethics and politics in a way Levinas would never have condoned. Viewed from a different lens, however, Levinas's engagement with power—beginning in his criticism of Heidegger—provides some clue as to how one might read a number of binaries that inflect Levinas's writing—from ontology and ethics to ethics and politics to the abstract and the concrete—in a way that insists upon their simultaneity even as it troubles it.

The association of Heidegger's thinking of Being with a kind of ontological violence justifies a number of subsequent moves on Levinas's part—from ontology to power to violence to totalitarianism to tyranny. Rhetorically, there is no question that Levinas's association of the power of ontology with imperialism is effective. This much seems clear given the influence it can claim on subsequent generations of philosophers. The valid- ity or lack thereof of Levinas's critique is not so much the issue here as the legacy that this theoretical encounter can claim. The Levinasian critique of Heidegger has had the effect of ontologizing power and violence, of making it difficult, if not impossible, to conceive of ontology without violence. The inheritance of the engagement between these two continues to reverber- ate in many corners of contemporary French thought, specifically in the commonplace assumption that thought is always already practical, and that ontology itself can never be divorced from the consideration of power.

ONTOLOGICAL IMPERIALISM

The fact that Levinas's response to Heidegger overtly assumes the shape of an argument regarding first philosophy is not without irony, since it is an abiding suspicion of this figure—first philosophy—that seems to shape both of their philosophical aspirations. For Heidegger, Western philosophy has privileged a metaphysical tradition that has remained ignorant of the question of Being and ontological difference. Where metaphysics is given priority, the question of Being is ignored. Of course for Levinas the problem in part remains one of priority, albeit of a different order. Where Heidegger urges a return to the question of Being, Levinas suggests that Heidegger's thinking is ethically impoverished in the sense that his thinking of ontologi- cal difference conceals the primacy of the ethical relation. Even as Heidegger questions the primacy of metaphysics, he falters in submitting the Other to ontology, a gesture that cannot help but enact a claim to possession and so reduce the other to the same. *Totality and Infinity* suggests that Heidegger has unequivocally endorsed ontology as first philosophy, and following from this assessment are a host of claims about the kind of power ontology exercises, a power that becomes linked to violence, totalitarianism, and imperialism.

In "Metaphysics Precedes Ontology" Levinas is advancing the critique of Heidegger that earlier emerged in "Is Ontology Fundamental?" where Levinas describes the encounter with the Other as the "first contestation of the primacy of ontology" (BW, 10). Here Levinas renders Heideggerian ontology problematic in its subordination of the other: "In our relation with the other (autrui) is it a matter of letting be? Is it not the independence of the other (autrui) accomplished in the role of being summoned? Is the one to whom one speaks understood from the first in his being? Not at all. The other (autrui) is not an object of comprehension first and an interlocutor second. The two relations are intertwined. In other words the comprehension of the other (autrui) is inseparable from his invocation" (BW, 6). Levinas begins to mark his distance from an account that would have the relationship with the other reduced to either letting-be or comprehension. Neither captures the element of invocation or revelation that Levinas wishes to emphasize in the approach of the Other. Levinas illumines the manner in which the other is given in society with us, but this sociality cannot be reduced to a property of the given that is revealed in comprehension; indeed, Levinas claims that this ethical society of self and other is irreducible to comprehension and thereby profoundly distanced from the exercise of power (BW, 8). The link between comprehension and power is theorized in greater detail in Totality and Infinity, but already in this earlier essay, there is evidence of a parsing of ontology and ethics that is justified with reference to the possessive power (and violence) of ontology. Indeed, "Is Ontology Fundamental?" concludes with the claim that "the human only lends itself to a relation that is not a power" (BW, 10).[4] With this, an antipathy is established between power and ontology on the one hand and ethics on the other.

This opposition is magnified in the early pages of Totality and Infinity, where Levinas's criticism of Heidegger is furthered through an interrogation of Heidegger's understanding of the relationship between Being and the existent. In one guise, theory designates a relation with the other wherein the known being is allowed to manifest itself in the absence of any claim to possession by the knower. Of greater concern for Levinas is the fact that historically, "theory" tends to designate a different movement, comprehension—a move proper to most theories of knowledge in Western philosophy—wherein the known object is subsumed, claimed, or possessed in a cognitive relation that reinscribes the privilege of the subject. This latter way of approaching the known being enacts a disrespect or foreclosure of alterity and even more profoundly announces the conceit of a subject that

refuses to be limited, called into question, or disarmed by the approach of
the other. This movement of possession is crucially manifest through a third
term—a neutral term—which is itself neither being nor existent (TI, 42/32).
Levinas claims that this third term—the mechanism of possession—"may
appear as a concept thought," or yet—to use Heidegger's language—as the
thought of Being itself. "Being, which is without the density of existents, is
the light in which existents become intelligible" (TI, 42/32). This possession of the Other through the interposition of a middle or neutral term—
Being itself—is ubiquitous in Western philosophy as Levinas understands
it. It is present in the inheritance of the Platonic tradition as particulars
are illumined through their participation in the forms, and it is likewise
writ large in phenomenology, wherein the other is known only through
its appearance within a horizon drawn by the subject and illumined by a
constituting consciousness. For Levinas, such an appearance can only ever
be a claim to possession.

In Totality and Infinity, Levinas's critique of Heidegger iterates the
worry that the "letting be" of the other is in fact a ruse, as this moment of
passivity is ultimately suppressed in the possessive gesture of comprehension.
On this account, there is no intertwining of letting-be and comprehension
so much as a suppression of the other accomplished as knowledge. To be
given is to be exposed to understanding, comprehension, representation,
illumination in being, confinement within a horizon, and so on—all of
which for Levinas are commensurate with a kind of appropriation and suppression. As the phenomenological tradition is replete with references to this
gesture, wherein the other is illumined, recognized, and ultimately grasped
by consciousness, it stands indicted of a kind of injustice. The injustice
is justified with reference to Levinas's conflation of intentionality with a
kind of possessive violence that bolsters the ego and refuses to be alienated
or undone in exteriority. Levinas concedes that the thought of Being as
described by Heidegger melds both a possessive moment of comprehension
and a moment of critique: "To broach an existent from Being is simultaneously to let it be and to comprehend it" (TI, 45/35). He regardless claims
with some assurance that "Being and Time has argued but perhaps one sole
thesis: Being is inseparable from the comprehension of Being (which unfolds
as time); Being is already an appeal to subjectivity" (TI, 45/36). Levinas's
subsequent reservations concerning Heidegger's thought are grounded in this
critical contention. The bivalent nature of theory—its existence as comprehension and critique—is allegedly undone in Heidegger's privileging of
the moment of comprehension. Hence the thought of Being is construed
as a paradigmatic gesture of comprehension, and the critical impulse to let
being be is stifled. The critical capacity of theory collapses in the drive
toward comprehension and possession, where possession is "preeminently

the form in which the other becomes the same, by becoming mine" (*TI*, 46/37). In Levinas's eyes, this affirmation of the priority of Being (as concept and comprehension) over the existent announces a particular definition of philosophy. It decides the essence of philosophy. It is to subordinate the relation with the Other to the relation to Being; it is to renounce ethics in favor of ontology.

In the latter pages of "Metaphysics Precedes Ontology," this possessive gesture is linked explicitly to injustice, tyranny, and imperialism. Levinas moves *from* the consideration of a scenario wherein the other is reduced to the same through comprehension *to* the claim that this notion of ontology is itself an operation of power, one that issues in the tyranny of the State, unable to secure itself against its own foundational violence and, as a consequence, unable to interrogate its own freedom (*TI*, 46/37). This critical incapacity constitutes the injustice of ontology. While Levinas may be quite amenable to the Heideggerian impulse to critique the technological drive that enables the forgetting of Being, this gesture is not in and of itself radical enough. In ceding such power to Being, the Other is rendered subordinate to the anonymous force of neutralization, and so rendered vulnerable to tyranny and imperialist domination (*TI*, 47/38). Hence the remembrance of Being is rendered by Levinas as an anemic and inadequate gesture from the perspective of ethics: "Even though it opposes the technological passion issued forth from the forgetting of Being hidden by existents, Heideggerian ontology, which subordinates the relation with the Other to the relation with Being in general, remains under the obedience of the anonymous, and leads inevitably to another power, to imperialist domination, to tyranny" (*TI*, 48/39). Having advanced this criticism of Heidegger, Levinas moves to consider theory in its more redemptive—that is critical—dimension.

ETHICS AS CRITIQUE

As critique, theory has the capacity to undermine the conceit of ontology. If one movement of theory consists in the possession of the other that is proper to comprehension, the other consists in a redemptive critical moment, where the pretense of ontology itself is disarmed. In this more critical guise, Levinas concedes that theory can indeed accomplish a respect for exteriority and alterity. Precisely in those moments when theory is made to double back, to turn on ontology itself, it warrants the name "critique." Such critique applies scrutiny to the spontaneity and freedom of a subject who resists being displaced and called into question by the other. This claim would be relatively pallid if theory were to remain an ontological movement, but Levinas insists that theory in its critical instantiation consists in a move beyond ontology wherein the exercise of the same is called into question.

It is this interrogation that comes to define ethics as Levinas understands it. "We name this calling into question of my spontaneity by the presence of the Other ethics" (*TI*, 43/33). Concretely, the calling into question of the same by the other is "the ethics that accomplishes the critical essence of knowledge" (*TI*, 42/33). Ethics, then, is critique; ontology is comprehension. But what is the nature of the force of critique? And from whence does it derive this power?

Levinas's elevation of critique is justified with reference to the fact that critique undoes conceptualization, and the concept is the mechanism in which ontology traffics. If there is violence in approaching the Other through the mediation of concepts, Levinas situates ethics in opposition to this kind of generalizing gesture by insisting that my conscience in the face of the other is a "conceptless experience" (*TI*, 101/103). The absence of this kind of mediating, conceptual violence, protects the Other's alterity. This inaugurates a respect for the other that ontology cannot approximate. Moreover, to approach the other not through an act of freedom or appropriation, but rather through a metaphysical desire, through ethics, is to approach *without touching* (*TI*, 109/111). Such a rendering of the desire for the other at the heart of Levinasian ethics seems to carve a space for ethics that would be devoid of the operation of power, and with it the threat of violence and tyranny that accompanies the movement of comprehension. Whereas the "I can" becomes an "I do" in Levinas's critique of Heidegger—as intention collapses into possession—"Metaphysics approaches without touching. Its *way* is not an action, but is a social relation" (*TI*, 109/111).

Further in *Totality and Infinity*, Levinas describes critique as "the investiture of freedom" and claims that the activity of philosophy is importantly genealogical, involving a movement that "traces freedom back to what lies before it, to disclose the investiture that liberates freedom from the arbitrary" (*TI*, 85/83). In this sense, what is proper to theory as critique it not the possibility of grasping objects, but rather the capacity to penetrate beneath its own condition, a power of self-interrogation. (ibid.) "The knowing whose essence is critique cannot be reduced to objective cognition; it leads to the Other. To welcome the Other is to put in question my freedom" (*TI*, 85/83). If theory as critique involves a radical interrogation of the self—and with that an indictment of the spontaneity and arbitrary nature of freedom—this is because the Other is unable to be contained by the concepts in which reason, knowledge, and comprehension traffic: "The Other, whose exceptional presence is inscribed in the ethical impossibility of killing him in which I stand, marks the end of powers. If I can no longer have power over him it is because he overflows absolutely every *idea* I can have of him" (*TI*, 87/86). Comprehension, as possession, is inadequate to the Other, who transcends these attempts at assimilation. At still other moments, Levinas claims that the ethical relation transcends those concepts that can be applied to things:

"The welcome of the Other expresses a simultaneity of activity and passivity which places the relation with the other outside of the dichotomies valid for things: the a priori and the a posteriori, activity and passivity" (*TI*, 89/88). This would seem to imply that ethics and power are antithetical, so much so that ethics cannot be thought given a logic of activity and passivity that is proper to the calculus of power. One can exert no power over that which cannot be contained.

In "Ethics and the Face" the opposition between ethics and power is further emphasized. The face of the Other, claims Levinas, resists my powers; indeed the face erodes my capacity to have power at all. "The expression the face introduces into the world does not defy the feebleness of my powers, but my ability for power" (*TI*, 198/216). The Other "paralyses the very power of power" (*TI*, 198/216). The face is an invitation to a relation that is utterly incommensurate with power. Yet Levinas is quick to add an addendum. The face still remains exposed to power in a sense, but Levinas insists that it is "in a sense only," because the encounter with the Other modifies the very nature of power. In the domain of ethics, power can no longer take, it can kill. If there is something in the approach of the Other—concretely realized as a calling into question of oneself—that undermines power in turning freedom back against itself, there is also something in the ethical relation that alters that kind of power that is at stake. Comprehension is no longer the issue. The sense in which the face is exposed to power is in its vulnerability to annihilation. This is not the violence of ontology or comprehension simply magnified, for "to kill . . . is to renounce comprehension completely" (*TI*, 198/216). The power at play in the ethical relation is thus rendered as profoundly different in kind from the power of Heidegger's thought of Being, the power of comprehension, or the imperialism of ontology.

What sort of approach is this, that it may claim such power over us, but not touch us, that commands us in its refusal to be contained? *Otherwise than Being* construes this relation as a kind of obsession:

> The neighbor assigns me before I designate him. This is a modality not of a knowing, but of an obsession, a shuddering of the human quite different from cognition . . . Through the suppression of the singular, through generalization, knowing is idealism. In an approach I am first a servant of the neighbor, already late and guilty for being late. I am as it were ordered from the outside, traumatically commanded, without interiorizing by representation and concepts the authority that commands me . . . Consciousness is not interposed between me and the neighbor; or, at least, it arises only on the ground of this antecedent relationship of obsession, which no consciousness could annul, and of which consciousness is a modification. (*OB*, 87)

Levinas goes on to claim that this obsession is "unassumable like a persecution," implying once more that the approach of the Other undoes me
without mediation, without concept, and without touch. Levinas would
seem to be claiming that an other who does not touch me, who exercises
no power, holds me hostage. Then again, the "unassumable" nature of this
responsibility I have for the Other seems to imply extraordinary powers.
What is the nature of this summons without touch? And what power does
it claim over me, if any?

    In a passage from *Totality and Infinity*, Levinas claims that power has
the capacity to be transformed into justice, even though he insists that power
is "by essence" murderous: "The effort of this book is directed toward apper-
ceiving in discourse a non-allergic relation with alterity, toward apperceiv-
ing Desire—where power, by essence murderous of the other, becomes, faced
with the other and 'against all good sense,' the impossibility of murder, the
consideration of the other, or justice" (TI, 47/38). And yet this description
of power as "becoming" the other of comprehension and tyranny—that is ethics—is fundamentally at odds with Levinas's claim that the ethical relation is
"opposed to first philosophy which identifies freedom and power." How would
Levinas account for the metamorphosis? Does this bending of power in the
service of ethics gesture toward an important intersection of the domains and
ethics and politics? The meaningful question for Levinas concerns the very
nature of power as he understands it. Early descriptions of power consign it
to the realm of ontology and render it complicit in "ontological imperialism."
In still other places, Levinas implies that power can be bent in the service of
justice, though he never seems to relinquish the idea that power is essentially
murderous. In the later work—which is itself rife with the imagery of power
and violence—Levinas complicates matters by claiming that the obsession
and responsibility that are born in the approach of the other are unassumable;
they do not call for my power, but in fact undo my very capacity for power.

    If Levinas's own account of the relationship between ethics and power
ultimately remains ambiguous, the ubiquity of images of violence testify
to what Le Doeuff claims is a moment of theoretical tension of incoherence. Rhetorically, the ethical relation is inscribed again and again in scenes
of suffering, shame, and power. In this sense, the Levinasian ambivalence
regarding the relationship between power and ethics is not to be explained
away with reference to a strict parsing of the ontological and the ethical,
but is rather symptomatized in images marked by power, and frequently
violence. This contamination of the ethical and the ontological arguably
speaks to the impossibility of any first philosophy, if and when this philosophy carries with it the conceit of being foundational and sufficient for its
own justification. The fact that Levinas is forced to bend phenomenology
against itself would seem to buttress this concern, namely, that ethics does

not—and cannot—remove itself entirely from the domain of ontology and power. Along these lines, in "Violence and Metaphysics," Jacques Derrida famously argues that the thought of Being is both "foreign" to, and requisite for, every first philosophy, so it is not complicit in the degradation of ethics.[5] On this account, the thought of Being exercises no power and does not privilege certain kinds of discourse over others.

"AS CLOSE AS POSSIBLE TO NONVIOLENCE"

To rehearse in detail Derrida's argument in the section "On Ontological Violence" from Violence and Metaphysics is not necessary here, so much as to note that Derrida's strategy in this chapter is to illumine the very same tension to which Le Doeuff refers, namely, the idea of how to think the simultaneity of what is both requisite for and also foreign to philosophy. Derrida claims that there can be no thought of Being, "in its unveiling" that is ever foreign to violence. This is because Being "is always dissimulated," concealed in its manifestation in the existent. "This determination of the revelation of the existent (Metaphysics) is the very veiling of Being" (VM, 144). There is a retreat or withdrawal of Being in its disclosure as the existent, a perpetual movement of veiling and unveiling that conceals being just as the existent is illumined. The thought of Being must do violence to itself in order to appear. "A Being without violence would be a Being which would occur outside the existent: nothing; nonhistory; nonoccurrence; nonphenomenality." "A speech produced without the least violence would determine nothing, would say nothing, would offer nothing to the other" (VM, 147). In short, a speech without the least violence would approach the other with empty hands; it would be a gesture devoid of content and meaning. In its original possibility as a gift, language is nonviolent; when it assumes a place in history and owns its relation to totality, it traffics in violence. Hence there is unavoidable violence in the revealing of the thought of Being, in the very manner in which it announces itself; there is no such revealing that does not "pass through the violence of the concept" (VM, 147). Derrida's claim is simply that we err in attributing this violence to the thought of Being itself.

> Because if one does not uproot the silent origin from itself violently, if one decided not to speak, then the worst violence will still silently cohabit the idea of peace? Peace is made only in a certain silence, which is determined and protected by the violence of speech. Since speech says nothing other than the horizon of this silent peace by which it has itself summoned and that it is its mission to protect and to prepare, speech indefinitely remains silent. One never escapes the economy of war. (VM, 148)

It is not simply the case that the thought of Being is not an *archia* to which the existent is submitted; Derrida is not content to settle with this claim. His argument is more substantive. It is rather the thought of Being itself in which Derrida finds some redemption, for it is only the thought of Being that can make "the search for an *archia* tremble" and so attempt a liberation from violence. At best, traditional philosophy and metaphysics can only work for a lesser violence, using violence against violence, whereas "the thought of Being could not possibly occur as ethical violence" (VM, 142). Hence the thought of Being is the only thing that can gesture in the direction of a liberation from violence, by allowing for the possibility of letting the other be and hence respect. In a radical inversion of the Levinasian indictment of the violence of Heideggerian ontology, Derrida claims that "implied by the discourse of *Totality and Infinity*, alone permitting to let be others in their truth, freeing dialogue and the face to face, the thought of Being is thus as close as possible to nonviolence" (VM, 146). Not only is the thought of Being foreign to the imperialist exercise of ontology; it is altogether requisite for the ethical relation itself. The possibility of pure nonviolence foreclosed, the thought of Being approximates nonviolence as much as is possible.

A deconstructive reading—such as those advanced by Le Doeuff or Derrida—of Levinas's engagement with Heidegger betrays something about the nature of power in the Levinasian discourse on ethics. There is nowhere in "Violence and Metaphysics" the claim that ontology is not violence. Indeed, since violence is transcendental on Derrida's account—in this chapter and elsewhere—it is requisite for the generation of meaning, the condition for the possibility of identity's very emergence. Power is always at play, so there is radical sympathy with Levinas's concern about the power that is exercised as ontology. Derrida's more substantive claim is that the thought of Being must not be conflated with any first philosophy, whether that be ontology or ethics. This is why he claims that the thought of Being is at once foreign to every first philosophy and allergic to none. In this sense, the thought of Being has no agenda and cannot be credited with any design. In and of itself "Being itself commands nothing and no one" (VM, 141). Insofar as Levinas's critique of Heidegger conflates the thought of Being with first philosophy, Derrida argues that it is disingenuous. Again, the issue is not whether ontology is violent, or whether ontology exercises power, but the nature of the power that is exercised by any "first" philosophy. One might even suggest that to read Derrida, Levinas, and Heidegger together is to tarry with the illegitimacy of the very notion of any "first" philosophy. If this suspicion leads Derrida to a more sympathetic reading of Heidegger than Levinas would have allowed himself, it also leads to a reading of Levinas that suggests that an antipathy or allergy between ethics and power is ultimately untenable.

When Levinas argues that power—"by essence murderous of the other"—can morph into justice, can appreciate the impossibility of murder, he indicates that ethics and power are not entirely allergic. And even as he insists that the Other holds me hostage without touching me, the many images of force that animate his descriptions of the ethical relation testify to the impurity of the ethical domain. This, too, is what Derrida revealed when he claimed that the thought of Being is as close as possible to nonviolence, even as it is unrelentingly submitted to violence by its very nature. So too with ethics, which alters violence and is altered by violence. In this sense, the images of violence that pervade Levinas's engagement with Heidegger do indeed mark a point of tension, as Le Doeuff would have insisted. If the ethical relation can be meaningfully (if imperfectly) brought to bear on the realm of politics, it will of necessity submit itself to the various axes of ontological violence that animate the realm of the social. Of course it is no less the case that this ontological violence will itself be submitted to the interrogation of ethics. What the images of violence that circulate in Levinas's work indicate is that power itself is not a figure with which Levinas can break. If his descriptions of ethics can claim a concrete inheritance, they similarly must claim a complicity with power at some level. Power cannot be purged from the realm of ethics. Even as Levinas distances himself from the notion of power he associates with Heideggerian ontology, images of power continue to animate his descriptions of the ethical relation, even if the kind of power at play in this domain would be the kind of power that morphs into justice when confronted by the Other. It would thus be a power that is "as close as possible to nonviolence," to borrow Derrida's words, but never nonviolence itself.

SOURCES CITED

1. Michèle Le Doeuff, *The Philosophical Imaginary*. trans Colin Gordon (London: Athlone, 1989). Hereafter *PI*.

2. Emmanuel Levinas, *Totality and Infinity: An Essay on Exteriority*, trans. Alphonso Lingis (Pittsburg: Duquesne University Press, 1969); *Totalité et infini* (The Hague: Netherlands. Martinus Nijhoff, 1961). English pagination preceding the French. Hereafter *TI*.

3. Emmanuel Levinas, *Otherwise than Being*, trans. Alphonso Lingis (Pittsburgh: Duquesne University Press, 1998). Hereafter *OB*.

4. Emmanuel Levinas, "Is Ontology Fundamental?" in *Basis Philosophical Writings*, ed. Peperzak, Critchley, and Bernasconi (Bloomington: Indiana University Press, 1996).

5. Jacques Derrida, "Violence and Metaphysics" in *Writing and Difference*, trans. Alan Bass (Chicago: University of Chicago Press, 1978). Hereafter VM.

CHAPTER TWO

DREAMING OTHERWISE THAN ICARUS

_____

Heidegger, Levinas, and the
Secularization of Transcendence

Philip J. Maloney

In the series of lectures God and Onto-theo-logy, Levinas returns to a theme which inflects his work from the protoethical phenomenological analyses of *Existence and Existents* and *Time and the Other*: the distance between his thought and the thought which revealed for him the limits of the Husserlian problematic, Heideggerian ontology. In these lectures, Levinas seeks to make definitive a break with Heidegger that he had insisted upon since the 1940s but to which he rarely devoted more than rhetorical resources. In significant part, the clarity and precision of the break there detailed is due to a shared horizon: the need to contest the ontotheological character of the philosophical tradition. In this task, Levinas recognizes in Heidegger both a pioneer and a fellow traveler. However, as the course of lectures makes clear, Levinas is in profound disagreement with Heidegger concerning the substance and direction of the contestation.

Specifically, Levinas insists that Heidegger's attempted destruction of the ontotheological sway of metaphysics fails to radically question the dominance of being as the source of meaning, blinding it to a question which for Levinas is the question on which any attempt to contest this sway must turn:

"[D]id onto-theo-logy's mistake consist in taking being for God, or rather in taking God for being?" (*DMT*, 188/*GDT*, 163). This question, posed to us as much as to Heiedegger, has, like many of Levinas's questions, a ready answer. The remarkable thing about the lectures thus inaugurated is their willingness to sustain the question, to not rush to the answer which we all expect and instead to entertain the possibility that there might be more than one way beyond the confines of the ontotheological. This willingness is particularly evident in Levinas's renewal and reexamination of key terms from his lexicon. One of these terms, which gets considerable attention throughout the lectures, is particularly important in assessing the continued significance of Heidegger's thought for Levinas's work: transcendence. While no one would contest the prominence of transcendence to the discussion of "God, Death and Time," many might protest its significance for appreciating Levinas's relationship to Heidegger. It does not figure, after all, in the list of terms and concepts that Levinas highlights when asked about the significance of Heidegger's work for his own. Moreover, there is the fact that Heidegger himself abandons the term at the same time he abandons the project of fundamental ontology, finding it inextricably tangled with the ontotheological metaphysics he seeks to overcome. In spite of these rejoinders, and indeed precisely in light of the last, the present chapter locates a pivotal moment of Levinas's attempt to distinguish his own contestation of ontotheology from Heidegger's in the proximity and distance between his and Heidegger's conception of transcendence.

Concerned less to review the stages of either Heidegger's or Levinas's thinking of transcendence, the project undertaken here brings together Heidegger's criticisms of the notion with Levinas's reaffirmation, seeking to establish the terms by which our understanding of both Levinas's and Heidegger's thought on the subject can advance our own. If indeed we are living in the wake of the failure of ontotheology, if in that sense our thinking is irredeemably secular, then clarity as to the modes of thought which remain to us is urgently needed. And if, as both Heidegger and Levinas seem to understand, in its privative, positivistic sense, the secular is fundamentally insufficient to thought, how can transcendence, properly secularized, fail to compel our attention? The contribution to this effort takes as its limited goal delimiting the field for what seems to us an essential confrontation between two alternative approaches to a properly secularized transcendence.

I

In the lecture courses contemporaneous with the publication of *Sein und Zeit*, Heidegger struggled mightily with the issue that proved to be that work's undoing. This issue, as it is acknowledged in the course entitled The Basic

Problems of Phenomenology, develops in the recognition that "ontology cannot be established in a purely ontological manner" (*GP*, 26/*BPP*, 19). The recognition of the necessity for an ontic foundation for fundamental ontology is remarkable in as much as it seems to contradict Heidegger's continued attempt, in his early works, to ground the question of the meaning of being in fundamental ontology. Heidegger's strategy for overcoming this difficulty, already apparent in *Sein und Zeit*, is to radically reconceive the concept of ground itself. It is for this reason that in 1928, Heidegger's interests turned once again to logic and to the philosophy of Leibniz. In the "Second Major Part" of the course entitled Metaphysical Foundations of Logic as well as in the contemporaneous essay "On the Essence of Ground," Heidegger looks in particular to Leibniz's articulation of the "Principle of Reason." Heidegger's reworking of the principle in explicit conjunction with terms fundamental to the Dasein-analytic, particularly transcendence and freedom, opens up the possibility of an account of grounding proper to the ultimate aim of that analytic.

That this opening ultimately proved illusory is well known. By the time of Heidegger's self-critique of this attempt in the 1955–56 lecture course The Principle of Reason, the term *Grund* had taken its place within a substantially new register. Though freedom still figured prominently, it had been displaced from the Dasein-analytic and the fundamental ontology promised thereby. Completely absent from the history of being which had come to replace the aspiration for a fundamental ontology was "transcendence," a concept central to the 1928 treatment of *Grund* and to the problem of fundamental ontology more generally, in reference to which he insisted, "The transcendence of Dasein is the central problem" (*MAL*, 170/*MFL*, 135). Though the confidence of this statement was quickly replaced with dissatisfaction with its terms and aims, the illusory character of the opening announced in no way undermined the continuing relevance of Heidegger's work in this period. The story of the displacement of freedom and ground and of the banishment of "transcendence" from the thinking of being is well known, even as its terms and implications remain fruitful concerns of Heidegger scholars.

Of concern here are some of the implications of the eclipse of both the project of fundamental ontology and the transcendence in Heidegger's thinking and their relation to Heidegger's refiguring of the question of the meaning of being in terms of truth and the history of being. To contemporary ears, particularly to those sensitized by Levinas's reading of Heidegger, Heidegger's insistence on the centrality of transcendence to the Dasein-analytic, and thus ultimately to the project of fundamental ontology, can hardly fail to resonate. This resonance is amplified by the frequently discussed appendix to section 10 of *Metaphysical Foundations* dedicated to clarifying the nature of fundamental ontology. In this appendix, Heidegger returns to the problematic recognition of *Basic Problems*, here naming the complex of questions which it provokes "metontology." Suggestively, Heidegger announces that it is in the context of metontology that "the question of ethics may properly be raised for the first time" (*MAL*, 199/*MFL*, 157). This reference to ethics stands in contrast to his previous mention of it in section 10, which denies any relevance to ethics for the project of fundamental ontology (*MAL*, 171/ *MFL*, 136).[1] The consistency of this earlier mention with his later discussions of the concept (e.g., in "Letter on 'Humanism'") underscores the significance of the appendix. From this vantage it is possible to appreciate how Heidegger's self-criticism of the project of fundamental ontology conditions the particular character of his secularization of transcendence.

The discussions of *Grund* in *Metaphysical Foundations of Logic* and "On the Essence of Ground" have a common starting point. In both, Heidegger moves from a consideration of the complex signification and history of the "Principle of Sufficient Reason" to that which the complex points as its horizon: being.[2] In both, motivation for this development is found in the status of the principle as a logical one. Key to the project of making logic philosophical is the attempt "to loosen up the traditional logic," a dismantling (*Abbau*) with which "we shall gain immediate access to philosophy itself" (*MAL*, 7/*MFL*, 6). Moving from a discussion of Leibniz's doctrine of judgment, which demonstrated that this doctrine was grounded in a metaphysics of truth, Heidegger turns to a discussion of ground or reason. Drawing on Aristotle's elucidation of this concept of ground,[3] Heidegger points to the connection of ground with Being, taking this connection up as a pathway into fundamental ontology, "[T]he exposition of the dimensions of the problem of ground . . . is none other that the dimensions of an inquiry in the central direction of metaphysical inquiry as such" *MAL*, 7/*MFL*, 196/154). In other words, in the "dismantling" of the traditional conception of logic as exemplified by the work of Leibniz, Heidegger uncovers the primordial structures of Dasein itself.

Of course, Heidegger consistently underscores that the existential analysis of Dasein must be understood as merely preparatory; fundamental ontology is not the end of the project, but only, "the basic grounding of ontology in general" (*MAL*, 196/*MFL*, 154). In *Metaphysical Foundations*, Heidegger lays out the three movements of this founding: the analytic of Dasein in terms of *Zeitlichkeit*, an exposition of the temporal horizons of the question of Being in general, and the coming to self-understanding of fundamental ontology in the *Umschlag*.[4] In this overturning, Heidegger recognizes the fact that "fundamental ontology does not exhaust metaphysics" (*MAL*, 199/*MFL*,156). This recognition of the limits of the fundamental ontological project can be understood in terms of the centrality of Dasein to fundamental ontology, the fact that the existential structure of understanding-of-Being is grounded in the factual extantness of Dasein. Thus, along with fundamental ontology, metaphysics must contain a treatment of "beings as a whole," understood as the ontic totality of nature in which Dasein factually resides. This treatment is metontology. Metontology, understood as arising from fundamental ontology's *Umschlag*, is necessitated by the fact that, even at its most radical, fundamental ontology, as preparatory for general ontology, is rooted in the existence of Dasein.

Thus, the *Umschlag* arises in the movement of radicalization and universalization of the question of Being intrinsic to the fundamental ontological project itself (*MAL*, 201/*MFL*, 158).[5] In fact, Heidegger goes so far as to say that this overturning is the aim of fundamental ontology.[6] What we are to make of this statement is unclear; more than even some sort of structurally necessary recoil, the notion that fundamental ontology has as its goal its *Umschlag* would seem to problematize any description of fundamental ontology as establishing the possibility for the question of Being in general.[7] An important implication of Heidegger's discussion of metontology is the necessary connection he draws between the unity of fundamental ontology and metontology as a metaphysics of existence with the concrete existence of Dasein (*MAL*, 201/*MFL*, 158). Heidegger, by locating the possibility of *Seinsverständnis*, and thus fundamental ontology, in the existential structures of Dasein's Being, draws our attention to the fact that the necessity of the *Umschlag* is rooted in these structures. Indeed, Heidegger gives this grounding as much force as he can, indicating that the *Umschlag* is called for by these structures. It is this calling which Heidegger is pointing to when he says, "The metaphysical neutrality of the human being, inmost isolated as Dasein, is not an empty abstraction from the ontic, a neither-nor, it is rather the authentic concreteness of the origin" (*MAL*, 173/*MFL*, 137). As revealed in its ontological clarity, the Being of Dasein is the possibility of fundamental ontology and the necessity of its overturning.

In "On the Essence of Ground," Heidegger returns to the metontological concerns without naming them as such, though in this instance his concern with the factical possibilities of the *Seinsverständnis* turn not on the mutual implication of these possibilities with the *Umschlag* but on the relationship between ground and transcendence: "The occurrence of transcendence as grounding is the forming of a leeway into which there can irrupt the factical self-maintaining of factical Dasein in each case in the midst of beings as a whole" (*W*, 170/*EG*, 131). This relationship is not unremarked in *Metaphysical Foundations*, where, for example, Heidegger asserts that "the problem of transcendence must be posed as universally and radically as the problem of being as such" (*MAL*, 194/*MFL*, 153). However, the treatment of the relationship between transcendence and ground in "On the Essence of Ground" is both more systematic and more revealing of the difficulties posed by the relationship between the ontic and ontological moments of the project of fundamental ontology.

Taking up the relationship between these moments in the context of a distinction he pursues between "ontic and ontological truth," he identifies their essential unity in their belonging together to the ontological difference, and ultimately, as the ground of this difference, to the "*transcendence* of Dasein" (W, 134–35/EG, 105–06). In a development that has already been foreseen, this connection between truth and transcendence requires us to recognize that "the problem of ground too can be housed only where the essence of truth draws its inner possibility, namely, in the essence of transcendence" (W, 135/EG, 106). As such, inquiry into the essence of ground, and thus the possibility of addressing the question of the meaning of being in and through the project of fundamental ontology, requires an inquiry into the essence of transcendence. In a development which he will later implicitly criticize, Heidegger inaugurates the inquiry into transcendence by glossing transcendence as "surpassing" (*Übersteig*). While acknowledging that the term remains somewhat mysterious, Heidegger seeks with its employment to enfold the various traditional senses of transcendence in the being of Dasein. In a step with implications for Heidegger's later hesitations about the notion, the identification of transcendence as *Übersteig* leads Heidegger to the conclusion, already prefigured in *Sein und Zeit*, that "transcendence designates the essence of the subject, that it is the fundamental structure of subjectivity . . . to be a subject means to be a being in and as transcendence" (W, 137–38/ EG, 108). Though this step is both authorized and consistent with the project of fundamental ontology, particularly as it is pursued in *Sein und Zeit*, as well as having clear implications for the ethical possibilities of metontology, it is precisely its evidentness which calls it into question. It is to contest this evidentness that in *The Principle of Reason* Heidegger's first step beyond the formal-logical character of Leibniz's formulation of the principle is through reference to a verse by Angelus Silesius.[8]

How then are we to account for this dissatisfaction with the earlier analysis? To point to the abandonment of the project of fundamental ontology in favor of the history of being is at the same time to say as much as needs to be said and to say too little. One thing it leaves aside is an account of the displacement of ethics from its place in a "metaphysics of existence" to what is admittedly a more originary signification as "that thinking which thinks the truth of being as the primordial element of the human being" (BH, 356/LH, 271). What goes missing in this shift is transcendence. From the perspective of Heidegger's later work, the concept of transcendence, "remains captivated in a form of representation that belongs to the dominion of the oblivion of being" (W, 421/QB, 319). At issue is the complicity of transcendence with a transcendental-horizonal logic that for Heidegger imprisons the project of fundamental ontology, denying it the freedom of thought:

> Previously we had come to see thinking in the form of transcendental-horizonal re-presenting . . . [T]hus we determine what is called horizon and transcendence by means of this going beyond and passing beyond . . . which refer back to objects in our representing of objects . . . Horizon and transcendence thus are experienced and determined only relative to objects and are representing them . . . to suggest in this way that what lets the horizon be what it is has not yet been encountered at all. (DT, 63–64)

The implications of this captivity for thinking in general are spelled out in the "Letter on 'Humanism'" within the context of the overcoming of the Dasein-analytic and its ties to the ontotheological sway of Western metaphysics. There, in his discussion of the implications of specifying the essence of the human as ek-sistence, Heidegger explicitly warns against the mistake of treating this account of the being of the human, ".as if it were the secularized transference to human beings of a thought that Christian theology expresses about God" (BH, 327/LH, 249). This is a mistake, he goes on to suggest, that his earlier treatment of these issues had guarded insufficiently against, in no small part because of the "help of the language of metaphysics" (BH, 328/ LH, 250). This general observation does little to explain why "transcendence" is singled out in a way that neither "freedom" nor "ground" is, though clearly all of the terms have their own metaphysical heritage.

     Additional precision is offered by the discussion of transcendence in "On the Question of Being." This essay is important for the current discussion in a number of ways. The problem which animates the essay is the problem of ontotheology: in Heideggerian terms, how to think being other than as determined by metaphysics. The problem confronts us in this particular instance in light of Ernst Jünger's Nietzschean analysis of the "line" of nihilism and its ambiguous movement. Heidegger's own contribution to this analysis is his insistence on an appropriately fundamental answer to the question, "Wherein consists the consummation of nihilism?" (W, 388/QB, 297). As Heidegger attempts to show, Jünger's own answer to this question falls short of the appropriately fundamental in as much as its employment of the category of Gestalt "remains housed within metaphysics" (W, 395/ QB, 299) through its reliance on the notion of subjectivity.

Not surprisingly, it is at this point that Heidegger turns to the concept of transcendence. As has already been noted, fundamental ontology's reliance on the Dasein-analytic and its coordinate employment of transcendence in explicating Dasein's ecstatic being in the world was what first led Heidegger to question the possibility of sustaining this project. However, rather than merely rehearsing the by then standard objections to transcendence in terms of its complicity, in the form of the transcendental-horizonal determination of beings as representation, with the ontotheological character of Western metaphysics, Heidegger takes up transcendence as embodying ambiguously that character itself. In an argument whose form is familiar from post-Kantian idealism, Heidegger insists that the possibility of any representation is itself a representation of an authoritative ground for the representation. In the context of Jünger's analysis this argument supports the assertion that the "appearance of the metaphysical *Gestalt* of the human being as the source that gives meaning is the ultimate consequence of positing the human essence as the authoritative *subjectum*" (W, 397/QB, 300). Immediately drawing a general consequence from this particular example, Heidegger insists that "the inner form of metaphysics, which resides in what one can call transcendence, becomes transformed. Within metaphysics, transcendence is for essential reasons ambiguous" (W, 397/QB, 300). What is thus added to the criticism of transcendence is the insistence that it is, in and as metaphysics, fundamentally amphibolous.

In part, it is the danger posed by this amphibolousness that justifies abandoning the concept, "Where such ambiguity is not heeded, a hopeless confusion spreads, a confusion that may serve as the characteristic sign of the metaphysical representation that is still customary today" (W, 397/QB, 300). To demonstrate this, the disorienting position of transcendence as and in metaphysics is immediately returned by Heidegger to the question of the transcendent. From the perspective of the initial amphiboly, Heidegger glosses the tradition's multiply ambiguous significations of transcendence—as passage, as terminus and as excellence, a gloss which recalls his own earlier attempt to specify the sense of transcendence as *Übersteig*. Heidegger than proceeds to demonstrate how Jünger's own analysis betrays an indeterminacy with regard to these senses, limiting its significance. To choose one example that will resonate with the discussion of Levinas to follow, Heidegger remarks on the limitations of Jünger's analysis of technology, which, through its failure to adequately grasp that "[t]echnology . . . is manifestly grounded in that reversal of transcendence [resulting from its amphibolous character] into the recendence of the *Gestalt* of the worker" (W, 399/QB, 301) completely misses the fact that "the essence of technology . . . point[s] into still more originary realms" (W, 400/QB, 302). This "miss" is no accident, but is rather for Heidegger the unavoidable consequence of the amphiboly of transcendence.

It is this unavoidable failure which reveals the necessity of Heidegger's particular secularization of transcendence. Given the stakes that not only Jünger's but Heidegger's own reading of Nietzsche highlight, Heidegger can hardly avoid the force of this question: "What if the language of metaphysics and metaphysics itself, whether it is that of the living god or of the dead god, in fact constituted, *as* metaphysics, that limit which prevents a transition over the line, i.e., the overcoming of nihilism? If this were the case, would not crossing the line then necessarily have to become a transformation of our saying and demand a transformed relation to the essence of language?" (W, 405/QB, 306). As is the case with Levinas, capitulating to the modern forms of the domination of ontotheology, either as the blind maintenance of the traditional ambiguity or as the embrace of *Ge-Stell*, is not an option for Heidegger. Unlike Levinas, his analysis of the complicity of transcendence in the representational thinking of the transcendental-horizonal gestures of the grounding pursued in and through fundamental ontology, a complicity which is the unavoidable consequence of the amphiboly of transcendence, makes the ability to overcome ontotheology dependent on the ability to overcome transcendence. However, just as the fatality of transcendence is a syntactical one, so too is the overcoming. As late as the work of the 1950s, Heidegger continued to employ structures earlier identified with transcendence, like the ecstatic character of eksistence, and he continued to think the relation between the human and the divine in terms that explicitly evoke the tripartite conception of temporality central to fundamental ontology.[9] What has been overcome is the merely technical, instrumental, or transcendental-logical determination of these structures in favor of a philosophical-poetical determination. This difference is not trivial. In it is Heidegger's final word on the question of metontology, the basis for the movement from fundamental ontology to the history of being, and of the signification of ethics proper to that movement. In it as well is the basis for Levinas's attempt to distinguish his critique of ontotheology from that of Heidegger.

II

If Heidegger's thinking of transcendence undergoes transformation under the pressure of his increasing awareness of the gravity and implications of the ontotheological determination of Western metaphysics, Levinas's demonstrates a consistency of a thinker alerted from the beginning to this pull and its consequences.[10] By 1962, in the "Argument" which begins "Transcendence and Height," we find Levinas rejecting an account of transcendence rooted in the categories of traditional ontology. Starting from the recognition that metaphysical ontology has tended to suppress alterity by privileging the same, both epistemically and ontologically, Levinas moves, through the ideas of freedom and truth, to a sense of alterity which avoids the opposition of, and thus adequation to, the same. To readers of Levinas, this sense is a familiar one: the other opens up a dimension of height, a dimension in which is announced a transcendence other than that of knowledge, truth, and freedom. Lest we confuse this height with that of Olympus, Levinas, like Heidegger, specifies that the opening up of this dimension of height is accomplished in immanence by the putting into question of the subject by the other, a putting into question which can in no way be accounted for in terms of the spontaneity, powers, or capacities of the subject, "Instead of seizing the Other through comprehension . . . the I loses its hold before the absolutely Other, before the *Other*, and, unjustified, can no longer be powerful . . . The event of putting into question is the shame of the I . . ." (*TH*, 95–96/*TrH*, 17). Levinas identifies in the opening of transcendence in the shame of the I a "rediscover[y of] the Cartesian itinerary which moves from the Cogito to the world by passing through the idea of the infinite" (*TH*, 90/*TrH*, 12). In the discussion following "Transcendence and Height," Levinas makes clear what he finds so attractive about this notion.[11] There, he explains what he understands as the benefits of his rediscovery of the Cartesian itinerary in the fact that through this structure, "Cartesianism takes thought outside of immanence" (100/21), not by merely surpassing it in the movement of an infinite to which it never measures up, but by exposing it to "the inadequation par excellence of the idea of the infinite" (*TH*, 90/*TrH*, 12). The significance of Levinas's rediscovery of the Cartesian itinerary is evident also in the opening pages of *Totality and Infinity*. In the preface, Levinas makes an initial attempt to explain the relatedness of the subject to the infinite transcendence of the other by noting that this transcendence can be said to be produced both in the sense of being effected and of being revealed (*TeI*, xiv/*TI*, 26). As Levinas goes on to make clear, when properly understood, the distinction between these two senses collapses; the effectuation and revelation of the transcendence of the other are the same event. This transcendence is produced "in the improbable feat whereby a separated being fixed in its identity, the same, the I, none the less contains in itself what it can neither contain nor receive solely by virtue of its own identity. Subjectivity realizes these impossible exigencies" (*TeI.*, xv/*TI*, 26–27).

While the Cartesian infinite provides Levinas the means to specify the distance between his understanding of transcendence and that of the tradition of metaphysical ontology generally speaking, Levinas typically reserves more specific comments for the phenomenological critique of this tradition. For Levinas, as he makes clear in the beginning of *Otherwise than Being*, this critique is insufficiently radical, locating transcendence as it does in the movement of consciousness, what Husserl calls "immanent transcendence."[12] In contrast, Levinas insists on his own peculiar understanding of transcendence as a "[p]assing over to the other of being, otherwise than being" (AE, 3/OB, 3). Already, in the gap between this understanding and that which has, with phenomenology, become dominant, Levinas marks out the space of his departure from phenomenology. This "passing over" which is not death, not not-being, points to the possibility of a "difference over and beyond that which separates being from nothingness" (AE, 4/OB, 3), and thus, at least on the face of it, points to a difference between beings, between myself and the other, which is already outside of, as before, the identity of knowledge, consciousness, and being. Here, too, the break from the economy of being and nonbeing which "transcendence" names, requires, in response to the exceptionlessness and neutrality upon which this economy rests, the supposition of a unique and incomparable subject. In this context, it is not the Cartesian infinite, but the call to responsibility of the *other* which affords Levinas the resources to specify the possibility of this uniqueness, "Saying is a denuding, of the unqualifiable *one*, the pure *someone*, unique and chosen" (AE, 65/OB, 50). The other calls *me*, in my singularity, taking *me* hostage and demanding my, and no other's, response. This call to responsibility for the other "commands me and ordains me to the *other* . . . It thus diverges from nothingness as well as from being. It provokes this responsibility against my will, that is, by substituting me for the other" (AE, 14/OB, 11). It is with this distinction between the saying and the said, and the reworking of the phenomenological reduction into an ethical one that the distinction makes possible, that Levinas marks the distance between the phenomenological and ethical senses of transcendence.

In the lecture course God and Onto-theo-logy, Levinas returns to his critiques of the metaphysical and phenomenological treatments of transcendence, supplementing them with a discussion specific to the ontotheological determination of transcendence, a determination which he encapsulates under the rubric of "the sacred." In sight here too are the accomplishments and limits of Heidegger's critique of that determination. In response to this ontotheological determination, Levinas calls for a secularized transcendence, the "death of a certain God,"[13] one which corresponds to the possibility that the problem with ontotheology is its reduction of transcendence to a mode of Being, a reduction which deprives thought of precisely the resources to think outside this mode. The figure which Levinas introduces in God and Onto-theo-logy to signify the transcendence of the sacred, the transcendence that he seeks to secularize, is Icarus. This figure appears in Levinas's discussion of the common context of his and Heidegger's criticism of the ontotheological account of transcendence, a context which Levinas abbreviates by reference to conceptual thinking's need for a ground. Invoking as a *locus classicus* of this terrestrial conceptuality the cosmology of Plato's *Timaeus*, Levinas interrupts his exposition with a parenthetical which prefigures much of his secularizing work: "The interplanetary voyage does not shake the identity of repose, but it suppresses the transcendence of Height, which for the Ancients was an essential thing, for Height marked a distance impossible *to walk*; we should think, in this regard, of Icarus's dream. The gaze directed upon the stars is immediately adoration, idolatry . . . Interplanetary voyages . . . show these idols as common stones, on which one can *walk*—a sign that the divine assumes another meaning" (*DMT*, 150/*GDT*, 132). Icarus's dream, to reduce the distance which separates him from the heavens, is a dream the fatal end of which is the common fate of both the metaphysical tradition's and phenomenology's accounts of transcendence. It is also, as Levinas makes clear, a fate which Heidegger's rejection of transcendence in the name of the thinking of Being risks. For Levinas, Heidegger runs this risk not because he is unaware of the gravity which brings Icarus to earth. Levinas explicitly recognizes in Heidegger's rejection a form of secularization that, in its critical moment, is companion to his own. The risk emerges for Levinas in Heidegger's response to what was characterized above as the amphibolousness of transcendence. The overcoming of the transcendental-logical characterization of transcendence, which preserves much of the structure of the term as it was deployed in the context of the Dasein-analytic, may indeed provide access to the "more originary realms" with which Heidegger is ultimately concerned, but this access comes at the risk of missing something else: the concrete signifyingness which is, for Levinas, the meaning of transcendence. This is another version of Icarus's dream, a dream in which "the eyes turned toward the sky separate themselves in some fashion from the body in which they are implanted" (*DMT*, 188/*GDT*, 163).

Key, then, to understanding the distance that Levinas marks between his secularization of transcendence and Heidegger's is the recognition that whenever Levinas engages with Heidegger around the issue of transcendence he engages on precisely the terms that Heidegger specifies in the discussion of metontology in *Metaphysical Foundations*—Dasein's factical existence— though without fail this engagement is produced as a contestation. This is not an approach unique to the discussion in God and Onto-theo-logy. In the pre-ethical writings, for example, the factical ground of Heidegger's fundamental ontology was challenged with competing factical analyses.[14] In shame, insomnia, the feminine, Levinas identifies the concrete sense of transcendence distinct from that announced as the ecstatic-temporal horizon of Dasein's being-in-the-world. Though Levinas will return to some of these analyses in later works, reinterpreting them in the context of his ethical renewal of metaphysics, in his work from the late 1970s, he locates the signification of an appropriately secularized transcendence in hunger.[15] It is this trope which animates Levinas's secularization of transcendence in God and Onto-theo-logy.

Not merely another phenomenological mode affectively challenging those with which Heidegger specifies Dasein's being-in-the-world, hunger has the advantage for Levinas of insulating the hungry from the seductive warmth of the heights of ontotheology, weighing down transcendence which is for Levinas, even under the Heideggerian critique, too eager to leave behind its concrete signification and climb into the heat. Levinas's employment of this trope, if not its analysis, may strain credulity. Do we not see in the face of the hungry something ephemeral, even celestial, as if their lack of food, the emptiness of their bellies, spiritualized their being? It is not, however, the hunger of the ascetic that Levinas evokes in this context, but the hunger of the poor, which precisely refuses the silence of the category or the magic of spiritualization: "Perhaps there is no deafness that allows one to hide from the voice of the afflicted and the needy, a voice that in this sense would be disenchantment itself" (DMT, 194–95/ GDT, 169). There is in this refusal a paradox structured according to the *sens unique* of the ethical relation, a context that Levinas makes explicit in his occasional juxtaposition of hunger and desire, as for example in "Meaning and Sense." "The desirable does not gratify my desire but hollows it out, and somehow nourishes me with new hungers" (MS, 52). "Nourished with hunger" is admittedly a strange diet, and even more strange to insist that it is only thus fed that it is possible to avoid the fate of Icarus.

In order to clarify how the analysis of hunger authorizes a sense of transcendence which escapes this fate, escapes the horizon of ontotheology, as well as establishes an alternative to Heidegger's critique of transcendence, we must specify more precisely the significance of secularization and of the alternatives therein. For as we have already seen, there are other modes of disenchantment than that made concrete in hunger. The target of both Heidegger and Levinas, the disenchantment of the world accomplished by the positivistic, technologically enamored cultural forms which dominate our current experience is a mode of secularization, but it is not, according to either Levinas or Heidegger, one free of idols. There is, to be sure, a sense of transcendence operating in it. Indeed, it is nothing other than a mundanized form of the transcendence of consciousness, which is itself merely the perfection of a possibility inherent in the tradition of Western rationality (DMT, 190/GDT, 165–66). Just as surely, this transcendence is accomplished in the death of a certain divinity, but only in replacing it with another. "[T]he idolatry of transcendence becomes celestial geometry, astronomy, and ballistics; light becomes a chemistry of the untouchable; contemplation, a search for the truth . . . the given comes to fulfill the intentional aiming of the gaze . . . Thus die the visible gods" (SH, 8). Techno-scientism demonstrates the limits of one strand of the ontotheological confines of thought, and this secularization can legitimately be hailed as a stage in the progress of human self-understanding, but, as both Levinas and Heidegger are at pains to remind us, it is not the end of this progress.

Though techno-scientism is not the end of thinking, it is an end to the agreement between Levinas and Heidegger. As we have seen, for Heidegger the sway of ontotheology in the nihilism of modernity requires an abandonment of the project of fundamental ontology in its rootedness in Dasein's facticity in favor of the truth and history of being. This in turn leads Heidegger to a critical circumscription of modernity about which Levinas has reservations indicative of his understanding of the differences between his own mode of secularization and Heidegger's. The immediate context of these concerns is Heidegger's critique of technology, which for Levinas is wanting precisely in its own deafness to the voice of the hungry: "The condemnation of technology . . . has itself become a comfortable rhetoric, forgetful of the responsibilities to which a 'developing' humanity, more and more numerous, call and which, *without the development of technology, could not be fed*" (SH, 9).[16] At first glance, the thrust of this and similar passages seems to be a condemnation of a romanticized and depoliticized consciousness, confident in its self-possession and oblivious to the real plight of the less fortunate. However, this reading, unsupportable in the face of an even minimally charitable review of Heidegger's meditations on technology, completely misses the significance of the invocation of the hungry. When we approach the criticism from the ethical sense of hunger, a much more profound distance is opened between Levinas and Heidegger.

As we have seen, for Levinas transcendence signifies concretely. In this, he initially finds common cause with Heidegger's attempt to specify a sense of transcendence other than that of the ontotheological tradition. Though for both Heidegger and Levinas, the secularization of transcendence is produced as the subjectivity of the subject, for Heidegger this production remains inadequate. In the specific sense in which Heidegger understands the relationship between Dasein's factical existence and the question of being, the amphibology of transcendence, signifying concretely, remains complicit with the hidden metaphysical horizonality of fundamental ontology. Levinas, too, is wary of an overly subjective secularization, particularly to the extent that it becomes a pretext for the idolatry of a desacralized world. However, Levinas, rather than retreating from the specification of transcendence as subjectivity in a syntactical flight toward a poetics of being, weighs the subject down by locating it in the intrigue of responsibility. This is the significance of the voice of the hungry: "Such a voice would lead to an other secularization, whose agent would be the humility of hunger. A secularization of the world effected by the deprivation of hunger, which would signify a transcendence beginning not as a first cause but in man's corporeality" (DMT, 195/GDT, 169). In hunger there is no satisfaction. It is, as Levinas says, "*privation par excellence*," and as such already an-archy. The voice of the hungry is a cry without response, a vocative without a locative, in either ontotheological subjectivity or being. There is no poetry in hunger, at least in that "hunger that no music appeases, and that secularizes all that romantic eternity" (196, 170). In the intrigue of the infinite, hunger gives voice to prayer.

Does Levinas thus respond to Heidegger's syntactical secularization with a semantic one?[17] There is surely a boldness to a challenge to onto-theology—or to a poetics of being—that so readily invokes the *à-Dieu*. But boldness is not recklessness, and the prayer of the hungry is not necessarily a prayer for satisfaction. In the secularization of hunger, Levinas finds the resources for addressing the question he poses to Heidegger and us. For the prayerful voice of the hungry, in addressing itself *à-Dieu*, signifies mean-ingfully without signifying being. In what amounts to a final rejoinder to Heidegger's impatience with and suspicion of the apparently unavoidable reduction of transcendence to representation, Levinas agrees, "The inter-pretation of affectivity that holds that the latter rests upon representation is successful to the degree to which affectivity is taken as tendency whose aspirations can be satisfied in pleasure or remain unsatisfied in suffering" (*DMT*, 243/*GDT*, 214). His disagreement lies in his refusal to accept that this tendency exhausts the significance of affectivity. In his insistence that "in hunger . . . transcendence progressively appears," (*DMT*, 197/*GDT*, 171), Levinas marks the possibility of a meaning otherwise than being, as well as other than ontotheology, of, a "transcendence that can be called true with a diachronous truth, without synthesis, higher than the truths one confirms" (*DMT*, 254/*GDT*, 224).

Where then do we stand, the unavoidably but still not determinately secular? It is not, as one might suspect, in the face of a necessity to choose between poetry and prayer. The contingency of history (or perhaps the awkwardness of the presentation) certainly encourages the perception of succession, of one possibility superseded by another. In the face of the nihi-latingly idolatrous techno-scientism which daily extends its reach, seeking to reduce both our poetry and our prayer to its sway, there is surely an imperative to retain as many desperately needed modes of resistance as pos-sible. The present work has aimed at tracing the contours of the confronta-tion between poetry and prayer in the hope that clarifying its terms would reveal lines of addressing the challenge which Heidegger's and Levinas's disagreement about transcendence revolves. The first contour revealed, that the disagreement concerns in part the gravity of (metaphysical) language, should both hearten us and confirm the importance of our focus. Though Levinas balks at Heidegger's call to jettison the term "transcendence" in the face of its complicity with the ontotheological tradition of metaphysics, his hesitation is neither a refutation of Heidegger's concerns nor a simple rejection of the terms of Heidegger's maintenance of the structures which transcendence named. To the extent that he contests Heidegger's call to the thinking-of-Being, it is that for him such a call frees us from a certain terrestrial conceptuality only by reinscribing the Icarean dream. In response he points us back to the concrete signifyingness of transcendence as a "desire for the Good," in order both to highlight for us the risk of this reinscription as well as to acknowledge a risk, a "possible confusion" that his own account of transcendence runs (*DMT*, 253/*GDT*, 224). Responding to this possible confusion, the confusion of illeity with the neuter, requires more than just the *à-Dieu*. It is also, he insists, "necessary to return [his account of transcendence] to the signification of every ethical intrigue, to the divine comedy in which responsibility is implicated and without which the word 'God' could not have arisen" (*DMT*, 253/*GDT*, 224). This divine comedy is an origin no less obscure than the origins of comedy itself,[18] but it is as certainly an origin of poetry as it is for prayer.[19]

NOTES

I would like to thank the participants of the 2005 meeting of the Levinas Research Seminar, and particularly Eric Nelson, for their comments and suggestions on the first draft of this chapter.

1. Cf. also (21/17).

2. Cf., Martin Heidegger, *Metaphysische Anfangsgründe Der Logik Im Ausgang Von Leibniz*. Gesamtausgabe 26 (Frankfurt am Main: V. Klostermann, 1978), 144–45; Martin Heidegger, *The Metaphysical Foundations of Logic*, trans. Michael Heim (Bloomington: Indiana University Press, 1984), 117; and Martin Heidegger, "On the Essence of Ground," trans. William McNeill, in *Pathmarks* (Cambridge: Cambridge University Press, 1998), 126; Martin Heidegger, "Vom Wesen Des Grundes," *Holzwege* (Frankfurt am Main: Vittorio Klostermann, 1976), 100.

3. The first of the lecture courses devoted to logical topics, *Logik. Die Frage nach der Warheit* (GA, 21) was devoted to Aristotle.

4. The first of these movements, of course, was worked out in section 2 of part 1 of Being and Time, the second was to be section 3, which was never completed. The third is the topic of discussion of the appendix in *Metaphysical Foundations*, and it is seen almost nowhere else in the Heideggerian corpus.

5. On this point, see also Robert Bernasconi, "'The Double Concept of Philosophy' And the Place of Ethics in Being and Time," *Research in Phenomenology* 17 (1988): 51.

6. "Es gilt, durch die Bewegtheit der Radikalisierung und Universalisierung die Ontologie zu dem in ihr latenten Umschlag zu bringen." Heidegger, Metaphysische Anfangsgründe Der Logik Im Ausgang Von Leibniz, 201.

7. The uncertainty about when this appendix was written does leave open the possibility that this discussion was a product of Heidegger's later disillusionment with the possibility of fundamental ontology and that he is thus reinterpreting his strong

claims in terms of its impossibility. According to Bernasconi, "'The Double Concept of Philosophy' And the Place of Ethics in *Being and Time*," the proper response to this concern is to emphasize the preparatory character of fundamental ontology, in particular in relation to the unity of fundamental ontology and metontology in the metaphysics of Dasein, which must be understood as an articulation of the essence of Dasein itself. Fundamental ontology would then be a necessary first step for this analysis, a step which, despite its impossibility, must be carried out as if it were possible. It is not clear, however, whether this explanation accounts for the broader remarks made by Heidegger in *Metaphysical Foundations, Sein und Zeit*, and *Basic Problems* that indicate that he feels fundamental ontology has general ontological import and is not just directed back at the ontic-existentiell level. Perhaps, however, Heidegger is submitting himself to this necessary illusion as well.

8. Cf., "Lecture 5," Martin Heidegger, *Der Satz Vom Grund*, Gesamtausgabe; Bd. 10 ed. (Frankfurt am Main: V. Klostermann, 1997): 49–60; Martin Heidegger, *The Principle of Reason*, trans. Reginald Lilly (Bloomington: Indiana University Press, 1991), 32–40. The verse in question, "The rose is without why: it blooms because it blooms,/It pays not attention to itself, asks not whether it is seen" comes from Silesius's *The Cherubinic Wanderer*.

9. On the relationship between the four-fold and temporality, see Rex Gilliland, "The Fourfold and Temporality: Whence the Mortals?" (unpublished ms.).

10. This is not to suggest that Levinas's thinking on this issue is monolithic. As Bettina Bergo has ably demonstrated in her "Ontology, Transcendence, and Immanence in Emmanuel Levinas's Philosophy," Levinas's use of the term, particularly in its phenomenological/ontological employment, underwent substantial development from his earliest writings. Bettina Bergo, *Ontology, Transcendence, and Immanence in Emmanuel Levinas's Philosophy*, Available: www.philo.umontreal.ca/dept/documents/OntologyandTranscendence.pdf. However, a description of another transcendence, and in particular its distance from the phenomenological understanding, has been a feature of Levinas's work since *Existence and Existents* and *Time and the Other*. Cf., for example, Emmanuel Levinas, *Le Temps Et L'autre*, Quadrige, 43, 6e ed. (Paris: Presses Universitaires de France, 1996), 47–49; Emmanuel Levinas, *Time and the Other and Additional Essays* (Pittsburgh: Duquesne University Press, 1987, 64–66); Emmanuel Levinas, *Totalité Et Infini: Essai Sur L'extériorité*, Phaenomenologica; 8, 4e ed. (The Hague, Boston, Lancaster: M. Nijhoff, 1984), 20; Emmanuel Levinas, *Totality and Infinity: An Essay on Exteriority*, trans. A. Lingis (Pittsburgh: Duquesne University Press, 1988), 49; Emmanuel Levinas, "Langage Et Proximité," *En Découvrant L'existence Avec Husserl Et Heidegger* (Paris: Vrin, 1988), 226; Emmanuel Levinas, "Language and Proximity," in *Collected Philosophical Papers*, ed. Alphonso Lingis (Dordrecht, Boston, Lancaster: Martinus Nijhoff, 1987), 117; and Emmanuel Levinas, "Secularization and Hunger," *Graduate Faculty Philosophy Journal* 20–21, nos. 2–1 (1998).

11. The discussion in "Transcendence and Height" is a recapitulation and elaboration of comments made in Levinas, *Totalité Et Infini: Essai Sur L'extériorité*: 185–87, Levinas, *Totality and Infinity: An Essay on Exteriority*: 210–12.

12. *"The world of transcendent 'res' is entirely referred to consciousness and, more particularly, not to some logically conceived consciousness but to actual consciousness"* (Ideen I, §49, 115–16/92).

13. This formulation is from John Llewelyn's admirable *Emmanuel Levinas: The Genealogy of Ethics* (New York: Routledge, 1995), 149. It can also be found in a note by Jacques Rolland to "God and Onto-theo-logy," Emmanuel Levinas, *Dieu, La Mort Et Le Temps* (Paris: B. Grasset, 1993), 187n1, Emmanuel Levinas, *God, Death, and Time* (Stanford, CA: Stanford University Press, 2000), 275n1. The present discussion shares Llewelyn's concern to specify the distinct character of Levinas's contestation of the ontotheological tradition. In Llewelyn's discussion, Levinas's partner in the movement beyond this tradition is Nietzsche, and the question raised concerns the success of Levinas in avoiding a "post-ontotheological version of the theological transcendentalism." Llewelyn, *Emmanuel Levinas: The Genealogy of Ethics*, 155. As was suggested above, a similar question should be posed to Heidegger. The secularization of transcendence detailed in what follows can serve an affirmative answer for Levinas's part.

14. On this, see also Bergo, "Ontology, Transcendence, and Immanence in Emmanuel Levinas's Philosophy."

15. Most notably in "Secularization and Hunger." This analysis is repeated, often verbatim, in "God and Onto-theo-logy."

16. This criticism of Heidegger is repeated, more or less explicitly, in a number of places; for example, "For [Heidegger's critique of modernity] . . . is tied to a denunciation of technology. I claim that without technology, we would be in no position to feed the Third World" ("In the Name of the Other," in *Is It Righteous to Be?*, 190).

17. "[T]hat is the great novelty of a way of thinking in which the word God ceases orienting life by expressing the unconditional foundation of the world and cosmology, and reveals, in the face of the other man, the secret of his semantics." Emmanuel Levinas, *Alterity and Transcendence* (New York: Columbia University Press, 1999), 96.

18. Aristotle, *Poetics*, 1449aff.

19. Hent de Vries, in his *Minimal Theologies: Critiques of Secular Reason in Adorno and Levinas*, argues for a similar complication at the heart of Levinas's thought. Cf., in particular, Hent de Vries, *Minimal Theologies: Critiques of Secular Reason in Adorno and Levinas* (Baltimore: Johns Hopkins University Press, 2005), 459ff.

WORKS CITED

Bergo, Bettina. "Ontology, Transcendence, and Immanence in Emmanuel Levinas's Philosophy." *www.philo.umontreal.ca/dept/documents/OntologyandTranscendence.pdf*.

Bernasconi, Robert. "'The Double Concept of Philosophy' and the Place of Ethics in Being and Time." *Research in Phenomenology* 17 (1988): 41–57.

Heidegger, Martin. "Brief Über Den Humanismus." *Wegmarken*. Frankfurt am Main: Vittorio Klosterman, 1976, 313–64. Referred to as BH in the body of the text.

———. *Der Satz Vom Grund*. Gesamtausgabe 10. Frankfurt am Main: V. Klostermann, 1997.

———. *Die Grundprobleme Der Phänomenologie*. Gesamtausgabe 24: Abteilung 2, Vorlesungen 1923–1944. Ed. Martin Heidegger. Frankfurt am Main: V. Klostermann, 1975. Referred to as GP in the body of the text.

————. *Discourse on Thinking: A Translation of Gelassenheit.* New York: Harper & Row, 1966. Referred to as *DT* in the body of the text.

————. "Letter On "Humanism."" In *Pathmarks.* Cambridge; New York: Cambridge University Press, 1998. 239–76. Referred to as LH in the body of the text.

————. *Metaphysische Anfangsgründe Der Logik Im Ausgang Von Leibniz.* Gesamtausgabe 26 : Abteilung 2, Vorlesungen 1923–1944. Ed. Martin Heidegger. Frankfurt am Main: V. Klostermann, 1978. Referred to as *MAL* in the body of the text

————. "On the Essence of Ground," trans. William McNeill, in *Pathmarks.* Cambridge; New York: Cambridge University Press, 1998. 97–135.

————. "On the Question of Being." In *Pathmarks.* Cambridge; New York: Cambridge University Press, 1998. 291–322. Referred to as QB in the body of the text.

————. *The Metaphysical Foundations of Logic,* trans. Michael Heim. Bloomington: Indiana University Press, 1984. Referred to as *MFL* in the body of the text.

————. *The Principle of Reason,* trans. Reginald Lilly. Bloomington: Indiana University Press, 1991.

————. "Vom Wesen Des Grundes." In *Holzwege.* Frankfurt am Main: Vittorio Klostermann, 1976. 123–75.

————. *Wegmarken.* Gesamtausgabe 9. Frankfurt am Main: Klostermann, 1976. Referred to as *W* in the body of the text.

Levinas, Emmanuel. *Alterity and Transcendence.* New York: Columbia University Press, 1999.

————. *Autrement Qu'être Ou Au-Delà De L'essence.* Dordrecht, Boston, London: Kluwer Academic Publishers, 1991. Referred to as AE in the body of the text.

————. *Dieu, La Mort Et Le Temps.* Paris: B. Grasset, 1993. Referred to as *DMT* in the body of the text.

————. *God, Death, and Time,* trs. Bettina Bergo. Stanford: Stanford University Press, 2000. Referred to as GDT in the body of the text.

————. "Langage Et Proximité." In *En Découvrant L'existence Avec Husserl Et Heidegger.* Paris: Vrin, 1988. 217–36.

————. "Language and Proximity," trans. Alphonso Lingis.In *Collected Philosophical Papers,* ed. Alphonso Lingis. Dordrecht; Boston; Lancaster: Martinus Nijhoff, 1987. 109–26.

————. *Le Temps Et L'autre.* Quadrige, 43. 6e ed. Paris: Presses Universitaires de France, 1996.

————. *Otherwise than Being or Beyond Essence,* trans. Alphonso Lingis. Dordrech,; Boston, London: Kluwer Academic Publishers, 1991. Referred to as OB in the body of the text.

————. "Secularization and Hunger." *Graduate Faculty Philosophy Journal* 20-21.2-1 (1998): 3–12. Referred to as SH in the body of the text.

————. *Time and the Other and Additional Essays.* Pittsburgh, PA: Duquesne University Press, 1987.

————. *Totalité Et Infini: Essai Sur L'extériorité.* Phaenomenologica; 8. 4e ed. The Hague, Boston, Lancaster: M. Nijhoff, 1984. Referred to as *TeI* in the body of the text.

————. *Totality and Infinity: An Essay on Exteriority,* trans. A. Lingis. Pittsburgh: Duquesne University Press, 1988. Referred to as *TI* in the body of the text.

————. "Transcendance Et Hauteur." *Bulletin de la Société Française de Philosophie* 56.3 (1962): 89–113.

————. "Transcendence and Height," trans. Simon Critchley. In *Emmaunel Levinas: Basic Philosophical Writings*, ed. Adriaan T. Peperzak, Simon Critchley Peperzak, Robert Bernasconi. Bloomington; Indianapolis: Indiana University Press, 1996, 11–31.

Llewelyn, John. *Emmanuel Levinas: The Genealogy of Ethics*. London, New York: Routledge, 1995.

Vries, Hent de. *Minimal Theologies: Critiques of Secular Reason in Adorno and Levinas*. Baltimore: Johns Hopkins University Press, 2005.

CHAPTER THREE

HEIDEGGER, LEVINAS, AND THE OTHER OF HISTORY

Eric S. Nelson

INTRODUCTION

In the early work *The Theory of Intuition in Husserl's Phenomenology*, Levinas upheld Husserl's critique of historicism, which he interpreted as the reduction of validity to empirical historical contingencies. But Levinas also noted the need to pursue the "origins of reality," including the origins of consciousness, perception, and the sciences, in the historical situation of life: "Historicality and temporality form the very substantiality of human substance."[1] Although Levinas employed the hermeneutical language of returning to "historical life" as the context of intuition and theory in 1930, he did not adopt the more existential or life-philosophical strategy of intensifying the feeling of life and its historicity in historical decision and resolve. Instead Levinas would soon criticize this strategy as the destruction of the freedom and personhood of the individual in his initial reflections on Hitlerism.[2] In these reflections, historical facticity and finitude become the brutal fact of being and the "being there" that assaults and traumatizes human freedom and the person's dignity.[3]

In this context, facticity is an inappropriable oppressive presence without refuge or escape. Philosophy is not about finitude in phenomena such as shame, Levinas maintained in 1935, but about the "I"; later, it is separation that is radically contrasted with any thinking committed to finitude.[4]

The anonymous and impersonal "there is" precludes the temporality and individuation that can only occur through the diachronic and asymmetrical relation with the other.[5] Lost in its own historical and ontological immanence, finitude is the nonrecognition of the infinite. Heidegger's finitude, an atheistic and cruel oblivion to the other, is "a regime of power more inhuman than mechanism."[6]

With the exception of the conclusion of *The Theory of Intuition*, in which the historicity of life is distinguished from reductive historicism, and occasional remarks on the interpersonal and potentially ethical character of history, Levinas is persistently wary of philosophical discourses of history and historicity and, particularly, how they are employed in Heidegger's writings.[7] For the most part, history is totality; it is the order wherein suffering is justified, justice left undone, the other effaced, and the personal sacrificed for the impersonal.[8] The philosophy of history, secularized theodicy which is already injustice to both humans and God for Levinas, is contrasted with the ethics of alterity that interrupts the historical and its compulsive repetition in answering the other's need and demanding justice. Whereas history contextualizes and relativizes, the other person is irreducible to contexts and conditions:

> History as a relationship between men ignores a position of the I before the other in which the other remains transcendent with respect to me. Though of myself I am not exterior to history, I do find in the Other a point that is absolute with regard to history—not by amalgamating with the Other, but in speaking with him. History is worked over by the ruptures of history, in which a judgment is borne upon it. When man truly approaches the Other he is uprooted from history.[9]

REPOSING THE QUESTION OF HISTORY

Levinas interprets Heidegger as the culmination of a thinking of history that does violence to the other by relativizing the ethical to the historical.[10] Levinas, like Leo Strauss, criticized how Heidegger radicalized historicism without in the end overcoming it. In this chapter, I repose the question of Heidegger's thinking of history as decision and event in the 1920s and in the posthumously published works of the late 1930s. The importance of the question of history to Heidegger's thought is undeniable, and yet its import remains underappreciated. Beginning with the early Karl Löwith and Herbert Marcuse, Heidegger's facticity was interpreted as "pseudoconcreteness" to the extent that approaching history through the history of philosophy distanced thought from the materiality of real historical processes, structures, and agents. In Heidegger's analysis, however, philosophy does not signify a derivative or superstructural intellectual history but concerns questions of how human beings exist, that is, the basic comportment and disposition of human existence as being-there (Dasein) in-the-world. Heidegger's destructuring confrontation with the history of ontology and metaphysics has a critical and transformative dimension to the extent that it engages ordinary and everyday ways of behaving, as structured by tradition and average public life.

Heidegger's path was repeatedly impacted by historical events that elicited further historical reflection. After notoriously actively and enthusiastically supporting National Socialism in its initial years in power, a well-documented commitment deserving the compelling criticism that Levinas pursued from the 1930s to his death, Heidegger began by the mid-1930s to confront (*if insufficiently*) its destructive giganticism, machination, racial biologism, and totalitarian integration in the context of the unfolding of Western metaphysics.[11] Heidegger's reflections concerning historicity and history are informed and distorted by the crisis of his times. They are problematic and should be interpreted within the ethical and social-political parameters indicated by Levinas's critique of Heidegger. Nevertheless, in their questionability, they also reveal a questioning of previous and contemporary approaches to and stagings of the historical that continue to speak to our contemporary situation.

Heidegger's works of the late 1930s resonate with and transform his more "existential" account of history developed in the 1920s. They radicalize his earlier distinction between history as an external object of inquiry and history as an event and performative enactment of being. In his historical writings, readers can observe how Heidegger practiced history. Although primarily oriented toward the history of Western philosophy and its modern consequences, including basic features of modernity such as technology and bureaucracy, they can be interpreted as an exemplar or conditional model for historical inquiry. Heidegger attempted in these works to encounter the past not "as it was"—as a retrieval of the past in its past presence, the identity of pure unsullied origins, or the "first beginning"—but from the nonidentity and interruptive force of what he called the other beginning (*der andere Anfang*).

Heidegger articulated this other beginning as accessible only in its relation to and difference from the first. This "confrontational" strategy (*Auseinandersetzung*) would challenge both reifying the past in its empirical factuality and reducing it to a construct imposed on it by the present. Heidegger accordingly unfolds the temporal relationality and dynamics of the historical as well as the possibility of a different relation with history in which the present can encounter and answer back to the past. Such historical responsiveness, a letting or releasement (*Gelassenheit*) allowing beings to be immanently encountered and engaged on their own terms, would move toward their past phenomenologically. The past would be welcomed to show itself from itself even as that past escapes and remains irreducible to present efforts—whether narrative or causal—to grasp and control it.

Descriptive-analytic approaches to history risk missing the present situation in which the past is received and interpreted, due to the historicity and temporal difference of past and present. Historical constructivism threatens the idealistic reduction of the past's alterity to the sameness of the present or a current system of signifiers such as consciousness, language, or society. Heidegger's works are a venture to rethink history through the possibility of encountering and responding to the past in its historicity, in both its continuity and discontinuity with the present, by pursuing the temporality of being as an inherently future-oriented—and not merely subjectively or objectively grounded—decision (Ent-scheidung) and event (Ereignis).

Heidegger's interpretation of history has implications for reflection on history and historical inquiry, since it entails that historical events have an ontological as well as ontic dimension. That is, history involves a relational way or manner of being as much as it concerns objectively and instrumentally available entities and structures. If the historical is both relational, as a between (Zwischen) or a nexus (Zusammenhang) from and to which understanding proceeds, and asymmetrical, such that there is an unavoidable alterity in relating past, present, and future, then it is insufficient to consider history as consisting of temporally equivalent factual occurrences or socially constructed objects. Historical works form, disclose, and allow a world to be encountered and engaged. They do not only descriptively reproduce events or replicate subjective and intersubjective interests and preferences. Beyond history construed as reproducing the empirically given or the socially constructed, and truth as consisting of correspondence with the actual or the coherence of a system of statements, the historical more fundamentally and constitutively occurs as the performative enactment, disclosure, and appropriation of a world. In disclosing and concealing, gathering together and dispersing, and closing off and opening up, historical works constitute a world and a way of being in that world.

"Being-historical thinking" (Seinsgeschichtliches Denken, as thinking history in the context of the history of being) is not a methodology or program for historical inquiry. It does have repercussions for such inquiry by diverging from history conceived of as the construction of first-person narratives and third-person causal explanations according to teleological, causal, and authorial schemas. This deviant history opens up and allows for hearing the other and unsaid of history and—mindfully and critically rereading Heidegger through Levinas—those silenced and victimized in history. Historically mindful reflection (Besinnung) elucidates a hermeneutical event of disclosure—via understanding, interpretation, and appropriation—in the context of its standing-outside-of-itself and expropriation in the facticity and possibilities of historical being.

ANOTHER HISTORY

Heidegger reconsiders the distinction derived from Dilthey and Yorck between lived *Geschichte* and conceptualized *Historie* in section 74 of *Being and Time*, contrasting history as enactment and occurrence (*Vollzugsge-schichte*) and history as the representation and science of objectively present objects (*Objektsgeschichte*).[12] History as enacted (*Geschichte*) indicates the absolutely originary history (*ursprüngliche Geschichte schlechthin*) as the fundamental temporality of being and event of existence (Dasein). History as represented (*Historie*), however, objectifies, reifies, and forgets the *Geschichte* that Dasein essentially is. Whereas *Geschichte* refers to history articulated from the horizon of the question of the meaning of being, which is reart-iculated as the history of the event and truth of being, *Historie* refers to the models of history found in the ordinary understanding of history as presence and re-presentation, and which continue to inform historiography and the philosophy of history. These understandings of *Historie* presuppose the "vulgar concept of time" analyzed in *Being and Time* as underlying everyday and philosophical understandings of time—whether linear or cyclical. These understandings block access to the history of being, obscuring rather than clarifying the history that we ourselves are.

Heidegger first discussed history in terms of the priority of event (*Ereignis*) and enactment (*Vollzug*), which are used in his early lecture courses in opposition to the traditional concepts of subject and object, and in terms of the difference between "lived history" (*Geschichte*) and historical science (*Historie*) in the situation of crisis and engagement with *Lebens-* and *Existenzphilosophie* after the First World War. Heidegger insisted that his concern was with questions of "historical life" in its motility and facticity as opposed to the science and philosophy of history that presupposes that life without addressing it.[13] Heidegger proposed turning from historiology and object oriented history (*Historie* or *Objektsgeschichte*)—that for him is typical of previous historical inquiry—to originary history (*Geschichte*) as a lived or existential enactment (*Vollzugsgeschichte*).[14]

The intensification of the historical moment as an originary and absolute historicity is "unrepeatable" (GA, 60:88. Despite this life-philosophical rhetoric of the intensification and heightening of the singular and exceptional, Heidegger criticizes the irrationalist absorption in the pure immanence and brute singularity of factical historical life, which Levinas charges him with perpetuating. Heidegger emphasizes throughout the 1920s the necessity of abstraction, conceptualization, and formalization in regard

to life—via formal indication and hermeneutical anticipation—in order to
open up the concrete multiplicity of that life. Rather than celebrating the
intuitive self-certainty of life and its power, their fragility and uncertainty
are revealed. The singularity and uniqueness of the moment (*Augenblick*) is
a crisis calling for an individuating decision (*Entscheidung*) and resoluteness
informed by the situation. This dynamic and unstable moment destabilizes
pre-existing concepts and habits, evading and resisting normalization and
being subsumed under categories and universals.

The young Heidegger argues that the Neokantian focus on individuals
acting according to universal concepts never begins to access more fundamental questions of the historically singular being, which is in "each
moment" called to decide who it is by how it is, and the occurrence and
enactment of that being's individuation in relation to others, its world, and
itself. Whereas previous philosophy remains in the security and self-satisfaction of derivative *Historie*, *Geschichte* needs to be existentially broached
in relation to the life that it is. That life shows itself in the security and
questionability of the hermeneutical situation and generation to which it
belongs, and which does not only enable and open up concrete possibilities but also inevitably disquiets, limits, and shatters them. The historical
situation is an alienated burden as much as a fulfillment of life (GA, 60:31–
33, 37). Its disquiet threatens historical existence (Dasein) with its own
questionability and tendency toward ruination (*Ruinanz*) such that understanding agonistically occurs and is enacted through counterruination and
Auseinandersetzung, understood as an interpretive differentiation (GA, 61:2).

Critically reading Heidegger's thinking of history in the context of
Levinas's critique leaves us with significant questions: (1) How does Heidegger understand history differently than the everyday, traditional, and
scientific conception that he interrogates? (2) What alteration does the *Contributions to Philosophy* introduce with reference to Heidegger's earlier portrayal of history, in particular since he himself criticizes his earlier thought
as remaining caught within the paradigm of the philosophy of the subject?
(3) To what extent can we continue to think history with Heidegger in
light of the genuine ethical deficits and limits exposed in Levinas's forceful
evaluation of the history of ontology as a history of violence?

HISTORY AS DECISION AND EVENT

The historical does not denote a manner of grasping and exploring
but the very event (*Ereignis*) itself. The historical is not the past, not
even the present, but the future, that which is commended to will,
expectation, care.[15] Levinas's analysis of history in Heidegger is based

on writings published during his lifetime and does not take into account
the posthumously published writings; in particular, *Contributions to
Philosophy*, the basic task of which is to prepare for a possible decision
while reinterpreting "decision" itself.[16] Heidegger asks *what* this decision
is about and answers that it is about history and the loss of history,
belonging to being or to nonbelonging in the abandonment of beings
(GA, 65:44, 100). This decision is about historicity and the lack of
history and is a decision for or against history (GA, 65:13, 32, 504). It
is not a decision about history, neutrally evaluating or explaining it from
outside, but a decision enacting history in its historicity or the specificity
and singularity of its historical being.

Heidegger asks *who* is to make this decision and replies with seemingly
contradictory answers. It is being (*Sein*) who decides; it is the few and the
rare who decide (GA, 65:96); it is "everyone" who decides (GA, 65:100).
Who then decides? It is the singular, the few, and the many who decide
even in abdicating deciding and in not wishing to decide (GA, 65:97–100).
Heidegger inquires into *how* this decision is to be made. History is not
"made" or produced but occurs. It transpires in such a way that it can be
intimated and prepared for or not, as expectation is exposed to the unexpected. What then does this decision about history signify, and how is this
decision itself historical? Who decides history, and who is it that is thereby
historically decided? These are the guiding questions of Heidegger's thinking
of the history of being in the mid- and late 1930s. It is a time of distress
and of deciding and evading decision in reply to this distress and abandonment. More than this, to transit from Heidegger's to Levinas's idiom, it is
a moment of injustice and irresponsibility to the other that problematizes
Heidegger's thinking.
    Heidegger intensifies the strategy of historical destructuring (*Destruk-
tion*), first developed in his interpretation of early Christianity in the early
1920s and familiar from *Being and Time*, as confrontation (*Auseinandersetzung*) in the 1930s. *Auseinandersetzung* is a setting-apart-from-one-other and
differentiation through expectation and care, that is, the receptive releasement or letting of a nonviolent encounter and nondominating confrontation, which is suggestive in the context of Levinas's asymmetrical ethics
and critique of violence. Deeply concerned with issues of violence, power,
and domination during this period, Heidegger replied to the brutality of
his time not by abandoning the agonistic dimension of his thought but
by speaking of nonpower (*Ohnmacht*) as something other than a vice as
well as of a nonviolent and noncoercive contest and struggle that would
contrast with and contest its ideological deformation in the self-assertion of
the will and struggle for existence.[17] While Heidegger embraced the violent

language of the assertion of the will in 1933, notably in the *Rektoratsrede*, soon thereafter he rejected such self-aggrandizing of the subject. Heidegger would question the priority of its authorship and willing, arguing for the priority of the work over the agency, genius, and will of the subject and conclude that genuine willing is a letting rather than a forcing; "all willing should be grounded in letting" (GA, 45:40–41). It is not only Levinas that questions Heidegger's political commitments. Heidegger's growing questioning of power and violence, its gigantism, interventionism, and totalization, makes the *Contributions* a highly political and politically ambiguous work.[18]

Heidegger's articulation of history (*Geschichte*) as intimating an alternative to ordinary understandings of history and the dominant models of historiography and the philosophy and science of history (*Historie*) is crucial to the *Contributions*. Heidegger indicated the traces of the *other* of this history, an other history to the present history of totalizing and destructive machination. Contrary to the reduction of the past and future to the interests and projects of the present, Heidegger wagers to open up history through another history. This history is not "future-oriented" in the usual sense that the future will merely continue and reaffirm the prejudices of the present. It is oriented by the unfamiliarity and noncalculability of the futural always-still-other "not yet," a not yet that would not continue and reproduce the present but potentially place it into question. This other history, which lets history be open to the other of history that evades historical understanding and calculation, is the history of the "other beginning." The other beginning is articulated in thoughtful confrontation with the history of the first beginning, as it unfolds from the birth of metaphysics to the totalizing technological worldview of modernity. Heidegger's critique of the narratives and explanations of historiography and the philosophy of history point toward an-other history—history as the history of being rather than of beings, the history of the other beginning that begins to be heard and said through the historical encounter with and remembrance of the first beginning.

Heidegger begins *Die Geschichte des Seyns* from 1938–40: " 'The history of being' is the name for the attempt to bring the truth of being as enowning event into word for thinking, and familiarize the word and its sayability as an essential ground for historical humans."[19] Heidegger's enunciation of history through the question of the history of being, as the happening of the truth of being, is an alternative to the narrative and explanatory models of historiographical and philosophical approaches to history—with all their political implications—and their basis in the metaphysics of the first beginning that thinks being as constancy and presence and time as conforming with the present (i.e., presentism) (GA, 65:31): "But just as little [as it is the past] is this happening the present. The happening and the happenings of history are primordially and always the future, that which in a concealed way comes toward us, a revelatory process that puts us at risk, and thus is compelling in advance. The future is the beginning of all happening. Everything is enclosed within the beginning" (GA, 45:36–37).

HISTORIE AND GESCHICHTE

Heidegger's elucidation of history in the 1930s is less concerned with the question of existential individuation than with the history of being, which initially seems abstract and removed in comparison with his earlier, more emphatic and individualistic language. The distinction between *Historie* and *Geschichte* remains in play even as the meaning of these basic words changes. The history of being is ensnared in the history of its concealment and forgetting in metaphysics and involves the entangled difference between the calculability of historiography and the science of history (*Historie*) and the immeasurability and singularity of occurring history (*Geschichte*) itself.[20] It might appear as if historiographical history is more interested in the different, individual, and singular in focusing on empirical plurality and individuality, yet it is attentive to these for the purposes of comparison, categorization, and calculation (GA, 65:151).

The science and philosophy of history obstruct contact with the question of historicity, of the singular and unique in its occasion and happening. Heidegger therefore comments that "historiographical comparison grasps the differences only to place them into a wider and more entangled field of comparability. All comparison is essentially an equalizing, a referral back to the same that as such never even enters into knowing awareness but rather makes up what is self-evident in terms of which all explanation and relating receives its clarity" (GA, 65:151). It not only fails to broach but hinders questioning that which is singular and unique. This is not fortuitous, as the narratives and explanatory schemes of historiographical history are implicated in the calculable and designed world of modernity that culminates in the reduction of the meaning and truth of being (*Sein*) to being abandoned amidst beings (*Seiende*). This vision of history belongs to the history of metaphysics, in which this history emerged as ontotheology and theodicy and was subsequently secularized in humanism, beginning in the cyclical repetition of nature and the divine and concluding with the idea of progress, culture, and values.

In theodicy, traditionally the justification of God's justice in the face of worldly evil and suffering, history becomes the product of God's providence, whereas in humanist thought, history is the product of human activity. Despite their apparent difference and continuing conflict, both models share the presupposition that history consists of creating and producing. The model of history as something made and produced presupposes problematic notions of agency, design, intentionality, and decision. God reveals Himself according to monotheism through an ultimate narrative assigning meaning to all things. Humans produce narratives and explanations allowing them to consciously decide and practically design their world.

Adorno and Horkheimer contend in the *Dialectic of Enlightenment* that progress is identified with the increasing domination of nature and the rationalization of human society in which human freedom and happiness are undermined by efforts to realize them. After the Holocaust, and the problematization of history in thinkers such as Adorno, Heidegger, and Levinas, the philosophy of history is in crisis. History as a product or construct of divine and human activity, as the creation of an inherently meaningful and good order, has fallen into doubt even as such models continue to inform the ambitions of authoritarian leaders and their followers' dreams. Heidegger questions history as a creation, design, making, planning, and producing, since such models are inherently calculative in instrumentally reducing beings and their significance to a further being and its purposes. This questioning remains salient given the continuing power and violence of this instrumental paradigm that does not allow beings to have their own immanent and self-generating—rather than externally imposed—significance. Heidegger introduces the need for a different thinking of being, which begins to respond to beings from out of themselves in contrast with imposition by egos or a neutral schema of being. Levinas's analysis is complementary and incommensurable in so far as Levinas is concerned with the reduction of beings to "calculation, mediation, and politics," in which "the struggle of each against all becomes exchange and politics," and yet this calls forth a thinking beyond being that does justice to individuals in their singularity.[21]

Just as historicity is clarified through facticity in his early thought, a facticity that resists and withdraws from the intentionality of consciousness, history is articulated by Heidegger in the mid- and late 1930s beyond the activities of the subject through the self-generativity of *Ereignis*. In ordinary German it signifies "event" and, because of the verbal sense of *er-eignen*, it has been translated as the event of appropriation, propriation, and enownment. Heidegger envisaged history as the history of being—thus moving, at least on a surface reading, from the more Dasein-centered perspective of *Being and Time* to the being-centered perspective of his later thought—and explored this history as *Ereignis*, the "enowning event" of being in its disclosure and concealment.

Ereignis is the self-generating event of history itself, what makes history as the immanent event and enactment of a being—and thus historiographical narrative and explanation—possible. It furthermore names the other of history entering into and potentially interrupting and transforming existing historical life, which is a changing point of departure for reflection. It intimates the continuity of history, its epochal breaks, and the irremovable caesura between the history of the first beginning and that of the other beginning (GA, 65:177). Nevertheless, this does not imply the "end" of totalizing narrative and reductive explanation in history or the impossibility of history as theodicy or a determinate teleological order, whether in its divine or secular variants, because "we" historically situated finite mortals still dwell within this "end" having not yet crossed over to a "totally other" thinking and dwelling.

Western ontology's unfolding concerns history in respect to the history of the disclosure and concealment, the forgetting and remembering of being. This remembering, which is later described as the "step back" in opposition to the recovery and absorption involved in Hegelian recollection, does not make the past present but "is a matter of becoming aware of our essential abode in history."[22] It is a remembering oriented toward the future rather than the kind of remembering that "can only remember from out of and by appealing to something present and something that has been present" (GA, 65:257). Yet no orientation can adequately prepare one for the not yet and nonpresent future, which also concerns Levinas as eschatology and prophecy in *Totality and Infinity*.[23] Although Heidegger does not employ the ethical language of Levinas, he does challenge history and time conceived of as presence: "In the other beginning . . . a being is never actual in the sense of this 'being-present.' Even where this being-present is encountered in constancy, it is the most fleeting thing for the originary projecting-open of the truth of being" (GA, 65:257).

The dismantling of history emerges as both the possibility of confronting what is past and of being attuned and attentively oriented to the otherness of the unsaid. Hermeneutics concerns the possibility of individuation in relation to the tradition that it discloses and conceals; it occurs through a dialogue that inherently sets-apart. This strategy of receptivity through confrontation informs both the early Heidegger's thinking of facticity and his later thought of the event. For instance, in receptivity to the event, to think with the self-interrupting movement of Heidegger's *Contributions*, one comports oneself to the "origin" in order to think it in relation to the excess and other of that origin. This is the "other beginning" of the first beginning and the "always-still-other" of the same (GA, 65:52). The "other beginning" is the "origin" as interruptive break (*Ab-bruch*). It is not a cause, a reason, a motive, a principle, a mover or creator, nor is it a ground in the sense of condition. It is the ground that is an *Ab-grund*, an "inexhaustable abyss" (GA, 65:29). The origin as first beginning is never available and as the other beginning is never ready (GA, 70:187). Hence, the recollection

(*Erinnerung*) of an origin is inevitably a recollection confronted by difference. This difference calls for thoughtful remembrance (*Andenken*).

The "always-still-other," an alterity escaping thought and recollection,
hints at while transforming Heidegger's earlier formulations of temporality. Time is not a series of discrete now-points, identical repetition, nor
pure presence. The present today is not simply or self-identically itself to
the extent that it is structured by a past that it cannot retrieve and open
toward an unknowable future. Heidegger questioned the idea that the future
only continues the present, the calculable future of planning, in favor of
a divergent future springing from another history, that is, from the other
beginning (GA, 69:16). These writings articulate a more far-reaching temporal facticity than his earlier thought: that of a past that never was and a
future that is in each case other due to its discontinuity with the present.
Heidegger thus rejected the ordinary model of knowing and understanding in
the standard view of historiography. "Man is either ready for what is always
original, or he knows better. Knowing better also reigns where man seems
to subjugate himself to a divine world-plan. This knowing better begins in
Western historiological consciousness. The rise and universal currency of
historiological science and its varied utilization and exploitation, however,
are already the late development of man's calculating 'attitude' toward history" (GA, 51:6–7).

UNDERSTANDING AND INTERPRETATION

Knowledge is habitually interpreted as a "knowing better" from the perspective of a divine or human plan and its teleological or instrumental
outcome. Understanding is likewise "understanding better," which is most
clearly expressed in the traditional hermeneutical maxim that "one should
understand the author better than the author does" or "understand a tradition better than the tradition understands itself." This strategy, consuming its
objects and leaving them without their intrinsic significance, was developed
in the Christian interpretation of itself as the overcoming and fulfillment of
Judaism and Greek philosophy and is evident in the sublimating mastery of
the other in the prevailing practice of dialectics and hermeneutics.

Although there are multiple ways of interpreting the maxim of "understanding better," from the principle of charity and maximizing rationality to
immanent critique, the hermeneutic model of understanding better entails
for Heidegger that what is being understood "contains a content in which
we ourselves can grow."[24] "Understanding better" should not be the repetition and deepening of identity, indicating instead the need for a different
interpretation that does not make others understandable only by reconstruct-
ing their position from our own perspective. Understanding better can be a

careful attuning and responsive "understanding appropriately," or it is not an understanding of the other *as* other at all: " 'Understanding appropriately' as 'understanding better' is no mere rejection of what is understood but rather is giving it 'validity.' A philosophy truly has 'validity' when its own power is released and the possibility is provided for it to deliver a shock and to make a difference" (GA, 25:4–5).

Understanding better implies understanding differently from out of the difference, the material alterity, of what is to be understood. The validity given to it in my understanding is its own occurrence and self-generating validity. This involves giving oneself over to what is to be thought and understood. This *Hingabe* is a "letting" and releasement toward the being rather than a reconstruction or imposition of an extrinsic meaning. This receptivity is not an indifferent passivity, although for Levinas passivity in Heidegger is never passive enough to the point of being hostage to the other, as it happens in the struggle of interpretation. This interpretive *agon* leads to questions questioning not only the other but oneself, such that conflict and confrontation are involved in all interpretation precisely when it is most attentively responsive (GA, 25:4–5). To thoughtfully understand the other is to risk oneself and one's own understanding in encountering the other rather than "understanding better" from the self-certain security of one's own understanding.

The receptivity of understanding demands differentiating confrontation and destructuring if it is to genuinely respond to and be responsible for the question to be thought.[25] Heidegger's thinking of *Auseinandersetzung*, for which destructuring is preliminary, culminates after 1935 in his being-historical thinking of the originary confrontation of the first beginning, the truth of beings, with the other beginning, the truth of being.[26] Thinking from this other beginning places metaphysics, and its thinking of history from out of the presence of the present, into question (GA, 49:5, 10).

The hermeneutics of understanding the other better than the other understands herself is a questionable mastering of the other subordinating difference to the logic of identity and construes others as the raw material for one's own activities. Contrary to thinking history as historical confrontation with what is unique, or of a uniqueness beyond history, Heidegger and Levinas suspect dialectics of being a model in which the singular and the other is to be assimilated or excluded, mediated or canceled (*Aufhebung*) (GA, 66:75). This "mediating" way of enacting understanding risks refusing the question of its own self-understanding in encountering what is other. Against the risk of exposure to the depth of otherness—in the other, the world, and the self—it reinstates narrative and teleological representation against its breakdowns, failures, and limits. Every limit is "transgressed" in order to be "reappropriated." This model of reintegration remains at work in Heidegger, according to Levinas, insofar as the breakdowns—including death—are situations for the self to project its mastery and virility. This dialectical process, in which all alterity is revealed as conditional, privileges one moment of temporality over another and operates according to a line of development in which the other is to be sublimated and eliminated as a "lesser" moment or version of myself. In strong accounts of teleology, history is not interpreted according to its character of the facticity and possibility of an event. Its possibility, openness, and "being underway" stressed by Heidegger are subordinated to necessity of a final outcome.

Heidegger questions as much as Levinas strong teleological accounts of history as a narrative of purpose proceeding from origin to goal (condition to result), judging historical episodes and figures through an order of progress, regress, or cycles. In contrast to the setting up and reification of an external purpose governing history and time, "Seeking itself is the goal. And this means that 'goals' are still too much in the foreground and still take place ahead of being—and thus bury what is needful" (GA, 65:18). Not only does the reification of history as determined by an ultimate outcome do violence to all the moments of the past in denying them any inherent significance, but goal-oriented calculative thought misses the way and being underway of thinking, its very questionability. Being itself undermines these goals and projects, revealing their limited and conditional character in the interruption and breakdown of what can be explained (GA, 65:477).

Explanation, including its teleological and efficient-causal variants, is criticized by Heidegger for spatializing temporality (whether imagined as the line, cycle or circle) and repeating the "vulgar concept of time." Heidegger analyzed this vulgar concept as serializing time into equivalent and symmetrical moments and the destruction of ecstatic lived temporality in the monistic identity of the present. Although this critique is inadequately developed in Being and Time, it remains applicable: spatialized time condenses the spontaneity and receptivity of worldly relations of meaning and sense to an explanatory schema of those relations, such as found in causal explanation, eliminating the asymmetry, distance, and interval between occurrences and the temporal "ecstases" of past, present, and future. This critique of spatializing and solidifying time, although it never reaches Levinas's diachronic time of the other, is deepened in the late 1930s.[27]

The return in remembrance (Andenken, which should be distinguished from Hegelian Erinnerung) does not eliminate distance and difference in order to be submerged in the "origin," as this nostalgic strategy—which for Levinas Heidegger himself remains beholden to—stays within representational and explanatory thinking: "But returning into the first beginning (the 'retrieval') is not displacement into what has passed, as if this could be made 'actual' again in the usual sense. Returning to the first beginning is precisely distancing oneself from it. It is taking up that remote-position that is necessary in order to experience what began in and as that beginning. For *without* this distant-positioning—and only the positioning in the *other* beginning is a sufficient one—we always stay insidiously too close to that beginning, insofar as we are still covered over and pinned down by what issues from the beginning" (GA, 65:185–86). In the differentiating distancing encounter with the first beginning, the possibility of the other beginning and thinking steps forward from that difference and distance itself.

Heidegger depicts the way that such explanatory forms inhibit the recognition of the inexhaustible strangeness of the unfamiliar (GA, 51:82–83). The history of being opens up the possibility of encountering this strangeness and confronting totalizing accounts, including teleological reconstructions, in so far as "there is no privileged standpoint at the end of philosophy, simply a different standpoint, one that is as much defined by what it lacks—a word for being—as by its positive characteristics."[28] The history of being—being in its oblivion and withdrawal—does not itself operate as an explanation.[29] Instead of asserting history as identity or totality, thought exposes itself to the unfamiliar for the sake of genuinely encountering the historical *as* historical. Already in the early 1920s, Heidegger challenged the traditional hermeneutical model of "understanding better" with the practice of *Auseinandersetzung* (setting-apart-from-each-other) that entails attentive confrontation (GA, 25:3–5). It is a confrontation in dismantling reified structures and responsive in that it dismantles precisely to listen to what is said and left unsaid. This historical confrontation is intensified in his thinking of the upsurge and event of being (GA, 66:76–77).

HISTORICALLY MINDFUL REFLECTION

Heidegger distinguished the disruptive history of the "other beginning" from narratives and explanations (*Historie*) of the origin that culminate in calculative historicism (GA, 66:275; 70:179–80, 184). This restates the difference between historical understanding, as historically mindful reflection (*Besinnung*), and calculating explanation operating according to cause and effect and origin and goal. The "origin" sought in explanation operates as a condition and reduces phenomena and the plural givenness of things to a first cause or principle (whether divine or natural). In the history of the first beginning, God is the unconditional and infinite ground of being and cause of beings (GA, 66:242). It is this explanatory and reductive use of the absolute that Heidegger confronted in the destructuring of Western history as metaphysics, ontotheology, and technology, which even in confronting the questionability of the West continues to problematically privilege it.[30]

In confrontation with the first beginning, the prehistory of the other beginning emerges, the other beginning hinting at being as the enowning event and upsurge of the unfathomable nonground or abyss (GA, 66:242). Without hierarchical subordination to a first cause or condition, being is the open horizon and crossing of the "between." The "other beginning" elicited through mindful reflection (Besinnung) is the other of the "first beginning," the metaphysical origin. Interrupting the identity inspiring metaphysics, it is the "always-still-other" that can neither be explicated nor considered the condition of all phenomena (GA, 65:52). While Besinnung asks the question "who?" and concerns the who deciding its history in its distress, the question "why?" asks for a cause, ground, reason or condition reducing one phenomenon to another (GA, 66:271–74). Heidegger questions whether "the 'why' can still be made into a tribunal before which being is to be placed" (GA, 65:509) The "why" cannot approach being insofar as it already presupposes an answer to it. The why question is not the neutral beginning imagined by science, as it already presupposes an answer as "what"—essence and substance—and thus an interpretation of beings as entities. The priority of the "why" question demands the explanation of one event through another, one thing through another, linking modern calculative thought with metaphysics as "ontotheology." The question "what?" also resides in the dominion of the shrinking of being to the intelligible and calculable. In contrast to prioritizing the why and the what, the basic questions of Western metaphysics, Heidegger remarks that the question "who?" transformatively transposes the questioner into the belongingness of being's hiddenness (GA, 66:148).

The difference between Geschichte and Historie persisted from the early "hermeneutics of facticity" to Heidegger's later history of being. Historicity is crucial from Da-sein's uncanny historical finitude in the 1920s to his revised questioning of history as the history of being in the late 1930s. Uncanniness and violence are historically interconnected and emerge in a particular configuration in Western history. These issues continue to resonate in Heidegger's inquiries of the late 1930s, where there is a renewed effort to think the relation of preparatory thinking of Besinnung and history in the notion of event (Ereignis). Heidegger addresses the historical in these writings through "seinsgeschichtliches Denken" (i.e., thinking history from out of the history of being), Ereignis (the event of history and the "other" of history, the event of appropriation that expropriates human existence, and the disclosure and withdrawal of being in history), and the "always-still-other" (Immer-noch-Andere) disclosed in historically reflective thought (Besinnung) (GA, 65:52). In interpretive reflection (Besinnung), questions of the facticity and alterity of being come to the fore in challenging strong holistic and teleological models that totalize history according to a pre-established unity that dictates to historical phenomena. Yet another truth offers itself in the encounter.[31]

In encountering the historical as irreducible to such a project, understanding and interpretation must take other routes to questioning the sense of the historical and do so through asking "who?" It seems odd to inquire, "Who is the event?" Who is addressed by such a question, and what would it mean to answer it? The translation of *Ereignis* continues to be controversial, as some argue that translating it as "event" reduces it to an ontic occurrence, while translating it as appropriation or enownment makes it more mysterious. The word "event" is appropriate if it is equally the ontological and ontic happening of history and the other of history entering into the historical. The event indicates the continuity of history, according to a singular plural logic of Heidegger's thinking and its disruption and impossibility. Heidegger's eschatological and messianic language is not dissimilar to its uses in Walter Benjamin and Levinas, although it lacks their ethical and social-political inflection. His event shares the interruptive force of the messianic moment as well as its potential reification that—as Derrida notes—justifies violence and dominion in the name of the religious and the ethical, disciplining time and history anew.

Confronting the history of Western metaphysics reveals the history of the disclosure, concealment, and forgetting of being. Being is itself the ontological difference and intersection of being and beings, which cannot be included under the same concept or mediated without reaffirming metaphysical tendencies toward reduction, closure and instrumentality. This reductive conception of history means: "The ascertaining explaining of the past from within the horizon of the calculative dealings of the present. Beings are hereby presupposed as what is orderable, producible, and ascertainable" (GA, 65:493). Heidegger interrogates contemplative and instrumental-teleological conceptions of history, resisting the illusion of mediation, since transition is not mediation but *Ent-scheidung* ("decision" as the cut of differentiation) (GA, 66:405).

Heidegger distinguished history as *Geschichte*, as open to being's non-totalizable event, and history as totalized through an explanatory and narrative *Historie* that assumes complete intelligibility in order to establish and exercise dominion over nature and humans (GA, 65:493). The assumption of comprehensive intelligibility and calculability characteristic of metaphysics and modern social and technological organization closes off other possibilities for being and flourishing that continue to be hinted at in poetic works and interpretive reflection (GA, 66:63; 67:172). Historically mindful reflection transpires as a preparatory thinking that responds with care to what is other than itself. Historically mindful reflection lingers in the expectancy and tension of the "always-still-other" (*Immer-noch-Andere*) and "other beginning" seemingly absent in the always-still-identical and first origin that would condition all. Heidegger's "narrative" of the history of ontology is paradoxical in operating as a counternarrative challenging narrative and explanatory order. This strategy might defy rather than reaffirm narrative and teleology by remaining in the tension between history as event and history as the continuation of the first beginning in the history of metaphysics, and the differentiation (*Unterscheidung*) between being (*Sein*), which defies being narratively spoken or described, and the incomplete narratives of finite beings (*Seiende*) (GA, 69:59).

ENDINGS AND BEGINNINGS

History is essentially egoism and the struggle for existence and mastery for Levinas. It consists of the war and violence of the same against the other.[32] History lives from the narratives of the victorious and the silencing of the victims. There is not much potential for understanding history from out of itself, or thinking history otherwise from within history, insofar as the historical is constitutively alienation, betrayal, fate, and injustice for Levinas.[33] Despite the intolerable ethical and social-political aporias and limitations exposed by Levinas, and their overlapping distrust of a dialectic or teleology of history, Heidegger's approach to history has two features worth highlighting: (1) how it confronts and differs from teleological and instrumental historical models of calculation, design, making, and production (*Herstellung*), without abandoning the immanent self-generative counter-totalizing sense of the historical, and (2) how history is displaced from identity to event, unitary subject to singular-plural being, and from "what" to "who." This "who" is addressed and implicated in history as a historical being who must decide about the history that it itself is from within the situation and context of that history.

Decision, according to Levinas, is persistently too late and after the fact.[34] For Heidegger, it must be decided not as a pure initiative of a monadic freedom but as reply. The "who" decides in the context of a history of being that it did not itself choose. Nor does it provide a univocal narrative, since it involves instead a finitude between the open and the hidden, disclosure and withdrawal. Instead of a narrative about a beginning and end, origin and goal, history is the opening space of the question, the question of the first and the other beginning, of the "always already" and the "always still not" (*immer noch nicht*) or other. History is moved from the mastery of a calculating subject—whose domination is enslavement—to that being "who" is addressed through history and compelled to decide. History does not inevitably preclude the moment of personalization and individuation, even as Heidegger missed this moment's ethical import as Levinas justifiably maintains.

Dismantling the reification of the historical through *Auseinandersetzung* suggests both confronting how the past has been handed down by tradition and of attentiveness to what has been unsaid and covered over. In reserved and grateful receptivity to the expropriation of the enowning event, which challenges appropriation as mastery, one comports oneself to the "origin" for the sake of what exceeds and overflows that origin. This is the other beginning, which is the "origin" as break (*Ab-bruch*) and which resists being posited and manipulated as a cause, reason, motive, principle, or the result of production. It names a ground that is the lack thereof, an abyss or *Ab-grund*, entailing the recollection of an origin that is a remembrance faced by the differentiating cutting apart of decision (*Ent-Scheidung*). Such decision is not the "activism" or "decisionism" of a subject or its will, much less the self-striving *conatus essendi* or egoism that Levinas interprets as dominant in Heideggerian ontology. It is a historically situated preparation and readiness: "Readiness to confront the inception can originate as genuine only from the necessities of history into which we ourselves are placed" (GA, 51:9–10).

Decision is not solely a human "doing" or "making." Nor is it a "doing" and "making" of another being or being as such. Heidegger's critique of explanation and the paradigm of production place such categories of the done and the made into question. In contrast to Vico's axiom, the true is the unmade. If such explanatory and interpretive strategies are inadequate, then notions such as "decision" are in need of being thought differently. What is at issue in decision is not making and designing but how one responds or does not respond. The rejoinder to being in its historicity is at issue, and decision is the care and carelessness, the responsiveness and nonresponsiveness of Dasein to being and its abandonment, to the earth which it preserves and cultivates or allows to be destroyed, and the openness which it lets be open or encloses, enframes, and forgets. Levinas's identification of care for things with cruelty to one's fellow humans in his critique of Heidegger's naturalism is then overly hasty.[35]

Heidegger's thinking of historical beginning discloses the "other beginning" and the "always still not." This indicates a nonrelative alterity, even if not ethically formulated. It is more radical than an external contrast between opposites, as alterity is revealed as already permeating the immanence that tries to forget it. The other beginning is the other of metaphysics and the other of our history. It presents another possibility that is already at work in Western history that can be articulated in confrontation with it. This possibility of a "past that never was" is impossible to think without the future, "the always still not," that draws near without becoming present, disclosing other possibilities for contemporary thought. Even as Heidegger's thinking involves the reification of origins and a nostalgic absorption in archaic forms of life, aptly criticized by Levinas for their philosophical and political aura and implications, other deconstructive tendencies indicate different possibilities involving a thinking of a basic otherness in relation to the hardened presence of that which exists. As Levinas argues, these possibilities do not yet specify a relation with ethical alterity and are consequently inadequate to justice. But Heidegger's idiom is never purely ontological to the extent that it can escape the ethical, even as Levinas's thought cannot escape ontology in its movement toward an ethics beyond and otherwise than being.[36]

Although Heidegger discontinued explicitly using the language of facticity questioned by Levinas, facticity provides a clue about this relation between the old and the new, an old that is "before time," or at least any temporal horizon, and a new that is inescapably "after time." The old and new are present in their "nonpresence" and absence in time and history, as disruptive and unruly traces intimating what is other than that time and history. While Heidegger thinks through varieties of self-alterity, as the self is fundamentally other than and most uncanny to itself, Levinas's alterity occurs through a transcendent. Levinas specifies the need to judge history from a point outside of it, as persons give meaning to events rather than events providing meaning to persons.[37] Levinas also identifies this external judgment on history with Judaism, which raises complicated questions.[38]

Given the ambiguous bonds between the ethical and the historical, such that one does not find a clear break and coherent conceptual dichotomy between them, another option is needed. The possibility of an ethically infused historicity and an immanent transformative praxis challenges both the reification of alterity in the eternal and transcendent and the alienation of immanence in an imprisoning and debilitating historical relativity. This prospect leads beyond both Heidegger and Levinas. But it is intimated in reading Heidegger critically through Levinas's objections, in particular those appealing to the righteous demand for justice and goodness, without adopting Levinas's antihistorical position: the alterity of history to itself is irreducible to history; it is anarchic in being irreducible to a determinate totality or an efficient-causal or teleological order. Yet such challenging difference has neither definitive name nor identity and cannot be calculated or counted on. It defies being articulated as either a principle immanent to history or as an absolute transcendent point external to history.

NOTES

1. E. Levinas, *The Theory of Intuition in Husserl's Phenomenology*, 2d ed., trans. A. Orianne (Evanston: Northwestern University Press, 1995), 156.

2. E. Levinas, "Some Thoughts on the Philosophy of Hitlerism," in *Unforeseen History*, trans. N. Poller (Urbana: University of Illinois Press, 2004), 13–21; *On Escape*, trans. B. Bergo (Stanford: Stanford University Press, 2003).

3. *On Escape*, 49, 51.

4. Ibid., 6; E. Levinas, *Totality and Infinity*, trans. A. Lingis (Pittsburgh: Duquesne University Press, 1969), 103, 105.

5. E. Levinas, *Time and the Other and Additional Essays*, trans. R. A. Cohen (Pittsburgh: Duquesne University Press, 1987), 46–47.

6. E. Levinas, *Collected Philosophical Papers*, trans. A. Lingis (The Hague: Martinus Nijhoff, 1987), 52.

7. *The Theory of Intuition*, 156–58; *Time and the Other*, 79.

8. *Totality and Infinity*, 23, 52, 227–28, 243–45.

9. Ibid., 52.

10. Note that this interpretation of history in Heidegger further develops and deepens the one in E. S. Nelson, "History as Decision and Event in Heidegger," *Arhe*, 4, no. 8 (2007): 97–115.

11. Albeit a controversial claim given Heidegger's continuing anti-Semitic and fascistic tendencies, it is apparent that the works of the late 1930s involve a critical confrontation with National Socialism. I analyze the transition from enthusiasm to questioning in E. S. Nelson, "Traumatic Life: Violence, Pain, and Responsiveness in Heidegger," *The Trauma Controversy: Philosophical and Interdisciplinary Dialogues*, ed. K. Brown and B. Bergo (Albany: State University of New York Press, 2009), 189–204.

12. On Dilthey's hermeneutics of historical life and Heidegger's misinterpretation of it, see E. S. Nelson, "Interpreting Practice: Epistemology, Hermeneutics, and Historical Life in Dilthey," *Idealistic Studies*, 38, nos. 1–2, (2008): 105–22; "Self-Reflection, Interpretation, and Historical Life in Dilthey," in H.-U. Lessing, R. A. Makkreel, und R. Pozzo, eds., *Recent Contributions to Dilthey's Philosophy of the Human Sciences* (Stuttgart: Frommann-holzboog, 2011).

13. GA, 60: *Phänomenologie des religiösen Lebens* (Frankfurt: Klostermann, 1995), 32, 34.

14. GA, 60:84; GA, 61:*Phänomenologische Interpretationen zu Aristoteles* (Frankfurt: Klostermann, 1994), 2.

15. M. Heidegger, GA, 45: *Grundfragen der Philosophie* (Frankfurt: Klostermann, 1992), 40–41; *Basic Questions of Philosophy*, trans. R. Rojcewicz and A. Schuwer (Bloomington: Indiana University Press, 1994).

16. M. Heidegger, GA, 65: *Beiträge zur Philosophie: (Vom Ereignis)* (Frankfurt: Klostermann, 1989); *Contributions to Philosophy: From Enowning*, trans. P. Emad and K. Maly (Bloomington: Indiana University Press, 1999).

17. Compare Robert Bernasconi, "Levinas and the Struggle for Existence," E. S. Nelson, A. Kapust, K. Still, eds., *Addressing Levinas* (Evanston: Northwestern University Press, 2005).

18. See R. Schürmann, "Riveted to a Monstrous Site," T. Rockmore and J. Margolis, eds., *The Heidegger Case: On Philosophy and Politics* (Philadelphia: Temple University Press, 1992), 313–14.

19. GA, 69: *Die Geschichte des Seyns* (Frankfurt: Klostermann, 1998), 1.

20. Compare GA, 66: *Besinnung* (Frankfurt: Klostermann, 1997), 75–76 / *Mindfulness*, trans. P. Emad and T. Kalary (London: Continuum, 2006); GA, 70: *Über den Anfang* (Frankfurt: Klostermann, 2005), 183–85.

21. E. Levinas, *Otherwise than Being or Beyond Essence*, trans. A. Lingis (Kluwer: The Hague, 1981), 4.

22. GA, 51: *Grundbegriffe* (Frankfurt: Klostermann, 1997), 92–93; *Basic Concepts*, trans. G. Aylesworth (Bloomington: Indiana University Press, 1993).

23. *Totality and Infinity*, 209–11.

24. GA, 25: *Phänomenologische Interpretation von Kants Kritik der reinen Vernunft*, 3rd ed. Frankfurt: Klostermann, 1995, 4–5; *Phenomenological Interpretation of Kant's Critique of Pure Reason*, trans. P. Emad and K. Maly (Bloomington: Indiana University Press, 1997), 4–5.

25. On Heidegger's reinterpretation of responsibility, see F. Raffoul, *The Origins of Responsibility* (Bloomington: Indiana University Press, 2010), 242–81.

26. GA, 66:68fn; GA, 49: *Die Metaphysik des deutschen Idealismus (Schelling)* (Frankfurt: Klostermann, 1991), 189–90.

27. GA, 67: *Metaphysik und Nihilismus* (Frankfurt: Klostermann, 1999), 127.

28. R. Bernasconi, *The Question of Language in Heidegger's History of Being* (Atlantic Highlands: Humanities, 1985), 7.

29. Ibid., 8.

30. On the issue of ontotheology and its contemporary consequences, see I. D. Thomson, *Heidegger on Ontotheology Technology and the Politics of Education* (New York: Cambridge University Press, 2005). On Eurocentrism in Heidegger's understanding of history, see L. Ma, *Heidegger on East-West Dialogue: Anticipating the Event* (London: Routledge, 2007).

31. On the *Entgegnung* in the *Begegnung* of another truth, see GA, 70:185–86.

32. *Collected Philosophical Papers*, 48; *Totality and Infinity*, 23.

33. *Collected Philosophical Papers*, 52.

34. *Otherwise than Being*, 180.

35. E. Levinas, *Difficult Freedom: Essays on Judaism*, trans. S. Hand (Baltimore: Johns Hopkins University Press, 1990), 231–32.

36. See E. S. Nelson, "Heidegger and the Questionability of the Ethical," *Studia Phaenomenologica* 8 (2008): 398.

37. *Totality and Infinity*, 241–44.

38. *Difficult Freedom*, 199–200. Judaism has been interpreted as radically transcending the this-worldly immanence of nature and history, as David N. Myers describes in *Resisting History: Historicism and Its Discontents in German-Jewish Thought* (Princeton, NJ: Princeton University Press, 2003). Another reading, developed by thinkers such as Moses Hess, understands Judaism as "the" historical religion, contrasting Jewish holism and historicity with Christian dualism and atemporality and articulating living history as the creative and transformative site of the prophetic and messianic. On Heidegger's resonance with Jewish thought, see A. M. Scult, *Being Jewish, Reading Heidegger: An Ontological Encounter* (New York: Fordham University Press, 2004); M. Zarader, *The Unthought Debt: Heidegger and the Hebraic Heritage*, trans. B. Bergo (Stanford: Stanford University Press, 2006).

PART II

TEMPORALITIES

CHAPTER FOUR

THE SINCERITY OF THE SAYING

Didier Franck

Translated by Robert Vallier

SYSTEM AND SUBJECT

The anticipatory resoluteness with which Dasein properly achieves its own being-able-to-die is at once both finite freedom and originary truth. "Our analysis of the anticipatory resoluteness," Heidegger recalls at the outset of the interpretation of the ipseity and temporality of care, "led us to the phenomenon of primordial and authentic truth. Earlier we showed how the understanding of being that initially prevails and for the most part conceives being in the sense of presence-to-hand and thus covers over the primordial phenomenon of truth. But if 'there is' being only insofar as truth 'is,' and if the understanding of being varies according to the kind of truth, then primordial and authentic truth must guarantee the understanding of the being of Dasein and of being in general. The ontological 'truth' of the existential analysis is developed on the basis of primordial existentiell truth."[1] Whether this latter truth is resoluteness, being-towards-death, or anxious freedom, the fundamental ontological truth rests on it. In other words, finite liberty is truth. But doesn't altering the meaning of finite freedom by making of it an irrecusably anarchic responsibility—"*the famous finite freedom of philosophers is responsibility for what I have not committed*"[2]—lead to a modification of the truth itself? What meaning will the truth have when finite freedom, with which it is in solidarity, is no longer ontological but preontological?

And how can we access it without once again proceeding from its properly ontological mode?

Let's return, then, to the beginning. The totality of being shows itself to itself of itself, and this self-showing or exposition [*ostentation*] is achieved as time, consciousness. "The truth can consist only in the exposition of being to itself, in self-consciousness."[3] Starting from this, phenomenality is essential to beings and also requires a consciousness to which to appear. From then on, the being of beings which is manifested in truth, and this truth itself, can in no way be imputed to manifested beings or to the particularities of the system that organizes them. There is consequently an indifference of the appearing being with respect both to its becoming-evident or appearing [*apparoir*] and to the consciousness to which it appears, which thematizes and identifies it: "[T]he term objectivity expresses this indifference and thereby the very being of that which is."[4] Inversely, by welcoming the manifestation, consciousness could not affect (not in a projective, hallucinatory, or even merely deformative mode) the being of what shows itself, precisely because it is the self-showing of being. In function of this latter, consciousness is pure diaphanousness, and if—in one way or another, beyond or on this side of this office that stems from the play of being—it came to play "for its own account," the essence of being would be obscured by it. Objectivity is thus the mode by which the truth of being or of essence is completed and, given that knowledge has not undermined what it has thematized, "subjectivity qua knowing is subordinated to the meaning of objectivity."[5]

Even though this latter, or phenomenality, does not belong to the quidditive or ontic tenor of the appearing being, the quiddity of beings is nevertheless brought to light. Objectivity is not proper to any particular being, but constitutes instead their common being. And because the being of each being is also the being of every other, being can only unfurl itself as that which relates beings to one another in their ensemble. "If in the quiddity of beings that show themselves their visibility and their being are not inscribed in the guise of an attribute, it is their grouping, their co-presence, that is—and this is something new—the position of one with regard to the other, the relativity in which each makes itself into a sign for the other—the reciprocal signifyingness [*signifiance*] of one in relation to another, which is equivalent to the coming to light of the qualified quiddities themselves. The regrouping of all these significations or structures into a system—intelligibility—is disclosure itself."[6] To understand is thus to show or to let be shown in "the shadowless noon of truth."[7]

What is this novelty and from where does it come? Above all from the existential analysis of worldliness in which the being of beings is no longer sought in their direct relation to the constituting subject but rather in the signifying relations that link them together, in which no separated being truly shows itself. "In accordance with their character of being usable material, useful things always are in terms of their belonging to other useful things."[8] Since the disclosure of the hammer as such in its thingliness (that is, as that which refers to nails which themselves refer to planks to be assembled, etc.) goes together with the preliminary disclosure of the world as an totality of references, a system of relations between terms, then signifyingness—the intelligibility which is the "systematic structure of totality"[9]—lets this structure appear by protecting it against all intrusion of the subjective gaze. But if signifyingness is the modality of manifestation, if appearing and signifyingness go together, or in other words, if the being of a term (Levinas doesn't speak of tools but only of terms, which at the same time makes evident what the existential analytic and the structural analysis have in common) resides in its relations with other terms, then the manifestation of these other terms is not only "the very way of impugning the interference of the gaze in the being as made manifest to it,"[10] but also the mode by which objectivity and truth are achieved.

Signifyingness—intelligibility—is both relation between terms, which taken in themselves have no meaning, and an evidencing of the totality of terms. What then happens to that which, within this totality, is not yet or no longer inserted in the system of relations? To ask this question is to recognize that "indifference with respect to the subjective regard is not assured in the same way as are terms, structures, and system." Or to say it otherwise, a thing is a being posited and identified, thematized, an other of appearing objectively in the full light of intelligibility. But if the brilliance of the coming-into-evidence here varies with this light, "we can . . . observe a divergence between separated simply thematized intelligible beings—if it is true that a phenomenon is possible without the kerygmatic *logos*, without phenomenology—and the state of the intelligibility of the system; we can speak of a passage from a simple *exposition* of a theme to its intelligibility. We can distinguish in the movement that goes from one to the other a hesitation, a time, the need for an effort, for good or bad luck, for the structures to be packed in. It is through this event, by this becoming open, in the intelligible itself that we can understand the subjectivity that would be here still be wholly thought from out of the intelligibility of being."[11]

How does subjectivity contribute to appearing qua intelligibility, that is, as an appearing that in principle is never that of an absolutely separated or transcendent being? Phenomenality does not occur without the simultaneous, synchronous, co-present, or immanent gathering and arrangement of elements with one another, and "the present, the privileged time of the truth and of being, of being in truth, is contemporaneity itself and the manifestation of being is a re-presentation."[12] And if representation rules over the truth, all meaning is ontological. Now, understood as a power to make present what is not present, representation is the power of a subject who, to be a subject of recuperable time, is able to gather within its present whatever is not yet or no longer present, and is therefore able to make signifyingness and appearing co-present, which for an isolated being is meaningless and obscure. This thinking subject (and to think is always in one way or another to gather and arrange) "is thus interpreted—despite its searching, despite its spontaneity—as a detour that being's essence takes in order to be arranged and thus to truly appear, to appear in truth. Intelligibility or signifyingness is part of the very exercise of being, of the *ipsum esse*. Everything is then on the same side, the side of being. This ability to absorb the subject to which essence is entrusted is what is proper to essence. Everything is enclosed within it."[13] We can thus give the name "reason" to this representation of a multiplicity of terms signifying (to) one another in the unity of a system, the operator or functionary of which is the representing subject.

"HERE I AM"

In function of intelligibility, of manifestation, and of an impersonal reason, the subject of the being who draws its being from the sole truth of being for which it is the sentinel is "without proper density."[14] On this basis, "the veracity of the subject would have no meaning other than this effacing before presence, other than this representation."[15] But the subject is not merely required by being as the site of its truth; the subject is also that which says this truth by communicating it to the other, that which relates, and in one manner or other, testifies to the truth. Does it still remain in this form included within being that "despite or because of its finitude . . . has an englobing, absorbing, enclosing essence"?[16] There would be no doubt whatsoever about this *if* saying means articulating adequate propositions about what shows itself, or if saying is, as the manifestation of manifestation, correlative to the said and is absorbed in it, or if in brief there is no diachrony between saying and the said. Effacing itself before the truth, the subject is veracious because it is diaphanous and "the veracity of the subject would be the virtue of a Saying in which the emission of signs—insignificant by themselves—would be subordinate to the signified, to the said, which in turn would be conformed to the being that shows itself. The subject would not be the source of any signification—independently of the truth of the essence that serves the subject. The lie would only be the price that being pays for its finitude."[17]

But why speak in the conditional unless because what is true for the subject of being is not also necessarily true for the subject of responsibility, or unless because, given that language (saying) signifies beyond being, the ontological truth (unveiling and representation) could not be the measure

of all truth. An-archic and unintentional responsibility signifies outside of
every context and beyond every system, neither refers to nor arises from any
correlation between subject and object or being, because it is signifyingness
itself. "One-for-the-other—that is, the signifyingness itself of signification,"[18]
Levinas wrote and proclaimed, interrupting with an exclamation point the
rigorously ordered course of his own discourse, an interruption that is ultimately the very content of the discourse. From then on, by its anarchy or its
radical diachrony that makes the "great present of synopsis in which being
shines with all its radiance"[19] fail, checks the gathering of being that, as
identification of the identical, is being itself in its truth, "the signifyingness
of signification is not brought about as a mode of representation, nor as the
symbolic evocation of an absence, that is, as a last resort or failure of presence."[20] However powerful it may be—it is power itself, the power of the
same—representation could not assimilate the responsibility for others that
signifies an immemorial past incommensurate with the present. Differently
from the subject required by being, the subject of responsibility, the *one* of
the one-for-another, is excepted from the train and the truth of essence,
and by reason of this exception, "the one-for-the-other or signification—or
sense or intelligibility—does not rest in being."[21]

Whatever the incommensurability of meaning is with respect to the
being that takes on meaning because of it—this is transcendence itself—the
truth of being must receive its meaning from the truth to which the one-
for-another is tied. And if the truth of the ontological subject is inseparable
from the logos, from the said, then the truth of the subject held hostage by
others must be sought in the saying. It is therefore a matter of describing
the intrigue of truth to which the responsible subject belongs. Responsibility signifies an irrecusable assignation to respond despite myself, without
any possible subterfuge (possibility is here subterfuge itself), it signifies an
alterity in identity that, as the animation of the body, is the psychical or
inspiration. Assignation thus signifies a commandment "exercised by the
other in me over me"[22]—it is substitution—and "to command continually
put forth only a 'here I am'" [*me voici*] can respond, in which the pronoun
'I' is in the accusative, declined prior to any declension, possessed by the
other, sick, identical."[23]

Does this "here I am" which is self-showing (*exposition*) to others,
"'extradition' of the self to the neighbor,"[24] not always imply an act, a "position"[25] and thereby the return of the unbreachable nucleus of the unity of
apperception? Probably, but this return will not be definitive if the "here I
am" is itself, as an inspired saying, passivity and exposition of the exposition,
the self-showing of self-showing. "For subjectivity to signify unreservedly,
it would then be necessary that the passivity of its exposure to the other
not be immediately inverted into activity, but expose itself in its turn: a

passivity of passivity is required and in the glory of the Infinite ashes from which the act could not be born anew. Saying is this passivity of passivity and this dedication to the other, this sincerity."[26]

What is this saying? It is not the transmission or the sharing of a said that always rides on or carries being, but rather a given sign of the givenness of the sign, a superlative exposition that consumes the prop or the substance of every position, the uncovering—denuding—of one to the other, an openness to the other more open than (and is the truth of) the openness to being. "The statement of the 'here I am' is identified with nothing but the very voice that states and delivers itself, the voice that signifies,"[27] pure signifyingness, "the very essence of the language before any tongue";[28] this saying over which the paradox of the liar has no hold is sincerity. "No Said is equal to the sincerity of the Saying, is adequate to the veracity that is prior to the True, the veracity of the approach, of proximity, beyond presence."[29] Absolutely anterior to being and to its time, to the synchrony of being or presence, "saying that does not tell anything, that infinitely, prevoluntarily, consents,"[30] sincerity is true of a truth that is not the truth of being and without which the truth being would have no meaning, because sincere saying is signification itself. "A fission of the ulti-mate substantiality of the Ego, sincerity is not reducible to anything ontic, or to anything ontological, and leads beyond or on this side of everything positive, every position."[31]

What does the sincerity that the saying accomplishes mean, and what relation does either have with the "glory of the infinite"—or inversely, what does this glory require of sincerity and saying? Saying responds to a com-mandment that consigns me to others from whom I am infinitely separated. From then on, "the more I respond, the more I am responsible, the more I approach the neighbor with whom I am charged, and the further away I am. This debit that increases is the infinite as infinition of the infinite, as glory."[32] But how must this be understood? Glory designates first what weighs heavily or confers values on, and next it characterizes the manifesta-tion of God to Israel—"*You [are] my servant, Oh Israel, in whom I will be be glorified*"[33]—that is, to the world and in the world as not being there. But even if glory belongs to theophanies, they go essentially together with the "radical irrectitude" that had already been a question concerning illeity. To Moses who asks to let him see his glory, Yahweh responds: "Behold, there is a place by me, and thou shalt stand upon a rock: And it shall come to pass, while my glory passeth by, that I will put thee in a cleft of the rock: and will cover thee with my hand while I pass by! And I will take away my hand, and thou shalt see my back parts: but my face shall not be seen."[34] In brief, if there is a phenomenological dimension or a moment of glory, the phenomenology concerned essentially and indirectly derogates the principle according to which all signification is monstration. As Levinas said several times with respect to the phenomenon and its light, glory is "a surplus of signifyingness."[35] Glory, "an excess over or exceeding of the present,"[36] "growing surplus of the infinite,"[37] is paradoxically the defection by excess of the phenomenon, a meaning that in a certain way contrasts with it in it or that, in an enigmatic manner, overwhelms it.

TESTIMONY

Can we now specify the relation between the glory of the infinite and the sincerity of Saying whereby one links itself to the other by freeing itself from itself for the other? My responsibility to the other does not result from a free decision, does not amount to the present of an initiative and grows infinitely, proportionately to it being exercised. As anarchic, it is a relation to an infinite that, because of this anarchy, bypasses the evidencing of which I am ontologically the constituting source and that, signifying beyond the phenomenon, is a glorious infinite. On this basis, this infinite could "not enter into appearing or become a phenomenon, not become a theme without being contained, without accepting limits in immanence. This refusal to appear is thus positively the very responsibility for the other, anterior to every memorable present, coming from a past that had never been present, that had never been the freedom of the subject, ordering me to the other, to the first to come along, then to the neighbor, without showing itself to me, but entering me by the simple effect of a traumatism, by breaking and entering. My responsibility for the other is precisely this relation with an unthematizable Infinite. It is neither the experience of the Infinite nor the proof of it: it is what *testifies* to it."[38]

How then must testimony be understood when it is neither an experience nor its account—which are always correlatives of a present, even the very form of presence and of gathering—nor a moment of the unveiling of being or of knowledge? My responsibility in testifying to the infinite—the glory of the infinite, its excess over the present—is nothing other than what I testify to the other by opening myself infinitely to it. And if this openness is the emphasis of all openness, the exposition of the exposition achieving itself as vulnerability until substitution, then it is the Saying itself. "The glory of the Infinite is the an-archic Identity of the subject flushed out without possible escape; it is the ego led to sincerity, making sings to the other for whom and before whom I am responsible, of this very giving of signs, that is, of this responsibility: 'here I am.' The Saying prior to anything said testifies to glory. This testimony is true, but of a truth irreducible to the truth of disclosure and does not narrates anything that shows itself."[39]

If testifying is Saying, in what sense can it be true, or what is the truth of Saying? As the mode whereby the relation between my responsibility for the other and the infinite that commands me is produced, testifying will be just as true or veridical as I will be without secret, "out of the dark corners of the 'as-for-me,'"[40] "without heavy zones propitious for evasion,"[41] open and to be discovered: sincere. By the saying whose every stated proposition carries its trace, by the sign given to the other for whom and to whom I answer, "I expose myself to the summons of this responsibility as though placed under a blazing sun that eradicates every residue of mystery, every ulterior motive, every loosening of the thread that makes the evasion pos-sible—already sincere, testifying for the infinite, not by relating it as a fact but rather by unfolding it, by the rupture of its silence, its very glory, by cracking the secret of Gyges, of the invisible-seeing-subject."[42] Sincerity—a truth that is neither a welcoming nor freedom but is rather the denuding of the denuding that becomes enucleating, substitution, and saying—does not arise from a spontaneous initiative; on the contrary, I am passively assigned to it, constrained by the weight of it, by the glory of a distinct sun of lead or, as paradoxical as this may seem, of the shadowless noon that character-izes the truth and the intelligibility of being and of the said because it is burdened by this weight, but every value of the good. If the truth of the ontological subject depends on the truth of being in order to be the represen-tation and gathering of it, that is, exercise itself, the sincerity or the veracity of the subject held hostage by the other testifies to the infinite without ever being able to represent it, and the truth is no longer evidence and unveiling but is instead the "witnessing of the infinite."[43] *Of* the infinite and not *to* the infinite, because it is not the infinite that belongs to testimony as the object belongs to the subject, but rather testifying belongs to the infinite, of which it alone is the very infinition, "there is witness—a unique structure, an exception to the rule of being, irreducible to representation—only of the infinite. The infinite does not appear to whomever bears witness to it. On the contrary the witness belongs to the glory of the Infinite. It is by the voice of the witness that the glory of the infinite is glorified."[44]

NOTES

1. Heidegger, *Being and Time*, trans. J. Stambaugh (Albany: SUNY Press, 1996), 292.
2. "As Old as the World?" in *Nine Talmudic Lectures*, trans. A. Aronowicz (Bloomington: Indiana University Press, 1994), 85. See also "The Temptation of Temptation," in *Nine Talmudic Lectures*, 8, and "Revelation in the Jewish Tradition," in *Beyond the Verse*, trans. G. Mole (London: Continuum, 1996), 142: "To be free is to do what no one else can do in my place."
3. *OTB*, 28 / *AE*, 35.

4. See "The Truth of Disclosure and the Truth of Testimony," in *Basic Philosophical Writings*, ed. A. Peperzak, R. Bernasconi, and S. Critchley (Bloomington: Indiana University Press, 1996), 98. Hereafter *BPW*.

5. *OTB*, 132 / *AE*, 168.

6. *OTB*, 132 / *AE*, 168–69; see also *OTB*, 165 / *AE*, 210.

7. *OTB*, 137 / *AE*, 175.

8. *Being and Time*, 64.

9. *OTB*, 132 / *AE*, 169. Levinas here takes up Heidegger's language of "totality," "structure," and of a "system of relations." See *Being and Time*, 82; see also "Martin Heidegger and Ontology," in *En decouvrant l'existence avec Husserl et Heidegger* (Paris: J. Vrin, 1949), 62ff (the partial English translation of this collection does not contain this essay).

10. "Truth of Disclosure," in *BPW*, 98.

11. *OTB*, 133 / *AE*, 169. The example of this "divergence" or of this packing in is furnished by the useless or broken tool; see *Being and Time*, 68–69.

12. *OTB*, 133 / *AE*, 170.

13. *OTB*, 134 / *AE*, 170–171. Beyond the existential analytic, the analysis is equally valid for structural thought, which thus presents a "significant convergence" with Heidegger's thought; see for example "No Identity," in Emmanuel Levinas, *Collected Philosophical Papers*, ed. and trans. A. Lingis (Pittsburgh: Duquesne University Press, 1998), 143–44 (hereafter *CPP*). It is moreover not impossible that by claiming that the subjectivity of the ontological subject always consists in "effacing itself before being," Levinas directly echoes the "Finale" of Levi-Strauss's *Mythologies*, where he speaks of the "effacement of the subject" and, after having claimed that the consciousness inherent in the work of knowledge "remains of the intellectual order," immediately specifies in a proposition whose ontological importance he underlines: "That is that it does not differ substantially from the realities to which it is applied, that it is these very realities accessing their own truth"; see *L'homme nu*, 561, 563; *OTB*, 134 / *AE*, 171; *OTB*, 96 / *AE*, 122.

14. "Truth of Disclosure," in *BPW*, 98.

15. *OTB*, 134 / *AE*, 171.

16. *OTB*, 134 / *AE*, 171. Being is finite because it is not manifested without the subject.

17. *OTB*, 134 / *AE*, 171.

18. *OTB*, 100 / *AE*, 126; see also *OTB*, 159 / *AE*, 202; and *OTB*, 177–78 / *AE*, 224.

19. *OTB*, 134 / *AE*, 171.

20. *OTB*, 136 / *AE*, 173. See also "From Consciousness to Wakefulness: Starting from Husserl," in *Of God Who Comes to Mind*, trans. B. Bergo (Stanford University Press, 1998), 21, where being is understood "as an event of the identification of the identical, as an event of identification that is only possible as a gathering into a theme, as representation and as presence."

21. *OTB*, 136 / *AE*, 173.

22. *OTB*, 141 / *AE*, 180.

23. *OTB*, 142 / *AE*, 180–81. Levinas here cites in a footnote the eighth verse of *The Canticle of Canticles*: "I am sick with love."

24. "Truth of Disclosure," in *BPW*, 106.

25. *OTB*, 142 / *AE*, 181.

26. *OTB* 142–43 / *AE*, 181–82. "To posit subjectivity in its responsibility," Levinas says elsewhere, "is to catch sight in it of a never sufficiently passive passivity of being consumed for the other. The very light of subjectivity shines and illuminates from out of this ardor, although the ashes of this consummation are unable to become the kernel of a being existing in-itself and for-itself; and the I does not oppose to the other any form that protects it or provides a measure to it. Such is the consummation of holocaust. 'I am dust and ashes,' says Abraham in interceding for Sodom (*Genesis*: XVIII, 27). 'What are we?' says Moses more humbly still (*Exodus*: XVI, 7)." See "God and Philosophy" in *CPP*, 168 or *BPW*, 143–44. "God and Philosophy" also appears in *Of God Who Comes to Mind*, 55–78.

27. *OTB*, 143 / *AE*, 182.

28. "Language and Proximity," in *CPP*, 122.

29. *OTB*, 143 / *AE*, 183.

30. "No Identity," in *CPP*, 147.

31. *OTB*, 144 / *AE*, 183.

32. *OTB*, 93 / *AE*, 119.

33. *Isaiah* 49:3.

34. *Exodus* 33:21–23. See Levinas's comments on it in "Phenomenon and Enigma," in *CPP* 68–69 or *BPW* 72–73. On the Talmudic interpretation of this text, see "Revelation in the Jewish Tradition," in *Beyond the Verse*, 144.

35. See "Bad Conscience and the Inexorable" in *Of God Who Comes to Mind*, 172–77; see also "Nonintentional Consciousness" and "From One to the Other: Transcendence and Time," in *Entre Nous*, trans. M. B. Smith and B. Harshaw (New York: Columbia University Press, 1998), 123–32, 133–54; and see also "Philosophy and Transcendence" in *Alterity and Transcendence*, trans. M. B. Smith (New York: Columbia University Press, 2000), 3–39.

36. See "God and Onto-Theo-logy," which is the title given to part 2 of *God, Death, and Time*, trans. B. Bergo (Stanford University Press, 2000), 121–242.

37. See "God and Philosophy," in *CPP*, 169 or *BPW*, 144.

38. "Truth of Disclosure," in *BPW*, 103; see also similar remarks in *OTB*, 144–45 / *AE*, 183–84.

39. *OTB*, 144–45 / *AE*, 184.

40. *OTB*, 144 / *AE*, 184.

41. *OTB*, 146 / *AE*, 186.

42. "Truth of Disclosure," in *BPW*, 107.

43. *OTB*, 119 / *AE*, 153.

44. *OTB*, 146 / *AE*, 186.

CHAPTER FIVE

TIME'S DISQUIET AND UNREST

The Affinity between Heidegger and Levinas

Emilia Angelova

> Can the nonrest of time, that by which time contrasts with the identity
> of the Same, signify otherwise than according to the continuous mobility
> that the privileged metaphor of the flux suggests? . . . This would suggest
> a disquietude that would be identified as indiscernible, or that would not
> be identified by any quality. To be identified thus, to be identified without
> being identified, is to identify oneself as "me" [moi]; it is to identify oneself
> internally without thematizing oneself and without appearing. It is to be
> identified without appearing and prior to taking a name.
>
> —God, Death, and Time, 109[1]

In his late lectures of 1975–76, Levinas returns to Heidegger, writing that—
behind the phenomenon of death in the analytic of Dasein in *Being and
Time*—it is "death" that "crouches like a question with no givens" (*GDT*,
38). Levinas grants Heidegger that death is an ending as well as being an
end, in the verbal and nominal senses. Moreover, he admits that Heidegger's
exploration of the transitivity of the existential verb "to be" constitutes his
"unforgettable" contribution (*GDT*, 122). Yet, for Levinas, to the extent that
"coming-to-the-end" and "coming-at-the-end" mark a signifying thought still

tied to logic, Heidegger remains preoccupied with the nominal sense of being, with an "epic of being." That is, Heidegger posits that the beingness of being and a certain reductive, that is, metaphysical comprehension of it, is at the origin of "all meaning" (*GDT*, 123). Levinas, who remains never too interested in the later Heidegger, leaves no room for departure from his early thesis. He is reluctant to see a change even as, after the mid-1930s, Heidegger shifts from the problematic of being-toward-death, recognizes that the epoch of philosophy itself has reached its end, completed and fulfilled in the dominance of European science, and embarks upon the opportunity to think differently, an opportunity for "thought to rediscover a possible thinking of being" (*GDT*, 126). As Levinas puts it, what the later Heidegger calls "*the thinking of being*" remains tied to a certain comprehension of being as having the transcendence of an entity, in the sense that "being is or does its business of being" (*GDT*, 124). In other words, Heidegger does not move beyond being and fails to think the *other of being* "as irreducible to the Same," which would imply a new notion of meaning and a certain ethical relationship, within which one may start out in this search. For his part, Levinas insists not on contrasting or opposing (*opposer*) being to its beyond, but on "separating" the Other from the Same. Only so will it be possible to think meaning—"what is meaningful does not necessarily have to be" (*GDT*, 125).

At first glance, it would appear that Levinas's explicit distancing from Heidegger offers no bridges, no connection between the two. It is instructive to note, however, that Levinas charges the later Heidegger with taking a "step backward," a procedure that is neither a negation nor a negativity of the substance that is thought itself. Levinas implies that the Hegelian term *aufheben*, which means that which *aufgehoben ist*, or what is sublated, is "at once rejected, preserved, and raised up" (*GDT*, 124), might apply to the later Heidegger's own critical distancing from the early thesis. There is something resilient in the early thought, Levinas seems to be suggesting, that does not easily give up. Might it be also, I ask below, that similarly there is more in common between Heidegger and Levinas, a resilience of a deeper order than individual thinkers are ready to accept. In this chapter, I suggest that on the point of taking a "step backward" there is a closer affinity between Heidegger and Levinas than Levinas might admit. Related to this point, there is more affinity than typically admitted between Heidegger's thinking of the withdrawal of Being and Levinas's thought of alterity. For Levinas, the Other "separates," evades, disrupts, yet only "within" my relationship with another (*autrui*), the very meaning of the "nonrelation" with the Other (and the Holy) is the openness and exteriority of its alterity that never closes in onto a "self" or immanence. As I show, the Other in Levinas—rather than repelling, opposing, and contrasting or confirming and exhibiting being—is a thought that enlarges a "dis-inter-estedness" (*GDT*, 125). But in this there is affinity with the later Heidegger's thought of the trace (*khreon*) of Being that does not appear. More significantly, I want to think the alterity and singularity of the "separated" in Levinas in proximity with what the early Heidegger, in the Freiburg lecture course of 1920–21, calls a kairological experience of time. On the basis of this rethinking of temporality, Heidegger revisits Western philosophy's conceptual determination of time and its temporal and temporalizing dimension already in *Being and Time*. Related to kairological time, I attempt to demonstrate that the resistance in the later Heidegger to his earlier problematic, and at the same time, his turning to language—as that spacing of the thought on which Being is founded; and to the "word," as that donation and meaning whose unfolding is "essentially a salutation"—offers more of a bridge to Levinas than is usually assumed.

Let us sketch the context of this main point. Levinas charges Heidegger's period of fundamental ontology (the inquiry into the conditions of possibility for any systematic ontology) from *Being and Time* with a turning to the hermeneutics of the questionability of being, a "what it is to be?" that is insufficiently radical. That is, for Heidegger, the existential imperative of the verb "to be" points to that sort of being whose own being is in question. Yet the mode of questioning is an abstract tautology, a circular hermeneutic faithful to the Greek and Modern sense of epistemological, attitudinal cognition, where to question being it is to posit being. Since Dasein's fundamental mode of being is that of projection—being-toward-death is projective being. The time of Dasein arises from out of projecting being to its own end, the project preceding time itself, as it were. Heidegger is obsessed with claiming the certainty and transcendence of being as possibility, as an "epic of being" (*GDT*, 123).[2] Accordingly, the epic or "repose" of being, being itself as "resting-upon," refers to a being secured onto a foundation whose transcendence has not been properly attended to and genuinely interrogated. After the *Kehre* or "turn" in the 1930s and World War II, Heidegger leaves behind his passing interest in hermeneutics and begins to think the "truth of Being" as practice and a delivery, a destining of Being, which announces European philosophy to be an epoch of the "forgetting" of the ontological difference between being itself and beings. That is, the forgetting of being has a foundation that is not in the form of a being. But Levinas is unambiguous that the safe "memory of logic," to which Heidegger now seeks to return, is not free from recuperative and transcendent Greek forms of metaphysical thinking; notably, the logician's being is taken for God. For Levinas, then, Heidegger's ties to "the manner in which being was translated as the Being of beings" still bear the marks of onto-theo-logy (*GDT*, 124).

This chapter asks whether it is really the case, as Levinas claims, that in Heidegger's analytic of temporality the "disquiet and unrest of time are abated" (GDT, 108, cf. epigraph). For Levinas, Dasein—by means of the fact that it receives its determination out of projecting its being toward its end (Dasein's being-toward-the-end is my "ownmost possibility")—confuses time and the real, and time and being. Levinas contends that existence is thought as synthesis and, therefore, rests upon being as given and as its own foundation. So Levinas attributes to Heidegger the flux or river model of time. In this model, the individual instant is "identified" by a synthesis. The instant flows past but is nevertheless "retained and protained," thereby constituting a time synchronous with itself (self-same) and coexisting "at the same time with" another (past) time. It is worthwhile to further attend to this difficult issue more closely. I take up this problem and show how time, in Heidegger, is tied to Dasein's being-in-the-world, with its facticity. Turning to facticity leaves us with a time model in which rupture is not abated, but rather emerges as a possibility of time itself, a futural "to-come" but one that comes both toward and behind us. Without including this rupture, and ontologically speaking, this "gap," into the utmost basic givenness of Dasein's determinate being-in and its facticity, Heidegger's existential analysis, especially the structure of "care," which implies encountering the Other in her Dasein and Being-with in the world, would remain misunderstood.

LEVINAS, OR AGAINST DEATH AS BASIS: THE ABSOLUTE ABSENCE OF THE OTHER BREAKS OFF

Below I focus on the objections that Levinas presents in the lectures appearing in God, Death, and Time. The aim is to give a succinct picture of Heidegger's premising of time upon the certainty of death as possibility, or, as Levinas puts it, a "being-toward-my-death." Against this premising, Levinas invokes his objection that Heidegger's is an altogether nihilistic, ontological rather than ethical stance and a complete denial of "all values."[3] These are objections predominantly concerning death, pointing to Levinas's alternative view of time as duration and diachrony. They bring time into focus as the problem that will keep Levinas and Heidegger distant from one another or bring them into proximity, as I contend here.

On Levinas's view, Heidegger reduces the affectivity of the Other to the "emotion" of anxiety, which demonstrates that the deepest desire driving the "human" is the "desire to be." Even if death is untimely, as he rightly argued, it remains nevertheless the being of man, for Heidegger, that is too short to cover desire—"my being cannot cover my desire to be: the coverage is too short." Originary time marks fundamental ontology, for in it desire originates. Yet since desire is understood on the basis of anxiety, time becomes the basis of mortality as the property of finite being. Being is reduced to the meaning of the mortality of finite being and is thus a "purely formal value." All values are reduced to the being mortal of man, thus entailing a denial of values, a failure to go beyond value and reach further than the individual will (*GDT*, 93). Levinas fully accepts from Heidegger the point that with death it is not a matter of asking a question as when one confines oneself in speaking about death, or of thinking about time as that moment when the impossibility to be arrives upon man. But for Levinas, contra Heidegger, death introduces a dimension of the Infinite and a radical Other, that is, the social intensity of a meaning that evades and surpasses finite being. So death is a "form that borrows nothing from some information [*renseignement*] about the beyond," and death is a "basis from which 'information about the beyond' could itself take on meaning." Before one can arrive at death as a basis, one must first of all arrive at time as that which takes on meaning. Time first allows for death to be a basis, or figure, a measure of the finite at all. But time, therefore, must be understood in its "duration and its diachrony as deference to the unknown," a deference to the social radicalism of the Other (*GDT*, 38).

Thus the idea of death, for Levinas, relates only to the death of the Other. Moreover, relating to it—if at all—is indeed a "scandal," a disquietude of the "first" death (Eugen Fink). Now for Heidegger, Dasein's being-out-ahead-of-oneself is a mode of there-being, which simultaneously also grasps, understands Being (*Seinsverständnis*). The latter is so because being-toward-death is Dasein's outstanding possibility (horizon), to be seized upon in advance of relating to self as given or determinate being. In this individuating structure, Dasein not only exposes the individual to dying. It exposes it above all to its death as both a phenomenon and condition of possibility that is mine alone, one that involves attestation to my ownmost potentiality for being. Concerning the transitivity of "to be," death is the ecstatic openness that is given to me directly, yet never in the same time and together with dying itself. Death's individuating instant (*Augenblick*), its intransitivity, is not identical with dying but precisely escapes conceptual determination. As both *the* end and an ending, death, in its pure projectivity, by itself precedes (*Vorlaufen*) being as given and as being-in. Death refuses grasping by understanding and illustration; it refuses figuration. For example, it refuses the sort of figuration that we find in the half-full moon, the other half of which is "elsewhere," "outside," and "withdrawn" or missing. Death is the outstanding possibility in the sense of time itself that is not yet. Since it is an ontological structure, death's not-yet never passes in the manner of calculable time (e.g., the fruit that is as yet unripe and waiting to mature). Thus the constancy of dying (*absterben*) is quite other than the decisiveness and difference (*Unterschied*) that the instant of death brings, as it were, with itself. The instant makes death appear as a pure phenomenon of mortality, a certain belongingness within Dasein. Dasein is able to die, for it contains its death within itself, a "distance" that is relative only to itself, a peculiar relationality without entailing a "relation" proper. In qualifying this peculiar distance, containment, and belongingness, then, Heidegger calls death my "possibility" for "being." One thinks the relationality of Dasein's death by analogy with the *Ausstand*, an "outstanding debt." Like borrowed money, one owes it, can withdraw it, yet unlike simple debt, it is the debt that will have been paid, a most certain and definite "possibility" (SZ, paragraph 48; cf. GDT, 39). Dasein's harboring within itself of the distance of the not-yet of its end is, therefore, Dasein's "ownmost possibility" for Being. But how indeed does Heidegger understand that? For Levinas, Heidegger thinks the end "in the very order of Dasein," a present-at-hand, *Vorhandensein*.[4] That is, for Levinas, the "not-yet" inheres in the there-being of Dasein, quite simply as a mode of individual being correlative to thought. The "that" there-is or "there-being" of the *Da-* of Dasein indicates a "content proportionate to its thought, a correlate of thought" (GDT, 115). The demonstrative property of the pronoun "Da-" cuts short the clandestine transcendence of the name and noun (the Other). Even as he follows Heidegger, arguing that death emerges as pure phenomenon, as within the relationship in which life doubles upon itself in death, the provocation entered by Levinas concerns whether this relationship "of thought to the beyond-measure" can "still be called thought" (GDT, 115).

Specifically, Levinas charges that Dasein approaches its own end as my-end, on the model of death as appropriation of the self-same, or my-death: the "suppression of the experience I could have of it [death, my end]" (GDT, 38). The problem that Levinas finds with Heidegger is at least three-fold. First, Dasein "assumes"—from the moment that it is, or is born—that it is ready to die. To Levinas, this indicates that for Dasein, also death is a way of being (*ist der Tod eine Weise zu sein*). It reduces something nonabstract and nonconceptual, a nearness between life and death, to something ontic and available, at Dasein's disposal (GDT, 40).[5] Second, Heidegger allows that in its death Dasein is no longer there, loses its structure. But for this to be so, it is the thinly disguised being of Dasein that masters the scene and masters itself in exiting this relation to itself. Dasein does not really dissolve or set structures free; it rather gestures at a dissolution while remaining closed up, in denial, firmly grounded in the self-sameness of being that is its own foundation. Third, Dasein's coming-to-the-end, which is coincidental with being-at-the-end, is the most proper, untransferable, and most inalienable possibility of Dasein. For Levinas, this coincidence attests to a circular teleology. Dasein sets up a relation to its own end if only to be able to figure it, imagine it, realize it by way of reliving it, in order then to reestablish its being-in-the-world at the basis of its own foundation. Dasein's self-assigned belongingness to death first enables its own relation to itself. It first asserts its "mineness" (*Jemeinigkeit*): thus "one cannot take the other's death from him [*dem Anderen seinen absterben abnehmen*]" (SZ, paragraph 47; cf. GDT, 39–40). The death of Dasein, hence, is something more clearly related to the purely formal value of being as something ongoing—never to stop—than to the "affair" of the Other that is my responsibility. As Levinas summarizes, for Heidegger, the possessive relation to being becomes something metaphysical, a determination of being *qua* being as never ending: "[T]ime is, in its origin, *zu sein* [to be], that is to say, *zu sterben* [to die]" (GDT, 41). "[I]t is on the basis of the to-being [*l'a-être*] of existence that the to-death [*l'a-mort*] that is Dasein must be grasped" (GDT, 40–41).[6] Considering his philosophical inheritance, Heidegger's error lies in resorting to a thought nurtured by Husserl's thematization of synthesis and the contents of consciousness. First Husserl allowed for a thematization of an "as-yet-unfulfilled future" that is certain of the stability of being, which is metaphysically overarching and self-identical with itself. Like him, Heidegger subordinates the instant's stability to the synchrony (i.e., meaning) of the present. Husserl posits a self-abiding time identical with itself, inherent in being, to be possessed. Being appears as time's own predicate, secondary to time, where time alone is what is or is-not, it is full or empty. Both Heidegger and Husserl premise the stability of time and the instant ultimately upon the thinker's own act of self-positing. Being is not more than self-relation, a presupposition resting on the self's synthesis with itself. For Levinas, the philosophy of presupposition is merely mathematically certain, confirming the identity of the term—"time as entity"—as self-referential with itself. Extrapolating to Heidegger, Dasein's death is not more than a relation mirroring a calculable grammar of relations, reducing to mere insignificance both self and the other. Possessive or attitudinal being takes beings for granted, while itself lacking all grounding in alterity: it is nihilistic and merely presuppositional, identical only with itself (cf. GDT, 108).

The charges against Heidegger amount to the basic objection that death is thought on the plane of positing a "question to oneself." A nihilistic ontology of Dasein commits Heidegger to the idealist model of entering a dialogue of the soul with itself. Precisely the structure of the "question" (even the "question questioning itself") fails to improve on Heidegger's philosophizing about being-toward-death. The ontological condition that Dasein elaborates upon fails to arrive at a structure that would succeed in staying open, awakening and disclosive. For Levinas, then, the pure "question mark" is rather a problem surpassing the tautology of the metaphysics of being and finite being's successions of self-positing. Heidegger's questioning "would never be possible unless the relationship with the Other [*Autrui*] and the question mark of his face had come about" (*GDT*, 114). Thus, the challenge is to think rationality and meaning without having to hold onto a model of fulfillment (*Erfüllung*, whether of intuition or conscious synthesis) where the "meaningful is the fully possessed." The lasting of "consciousness"—as Levinas belittles Heideggerian Dasein—might indeed appear in the mode of a question. Yet Heidegger lightens being of its weight and of its alterity. That Dasein "lasts" in the question is the wonder that ought to be rethought. So Levinas calls for approaching Heidegger's hermeneutic of openness and resoluteness from the alterity of the other that "uproots" all essence (*essentia*). Heidegger inevitably reduces being to the economy of contradictory predicates, vindicating a logic of opposites, and equates Being to death, "on the basis of the play of being *and* nothingness" (*GDT*, 114). Levinas, in responding, claims even death for alterity's alliance: death is a question mark that "might nonetheless have a meaning, and a religious meaning, the meaning of a deference to the Infinite" (*GDT*, 115).

Contrast the "now" based view of Heidegger's metaphysical being to Levinas's ambiguous notion of time, of which there are two kinds. Aside from the time that offers itself to construction—for example, the synthesis of existence, the unity of apperception, and so on—there is a time of suddenness, of disproportionate transcendence, provoking a destruction and disquiet, an undoing, unsaying, and "uprooting," a time of an "obsession," in which "the other besieges me." The time of ethics is what Levinas calls the "time of suddenness." Ethics is the relationship with another [*autrui*], a relationship (without a relation, not considering the protections of the concepts of ethics as protected in legal society and everyday life, for example, rights and freedoms of the I) construed on the model of the time of suddenness (*GDT*, 138). This emphasizes the contingent and gratuitous character of a relationship with the other, for the "other is the first to come." In this relation we speak of the blow or stroke of the Other, since the obsession (the nudity of the exposure of the face in which I see the death of the Other) is that which wholly structures my relationship with the other. The blow is sudden, since the transcendence of the Other is impossible "to see." She is the "invisible, and of whom one awaits no fulfillment." And it is sudden since the thought that thinks it is broken off, "separated" before the "before" of time signing the temporality of being. Levinas understands the exteriority of time as inaugurating the social figure of an ethics and the outside of the Other. But this inauguration is a disquiet, rupture—an uprooting from essence—and therefore is quite different than constitution (which would imply self-constitution) by the "hand of Dasein" (*fassen*, grasping in the manner of illustration, representing the Other). The Levinasian time model of ethics does not afford fulfillment since ethics evades the thetic standpoint or position-based view of the present as a pure "now." With Levinas, the awaiting sets forth the precedent of a "before" "without something awaited (time itself)" (*GDT*, 139). Finally, patience—not receptivity, contra Husserl, but also not impatience, contra the "eros" of what Levinas calls the "feminine" other[7]—is that which is in the manner of my relation to it a meaning as nonthematizable, disproportionate, and in excess of thought (*GDT*, 138).

To sum up: For the Levinasian subject, it holds that I/ It (the neutrality, anonymity, impersonality of the *es gibt*, *il'y a*)[8] participates in the reversibility of the infinite living of the Other always in the manner of contemporaneity. Participation defines the nameless subject in an untimely fashion, without ever yielding a confirmation, or a check sign, determining this subject before the fact, as both a late coming and arriving too early at the crime scene. For now we have established that, contra the Heideggerian epic of referentiality, of time, space, and Dasein's clinging to being even in being-toward-death, the Levinasian subject shakes off the centrality of my-death at the heart of being, with death itself losing its significance in being traversed, achieved, conquered, or surpassed. Were we to follow Levinas, one ought to revise Heidegger's thought of death as experience of the "end in its mode of being-there," as gathering up the totality of being. The objection from Levinas—that only in creating an "other relation" with the death of another, "can" we die—comes down to the contrast in method, contrasting ontology to the ethical relation and projection to inscription. However, Heidegger's thought, as will be discussed in the next section, is closer to inscription than Levinas would admit. Heidegger's assertion of mineness is not necessarily bound to a sense of the proper (*Eigentlichkeit*) nor a sense of totality, as Levinas wants to claim.

HEIDEGGER'S RELATIVIZATION OF DEATH: THROWNNESS AS POSSIBILITY TO BE REPEATED

I organize this section according to two objectives. I begin with some claims from *Being and Time*, with an eye toward a possible reply to Levinas's objections discussed in the preceding section. I end with observations on the role of kairological time in Heidegger.

In *Being and Time*, the "Preparatory Fundamental Analysis of Dasein" introduces the object of philosophy in such a way as to show that the starting point of philosophical inquiry is temporal, since philosophy has nothing in common with an "understanding of being" (*Seinsverständnis*), but rather presupposes it. This object is deepened into a fundamental ontology of being that would comprehend the Being of Dasein as "being-as-a-whole" and so the "meaning of being." Such an object—part of the analytic of Dasein, which in turn lends this object structural support—is and remains projective: the inquiry is "ontically rooted [*verwurzelt*]" (*SZ*, 13) in the radicalization of that everyday yet "essential tendency-of-Being which belongs to Dasein itself" (SZ, 15), such that Dasein has to question the meaning of its being.[9] For Heidegger, without the Da- of Dasein ("that it is" and "there-being"), life (das Leben) is not accessible. However, the there-being of Dasein is not anything like a "human reality"; such an assumption would mistakenly suggest a proximity between fundamental ontology and a philosophical anthropology. To make life accessible, on the one hand, Heidegger must subtract from there-being its strictly ontic empiricism, which is the object of study of anthropology, biology, and chemistry. On the other hand, however, to make life accessible, in making accessible a relation to Being at its ontological-existential foundation, Heidegger must subtract from there-being "ontological nothingness," the impossibility of being as such.[10] The question is how to make life accessible as more than a mere fact to be affirmed but rather as a "need for philosophy"[11]—though quite other than the preinterpretation arrived at through Lebensphilosophie, for example, Dilthey's hermeneutics. As I want to show, by engaging in an "unheard of history of violence,"[12] Heidegger tackles the problem first by recovering the existential structure of "thrownness" (Geworfenheit) of Dasein.

Three figures of thrownness—Dasein's being brought into its "there," but "not of its own accord" (SZ, 284, cf. paragraphs 29, 38)—are examined in Being and Time: expropriation, being born[13] or projection; everyday "falling" into being or facticity; and ontological guilt. Far from reducing the analytic of Dasein to the epistemological enterprise that is "philosophy of life," as Levinas suggests, Heidegger scrutinizes rather the separateness, the facticity (which is not to be confused with "fact") of the "throw" that first renders perceivable the separation of the "there" of Dasein. The Da- of there-being demonstrates nothing objectively determined, especially not an objective description of a being-present-at-hand. Yet it points to and orients, "clears"—since it rather qualifies a subject always already implicated in connectedness to its others. The "object" (not a Gegenstand) of the analytic of Dasein is a temporal totality involving the transcendence of Being first as difference, a propriation of the essence of thought and event, and only then as identity. It is thought thinking over itself that arises out of the demand to take up the identity of this difference. Dasein is indeed endowed with understanding upon which builds its demonstration of the conditions of possibility for reflection on the "ontological ground" of ontology. But for this demand to manifest, the Da- of Dasein precisely involves a distancing from Being, in the very midst of connectedness and proximity to it. Since the analytic is itself always already (immerschon) an involvement of thought with itself, an "expanded" interpretive act of thought, enlarged by its ideals, that it so emerges is possible against the background of a removal from itself of anything that would approximate factical conditions of being as such.

This removal, expressed in an ex-centered drifting away, binds upon think-ing itself. The internal necessity of this binding amounts to what it means to elevate oneself to the open ground of being. The removal plays out of the self-incurred demands for a twofold procedure for verifying what the later Heidegger calls the "truth of Being." Heidegger's approach to facticity versus fact is taken up below in light of these overall concerns, which for us are definitive of his philosophical position.

Briefly recalling Levinas's first objection, we can say that indeed the temporal totality implying the object of philosophy, entails what Heidegger calls in the *Analytic*, the "mineness" of being-toward-death of Dasein: "Dying is something that every Dasein itself must take upon itself at the time. By its very essence, death is in every case mine, in so far as it 'is' at all" (*SZ*, 240). This is so since fundamental ontology is a concern with the "task" implied in Dasein's having "to be" its being (*Zu-sein*). The "task" character of "to be"—the demand to also interpret, understand, not simply live—is attested to in the title of the early work, *Ontology: The Hermeneutics of Facticity*. "Facticity," already in 1923, is conjoined with "mineness," the latter having nothing to do with objectively describing the being of Das-ein. The transitivity of the sort of being that is Dasein's own to-be sets it apart from the being of an object to be taken cognizance of and having knowledge. Dasein is that which *is* insofar as it is, "according to its being [*seinsmäßig*]." Dasein is the kind of being "that it is and has to be": "'Fac-ticity' is the designation we will use for the character of the being of 'our' 'own' Dasein. More precisely, this expression means: in each case [*jeweilig*] this Dasein . . . insofar as it is, according to its being [*seinsmäßig*] 'there' in the character of its being . . . *Seinsmäßig* Dasein means: not, and never, to be there . . . as an object" (GA 63, 13).[14]

Second, for Heidegger, taking charge of one's being thrown is corre-lated with the necessary and asymmetrical assumption of death, of a being-toward death. Assumption—this overtaking (*übernehmen*)—is a response, a "taking over" out of internal necessity (unavailable to either objective or subjective values of "truth" verification). Assuming one's being-toward is a demand arising out of the in each-case-character of Dasein: "[I]n each case Dasein is mine to be in one way or another. Dasein has always made some sort of decision as to the way in which it is in each case mine [*je meines*]" (*SZ*, 43). Overtaking presents a challenge that is not to be overcome. Chal-lenge (demand) is assumed, yet it originates with a more primordial origin, namely, the inaccessible mineness of existence, an ethical solipsism, as we see below. And third, the ontic-ontological structuring of the Da- of Das-ein's being determines an untransferable experience of existing and dying. This latter determinacy precisely elaborates on the hermeneutic rigor that Heidegger calls "need of interpretation" as a "taking up in existence" (*SZ*,

135), an effort at laying out the ground of facticity, out of the radicalism of the difference between Being and a being. This is so since a metaphysics of presupposition is further grounded upon an ungroundable ground of "experience," namely, the "taking up in existence" that in each case posits access to a more basic form of givenness. Giving, then, just is a structure of openness and a receptivity, without which there can be no "response" or responsibility.[15] "The self, which as such has to lay the basis for itself, can never get that basis into its power; and yet, as existing, it must take over being-a-basis" (SZ, 284).[16] In sum, facticity is the inaccessible ground of experience (Erfahrung versus Erlebnis) and is the need for philosophy other than preinterpretation. It is, in short, Heidegger's speculative figure of a more originary responsibility. Consequently, Jemeinigkeit is the mark that implicates Dasein not only in the return of Being. Dasein's return "from Being" is likewise the work of its mark. Out of this mark destines the Being of the Da- (being-toward-death but as well being-born) and opens thought up to the real meaning of a "privative interpretation" of Being, in a significant sense, the alterity of Being. Thus, no one can take the other's death from him. To better understand Heidegger, we must turn more closely to Heidegger's text, then, on its own terms, as we briefly do below.

Dasein is projective in essence. It is the sort of being that is never already realized, due to the structure of its being. One is one's own being—as the transitivity of the verb "to be" involves a direct object, an ontic being, a fact. But, nonetheless, Dasein "is" a comportment disclosive of the relationality of Being in the mode of a question ("Was ist das Sein des Seienden?"). Dasein is finite by its form; it is temporally extending, unfolding out of a self-relation that is in a mode of being-out-lying-ahead-of-oneself; yet the sort of relation to being, which is alone Dasein's own, is never a relating to itself as a mere fact. The self-relation of Dasein—far from being derivative from a transcendental a priori condition—is a mode of conditioning a relation to self as anticipation (Vorlaufen) and temporalizing instant.[17] It is a stepping back- and out of- and behind- being, a "fact" of philosophy that is not given, that does not belong to the order of intratemporal being. Dasein does not as such relate to factuality, to states of affairs: "Facticity is not the factuality of the factum brutum of something present-at-hand, but a characteristic of Dasein's Being . . . The "that-it-is" of facticity never becomes something that we can come across by beholding it" (SZ, 135). This is, hence, what the analytic extracts doubly: a pure phenomenon of philosophizing, Dasein's "falling prey," its facticity, and a need for philosophy, an internal need for interpretation, including "curiosity" (Neugier) as one of the modes of the falling.[18] For Heidegger, the birth of theory, a unique quest for origin, is a function of curiosity. Curiosity begins in a regional ontology, but its theory is simultaneously submitted to the demands of a fundamental ontology. It is not a quest into which one is thrown once and for all, but rather is that into which one is in-each-case born. Whatever the facts that one can enlist for a person's Dasein, these will be facts that are simultaneously "taken up," surely lived, in her Da-sein.

In saying this, Heidegger is closer than expected to time as a mediation of being: a time as its own "to-come"; a time temporally differentiating itself from itself; with an eye to Levinas, a time determined by a synchrony that is simultaneously also a diachrony. In Heidegger's problematization, facticity means not what it says, its sign pointing always to something else.[19] So facticity is implicated in a repeating and a retrieval without an objectively determinate end and telos, another formative structure of the Da-. Repetition (Wi(e)derholung) is a recapitulation that simultaneously transforms—a deeply ambiguous structure, first striking us in the distracted "listening" (without hearing) (Hinhören) to the They-self. Repetition is always a participation in language. In relating "to" language, it is, more precisely, rather aimed "at" language, an end-goal wherefrom the telos withdraws, thus an idealization, a neutralization, and therefore, engagement in a relation to what being is not or not-yet (that is, to what is not-nothing). Françoise Dastur characterizes neutralization, not accidentally with reference to Husserl, as a relationship without a "relation," which takes time beyond synchrony: "The very element of reduction is effectively language itself—that operates a spontaneous neutralization of all facticity . . . This deadly power of language is only the reverse side of its constitutive power: in putting facticity to death, language opens the infinite realm of ideality."[20] Because Dasein's possibility "as such," of making sense of being, does not determine as "cause" the conceptual grasp of relating to Being, the object of philosophy laid out in Dasein's analytic exceeds the being of any ontic entity as ground of ontology. Granting access to Dasein's questioning no longer satisfies philosophy as metaphysics, but depends on a concept of philosophy as double grounding, that is, an ontic-ontological grounding, even if that be merely the "effect" of one.[21]

To sum up: facticity—including the brokenness[22] of distracted listening, the Hinhören (SZ, 271)—unites both the phenomenon of being (life, being-born and being-toward) and the individuating, relational difference to which amounts Dasein's mode of being (interpretation, language). That it does so is testimony to its own ambiguous (self-) expression, a condition for possibility that is also its own precondition. The latter is part of what, in a moral philosophy, would present access to transcendence. Dasein is the doubling of life (the conditioned) upon itself, understood, nevertheless, as in need of being con- and destructed, as at each-time my own (the unconditioned), a project. Most emphatically, the existential structure of Care—corresponding with the "experience" of utter dissolution (a disclosure, openness and resoluteness, e.g., for "as long as Dasein is, Dasein, as care, *is* constantly its 'that-it-is'" [*SZ*, 284][23])—grants an opening up to Being's internal structure. Facticity, culminating in care, points to a deepening of Being's openness, a relationship without a subordinated relation. Being's openness is, it seems, more likely than not, affinitive with Levinas's alterity.

With this in mind, what gives rise to Levinas's objection against Heideggerian time as synchrony, as he puts it, the "ecstasy of Being," is rather in need of undisguising from engagement in various devices for partially obscuring the precarious phenomenon of attunement. Such obscuration (always happening at the price of radicalizing relations with Being) introduces, notably, the basis of the foreclosive mood, *Grundstimmung*, of anxiety, "no longer caring for itself"[24] and "it is boring for one": *es ist einem unheimlich* (*SZ*, paragraph 40) and *es ist einem langweilig* (*BW*, 101).[25] Anxiety's mood is obscurant for it reveals more than the "insignificance of the world" and reveals the "nullity of that potentiality-for-Being which belongs to existence and which is founded primarily upon one's objects of concern." As Rudi Visker has demonstrated, contra Levinas and Michel Haar,[26] for Heidegger anxiety *qua* impossibility of an authentic *Seinkönnen* (*SZ*, 343)[27] is revealed as that which halts, paralyzes the time of indifferent, distracted listening and inauthentic being-in-the-world, which "im-possibilizes at the same time as it possibilizes." Following Heidegger in the *Fundamental Concepts of Metaphysics* (1929),[28] boredom is a mood more originary or fundamental than anxiety. In withholding itself, since withholding my possibilities from me, boredom is that "something," or master—rather than Death as master—that undoes and unmakes. As Heidegger adds, "possibilizing" involves a relating "to" time (neutralization). Time is "that which properly makes possible the Dasein in me [*das eigentliche Ermöglichende des Daseins in mir*]" and is "*whatever it is that makes possible, sustains and guides all essential possibilities of Dasein*" (*GA*, 29/30, 216).

All told, I am insisting here on an alternative reading of Heidegger's words concerning the analysis of boredom, "*Alles Versagen ist ein Sagen.*"[29] The *Versagen* or "impoverishment," a "withdrawal" of Being, to the degree of "de-*persona*-lization," lies on a continuum with "extreme singularization, metaphysical loneliness." That is, the continuum or reversibility (*Versagen*) of the living is part of the concretization of abstraction and the universal; it links not on a privation, but rather on a generation and a generosity, a giving, a listening-to/ responding of authentic being (*Zu-sein*): "no one can take over my *Zu-sein* from me." What breaks off or ruptures or drops, in this *Versagen*, is the mode of inauthentic listening (*Hinhören*), i.e., a belonging to the public persona of the they-self. Despite loss, what is not lost for us—for Dasein—hence what is and must remain un-lost—is the "truth" of disclosive Being. Since Dasein is always at play in, participating in (its) Being, so unlost is the determinacy of the self in the constancy of its mode

as care, its "that-it-is." As Heidegger has it, in the telling refusal of boredom there lies a message, "there lies a reference [*Verweisung*] to something
else . . . of possibilities left unexploited" (GA, 29/30, 212). And further:
"in all its nakedness *to itself* as the self that *is there* and has taken over the
being-there of its Da-sein. For what purpose? *To be that Da-sein*" (216).[30]
This is certainly an emphasis on exposure and being as pointed to "something else," an extra-temporaneity. But still more tellingly aligning Levinas
with Heidegger is the evidence that "possibilities" are pointed to, revealed
as to be exploited—as these break off and singularize the Da- of Dasein.
These are rendered in 1929, and in *Being and Time*, as a "trace" or "link"
with Being. As I demonstrate below, it is not the case here and elsewhere,
that rupture depends, as Levinas suggests, on the ontotheological "one" or
the signifier (Being as God). In particular, it is not true that Dasein falls
first into ontotheological Being and then falls into the radical sociability of
the world, but quite the reverse. That is, rupture is a "specific possibility of
time itself": "The moment of vision [*Augenblick*] ruptures the entrancement
of time [*Bann der Zeit*], and is able to rupture it, insofar as it is a specific
possibility of time itself. It is not some now-point that we simply ascertain,
but it is the look of Dasein in the three perspectival directions we are already
acquainted with, namely, present, future and past . . . the look . . . of resolute disclosedness for action in the specific situation in which Dasein finds
itself disposed in each case" (GA, 29/30, 226).

   For Dasein to be there-being, it means for it to expose itself to the
nihilative essence of the "nothing" (GA, 9, 1–19)[31] yet understood not metaphysically, but precisely as a "specific possibility of time itself," one that lies
at the basis of its questioning mode ("What it is to be?"). That is, there-being
cannot be anything at all, unless it takes up and assumes all its attributes,
and that is, unless it exposes to existence the transcendence of essences,
and the essence of "man." As Dastur explains, that "I *alone* am responsible
for *opening myself* to what happens to myself," is internally necessitated by
Dasein's at "each time mine" character. "At each time" the contingency of
thrown-being into the world is to be taken upon itself: this contingency
is what doubles upon itself. The gap is impossible to close between being
and a being, for its openness belongs with the "facticity of Dasein's being
brought before itself."[32] Contra Levinas, it seems, the three modes of "falling" of Dasein in its everyday-being have everything to do with Heidegger's
own staying higher and above moralizing critique or ideological critique or
a dogmatic religious account of the "fall" from an original condition.

   To prejudge Being as a formalism, a purely formal value, and individualistic will to power, as Levinas has suggested, it is to take lightly precisely
Heidegger's own distancing from ontotheology and insistence on approaching neutrality and neutralization differently. It is to misunderstand the

qualifier "fundamental" in Heidegger's "fundamental ontology," an inquiry into Being-in, the "phenomenon of equiprimordiality" (underivability from other phenomena), and into a "multiplicity of characteristics of Being" as its constitutive items (SZ, 131–132). It is no accident that also in *Metaphysical Foundations of Logic* (1928), interest in the "neuter," and a certain "in-exappropriability" of the event of Being, to use Derrida's word, guides Heidegger's inquiry. As Derrida takes this up: "To pass from *Mensch*, indeed *Mann*, to Dasein, is certainly to pass from the masculine to the neutral, while *to think or to say Dasein and the Da of Sein from that transcendent which is das Sein* . . . is to pass into a certain neutrality."[33] The passing from the incoherent transcendence of Being to a certain neutrality is tied to the very "requirement of an analytic of *das Dasein* in its very neutrality," i.e., to a "falling" that is a mode of comportment of Dasein to (its) Being as a radical question mark. Neutrality is the "effect" of inscription, in the absence of "cause," but also a silent violence. Falling is a neutralizing and a sheltering, but as well a genesis of ideas, a generating of the idea of inscription itself in the absence of transcendence. Falling simultaneously incurs a surplus over the ontic, deferring appearance, and renders classical ontology questionable, while mandating in its stead a self-relational, malleable, material substance subject to destinal vanishing. The generative openness of Dasein's falling ought to be thought as participating in the reversibility of the sort of Being which determines Dasein's relationality, all the way down, including the relation welcoming the successive "forgetting of Being" and metaphysical erasure. The lost-ness in the "they"—the falling and "throw" of average everydayness, *das Man, Verdeckungen, Verstellungen, Uneigentlichkeit*, in which we recognize traditional disciplines' concerns with falsehood and error, and evil and sin—is a neutrality that is itself not of the order of negativity. Rather, it is in the preinterpretations of Being that these "value judgments" engage in necessary movements of the history of Being and its interpretation. Thus neutrality is a requirement of Dasein's "determinate modes of being-in." However, as tying not-yet positions and points of view to the irreducible multiplicity of spatial meanings: "The being-in-the-world of Dasein is, with its facticity, always already dispersed [*zerstreut*] or even parceled out [*zersplittert*] into determinate modes of being-in" (SZ, 56).[34]

To be sure, Dasein's dispersion as being-in, as well as its distraction—*Zerstreuung* in both the above senses, which is not a diversity correlative of homogeneity—is that of inauthentic selfhood. Being as "anyone" (*Manselbst*) is, then, distinguished from authentic and proper (*eigentlich*) selfhood (*Selbst*) as, albeit only as modes, repetitions and "accents" of differentiation of the same generative continuity. That is, dispersion is both a general structure of Dasein and a mode of inauthenticity: the "who" is both the neuter (*Neutrum*) and "the one" (of "it was no one") (SZ, paragraph 27).[35]If the general and the particular[36] never could become self-identical, it is because the *Neutrum* is also the "who." Equivalently, the spacing or imagining of spacing between Dasein and (its) Being, Being's behind or beyond, and for Heidegger, a figure of extreme singularization, is the index rather of a "certain corruption, of the figure of man" (not "human nature"), in which the impossibility of closing the gap recurs. So one cannot encounter the parallel figures of anonymity, impersonality and neutralization shared between Levinasian ipseity, the subjectivity of the subject, and the Heideggerian nonindifference, intransitivity, or absolute particularity of the "one" that is the "who"—without seriously contemplating a certain profound affinity, a rather close proximity between the two thinkers.

Furthermore, this in-exappropriability of the *Neutrum*, the force of the "who" ("*Wer sind wir?*"), will resurface in the later Heidegger. There it is taken up as *Verwesung*,[37] but more precisely as force or a giving, granting as well as attestation, an ability to call into question every paradigm of "forgetting," of enframing or totalizing, that is, technologically making and producing (using, e.g., "religious, ethical and dialectical schemas"). In short, this powerful recourse to a "who"—reducible to neither private nor public self—aids Heidegger against deriving the "fundamental metaphysical character of Dasein" from "any generic organization or form of community of living beings as such." Because of this, *Being and Time* understands the more primordial givenness of the community of being-with, Mit- ("with") of Dasein's Mitsein ("being-with") with another Dasein as an existential structure (not a categorical). To speak with Derrida, a certain "generic drive of gathering together . . . has as 'metaphysical presupposition' the dissemination of Dasein as such, and thereby Mitsein."[38] Neutrality and neutralization—as well as boredom and anxiety as links with the anonymity of Being—have here been shown quite in contrast to what is attributed, including by Levinas, to Heidegger's "privative interpretation" of Being.

In this, no theme is more pervasive in the above reasoning than that of the trace, inscription, and Being as salutation. As recent commentators have noted, *Being and Time*'s mode of the "withholding" of Being—refusal to appear yet without entailing a "privative approach"[39]—is a mode of the revealedness of openness and resoluteness of Care. Being's "withdrawal" is continuous with the "trace" of Being in the later Heidegger, for whom "oblivion belongs to the self-veiling of Being" (*HW*, 336).[40] The idea of Being's withdrawal is taken up in work on the "early" trace—*unerscheinlich*—of which Heidegger speaks in "Anaximander's Saying."[41] The trace is "older" than Being, it can never be appropriated in the *as such* of its name, given it by Greek metaphysics, or of its appearing. Heidegger calls the trace a "unique word"—it is the first word of Being: *to khreon* (*HW*, 334, 337ff). This is translated by Heidegger in German by *Brauch*, usage—trace is the relation to what is present and that (relation) rules in the essence of presencing itself as a unique one (*ist eine einzige*). In the manner of the brokenness and singularization of Dasein—trace belongs to the uniqueness of Being itself. That is, because Dasein is broken up by Being as trace, as its unique possibility, it is not im-possible for language to find a single and unique word (*das einzige Wort*; *HW*, 337). Since Dasein is broken up or claimed by Being, the single word is addressed to Being. The word breaks up, singularizes, since every "thoughtful word" (*denkende Wort*) addressed to Being listens-to/ responds "on this side." It "speaks" "always and everywhere throughout language (*HW*, 338)." Language is devoted to "receiving that which asks to be opened up,"[42] listening/ responding to Being. Language is not a sign structure, in its essence it is a listening-to in which unfolds Being "itself," on condition of "being docile toward that which lays claim to it"—the voice of Being in its withdrawal.[43]

Above I maintained that Heidegger makes legible a transcendence of Being. It is a presence of thinking in excess of metaphysics: Being is not a content-question as the Greeks thought it. Instead, retrieved as a form(alization)-question, Being becomes the mode of the coming back of thinking to the essence of thinking itself. It is a renewal of a problem toward the mode of presence of the "unthought"—not as an "elsewhere" but as within relationship with being's other: what had remained external to Western thought, in excess of "logic," is first expanded to the subject as history of the "act of thinking itself." It is one of its essential possibilities as a giving. This coming back amounts to a redefinition of thinking as that meaning on the basis of which the opening out of another essence or transcendence becomes possible—"to respond to the promise, to hear, obey, call, remain faithful, to be grateful."[44]

To support this latter claim, I want to engage by way of concluding, Heidegger's early work on kairological time. Making sense of time as temporal totality—a kairological time, from the Greek *kairos*, "the appropriate time for decision"—complicates the objections by Levinas. In *Phenomenology of Religious Life*,[45] reflecting on St. Paul's letters to the Thessalonians and to the Corinthians, Heidegger is interested in the kairological experience of time, and what sets it aside as different from chronological time.[46] The suddenness of *kairos* comes to be remarkably close to the suddenness of the later Heidegger's *Ereignis*, the event: "Only he who is constantly 'available' to the unforeseeable temporal event can welcome, in the moment of decision, that which comes to meet him."[47] Heidegger retains the theological content of the Christian concept of the second coming, but as a way of commitment to ontic content as correcting, adapting to itself, the ontological condition: "faith" (*GA*, 60, 152) is a model of self-relation as carrying its justification in itself, experience turning to its own situation—for the sake of taking up that which is retained.

Faith is a self-relation that repeats itself as a meaning set out from the start—a meaning upon which life is based. But faith's relationality is a repeating on the order of the linguisticity of Being ("the *How* of the factual!")—"Because you *are* called the basic sense of your *Being is*" (GA, 60, 152; 150). The kairological determination of time is at once the form of suddenness (of what is to come) and a specific determination of existence as availability and vigilance (of those who await it).

In faith's repetition, without it being a repetition of something with a genus and the specificity of an entity, we must note once more the affinity between neutralization and effacement, as pursued above. The time of *kairos* interrupts the life of man. It is a nihilation of the day to day determination of existence upon which life is based as "secured and accessible." But it also is a replacement with, indeed displacement upon another, a more basic givenness. The replacement (a setting free) is sourced in life's own determination, as the always inaccessible, but also as wholly oriented by the stroke of suddenness transformatively announced with the coming of the temporal event. To the suddenness of this event that is coming corresponds the human behavior of vigilance. To sum up:

1. Suddenness characterizes the way by which it is given; the given is not a content but the event as the temporal totality of the coming.

2. The event interrupts from that which is absolute absence, that is, the future, as the unforeseeable and the unknown, so the present is placed "under the threat that comes to it from the future."

3. The threat coming from the future renders the present into the moment of "*decision*, at the same time that the decision is the affair of the moment." The wholly transformative effect of what is coming is the moment in which "everything" is in play: "The *kairos* can neither be awaited, nor grasped, for the importance of its ungraspable quality would be broken in the representation of a present prolonged into a future that we fundamentally already know."[48]

That is, the threat from the future is a threat to "all" of time. It is not the "end" of man as finite being, death's coming to-an-end and coming-at-the-end, as in Levinas's challenge to Heidegger. All (*das Alles*) of time, "everything" is in "play" and up for decision. The mode of coming of threat (the future, the Lord, the Messiah) is that of passing toward and a passing behind us. This thus stresses the donative aspect of what is coming as well as the ungraspability, unrepresentability, yet thinkability, of the future. The internal relation (filiation) between appearance and predication, memory and logic is that which cannot be decided by way of a thinking as comprehending, through reason or that which presents itself. The filiative relation is "older." The mode of presence of the to-come is a withdrawal and a welcome. It is not the withdrawal of thinking (negativity) but rather its presence in history, the presence of another rationality, another relationship: for Heidegger, this is the transformative experience of a more primordial religiosity of the community of the early Christian life.

Likely the young Levinas attended the lecture course of 1928, in which, as pointed out above, neutralization and neutrality, the withdrawal into unobtrusive concealment of the presence of Being, including the neutrality of "sexual difference" (*Geschlechtlosigkeit*) (noted by Levinas in *Existence and Existents*) occupy Heidegger. No doubt Levinas has better succeeded in fulfilling the ethical responsibilities of thinking, giving the Other the concreteness lacking in Heidegger. Yet perhaps, learning from his teacher, Levinas shares with Heidegger not only a distrust of ontotheological notions of transcendence, but likely also shares the very idea of alterity, the idea of the "good beyond being." For both thinkers, this alterity accompanies a certain sense of metaphysics' own exhaustion and completion, to speak with Heidegger, "at the very beginning of metaphysics."

NOTES

1. Emmanuel Lévinas, *Dieu, la mort et le temps* (Paris: Editions Grasset & Fasquelle, 1993); *God, Death, and Time*, trans. Bettina Bergo (Stanford: Stanford University Press, 2000). Henceforth cited as GDT.

2. "*Das Sein west*" becomes for Levinas the "*geste de l'etre*," to suggest Being's repose.

3. The argument against Heidegger is here confined to GDT as this is the most complete work by Levinas on death and time in Heidegger. It contains transcripts of two lecture courses, Death and Time, and God and Onto-theo-logy.

4. Martin Heidegger, *Sein und Zeit*, 19th ed. (Tübingen: Max Niemeyer Verlag, 2006); *Being and Time*, trans. John Macquarrie and Edward Robinson (San Francisco: HarperCollins, 1962). Henceforth cited as SZ. Cf. SZ, 42: "The instance or special case of some genus of entities as things that are present-at-hand, is indifferent to its mode of being."

5. Cf. SZ, 245.

6. Levinas implies a sense of farewell to God, a departure unto God and a giving over to the Infinite, a to-God [*à-Dieu*]. This implies also a giving over to

time, an awaiting for that which cannot be a term and which always refers from the other to an Other [de l'Autre à Autrui]. Cf. GDT, 115.

7. Eros is distinguished from agape, the Good or God that turns-toward, which is in turn attributed, controversially, to the masculine, throughout Levinas's work.

8. Since there is no generosity or fecundity to the il y a, Levinas levels against Heidegger objections against the neutrality of the es, "it"—"es gibt."

9. Cf. Steven Crowell, "Metaphysics, Metontology, and the End of Being and Time." Philosophy and Phenomenological Research 60, no. 2 (2000): 307–31.

10. Reiner Schürmann, Heidegger on Being and Acting: From Principles to Anarchy, trans. Christine-Marie Gros (Bloomington: Indiana University Press, 1987), 141ff.

11. This point is developed in 1921 in Phenomenological Interpretations of Aristotle. See on this Raffoul's excellent essay, in François Raffoul and Eric Sean Nelson, eds., Rethinking Facticity (Albany: State University of New York Press, 2008), 69–85.

12. Cf. Derrida's "Preface," in Catherine Malabou, The Future of Hegel: Plasticity, Temporality, and Dialectic, trans. Lisabeth During (London: Routledge, 2004), ix–x.

13. Being-born is not leveled out to the present-at-hand. "Understood existentially, birth is not and never is something past in the sense of something no longer present-at-hand" (SZ, 374).

14. Martin Heidegger, Ontologie (Hermeneutik der Faktizität) (Frankfurt: Klostermann, 1988); Ontology—the Hermeneutics of Facticity, trans. John Van Buren (Bloomington: Indiana University Press, 1999). All references of the type (GA 63, 13) are to the pagination of the Gesamtausgabe. Translation corrected from the English publication, cited in Raffoul and Nelson, 178.

15. Cf. Françoise Dastur, Death: An Essay on Finitude, trans. John Llewelyn (London: Athlone, 1996), 45.

16. Cf. Raffoul's elaboration. in François Raffoul and David Pettigrew, eds., Heidegger and Practical Philosophy (Albany: State University of New York Press, 2002), 205–19.

17. I borrow this idea from Malabou, 13–16.

18. Cf. SZ, paragraph 36.

19. This is reliant on Malabou, 16–20. But see also Jacques Derrida, Of Spirit: Heidegger and the Question, trans. Geoffrey Bennington and Rachel Bowlby (Chicago: University of Chicago Press, 1989).

20. In Françoise Dastur, "Finitude and Repetition in Husserl and Derrida," The Southern Journal of Philosophy 32, supplement (1993). See also Françoise Dastur, Heidegger and the Question of Time, trans. François Raffoul and David Pettigrew (New York: Prometheus Books, 1998).

21. See Robert Bernasconi, "The Double Concept of Philosophy and the Place of Ethics in Being and Time," Research in Phenomenology 18 (1988): 41–57; "Transcendence and the Overcoming of Values: Heidegger's Critique of Scheler," Research in Phenomenology 15 (1984): 259–66.

22. Cf. Raffoul and Nelson, 135. Eric Sean Nelson develops the point that singularization takes place "before" the before of Zu-Ende-kommen, "coming-to-be-at-the end," death. Cf. SZ 271: "If Dasein is to be able to get brought back from

this lostness . . . it has to find itself as something . . . which fails to hear in that it listens away to the 'they' [*sich selbst, das sich überholt hat und überhört im Hinhören auf das Man*]. This listening-away must get broken off."

23. Cf. "As existent, [Dasein] never comes back behind its thrownness . . . as some event which has happened to Dasein . . . [I]t *is, in its existing*, the basis of its potentiality-for being" (SZ, 284).

24. Using Visker's translation, in Raffoul and Nelson, 168.

25. Martin Heidegger, *Basic Writings*, ed. David Farrell Krell (San Francisco: HarperCollins, 1993).

26. This point is developed by Visker's essay "Intransitive Facticity?" in Raffoul and Nelson, 170–76.

27. Cf. SZ, 343: "[Anxiety] brings one back to the pure 'that-it-is' of one's ownmost individualized thrownness . . . brings one back to one's thrownness as something *possible* which can be *repeated*."

28. Martin Heidegger, *Die Grundbegriffe der Metaphysik* (Frankfurt: Klostermann, 1992); *The Fundamental Concepts of Metaphysics*, trans. William McNeil and Nicholas Walker (Bloomington: Indiana University Press, 1995). Cited as GA, 29/30.

29. Cf. GA, 29/30, 216. Not the Self, but only the name, status, etc., inauthentic being are drawn into indifference. As Visker notes, the English translation is inaccurate: "the Self" "which is *itself* drawn into indifference."

30. This 'that-it-is' of Dasein is what Levinas calls a "certain ecstatism of contemporary thought." Emmanuel Levinas, *Existence and Existents*, trans. Alphonso Lingis (Pittsburgh: Duquesne University Press, 2001), 138. I follow here Visker. On the "between" of Levinas and Heidegger, see further Dastur, 1996: 42–61.

31. Martin Heidegger, *Wegmarken*; *Pathmarks*, trans. William McNeil (Cambridge: Cambridge University Press, 1998).

32. Dastur, 44–45.

33. Cf. Derrida Jacques, "Geschlecht I: Sexual Difference, Ontological Difference," in *Psyche: Inventions of the Other*, ed. Peggy Kamuff and Elizabeth Rottenberg (Stanford: Stanford University Press, 2008). A similar but different view of death and sexuality is found in "The Tomb of Perseverance: On Antigone," in Joan Copjec, *Imagine There Is No Woman: Ethics and Sublimation* (Cambridge: MIT Press, 2002), 12–47.

34. Translation corrected, cited in "Geschlecht I."

35. Cf. SZ, 126: "The 'who' is not this one, not that one, not oneself [*man selbst*], not some people [*einige*], and not the sum of them all. The 'who' is the neuter (*Neutrum*), the 'they' [*das Man*]."

36. Cf. Martin Heidegger, *The End of Philosophy*, trans. Joan Stambaugh (Chicago: University of Chicago Press, 1973), vii–xiv. See further Joanna Hodge, *Heidegger and Ethics* (London: Routledge, 1995).

37. Heidegger on Georg Trakl's poem, cited in "Geschlecht I."

38. Cf. SZ, 120: "This Dasein-with of the Others is disclosed within-the-world for a Dasein, and so too for those who are Daseins with us [*die Mitdaseienden*], only because Dasein in itself is essentially being-with." This aspect of being-with is developed by Jean-Luc Nancy; cf. e.g., in Raffoul and Nelson, 113–29.

39. This concerns SZ, 42–45.

40. Martin Heidegger, *Holzwege* (Frankfurt: Klostermann, 1972), 296–344; *Off the Beaten Track*, trans. Julian Young and Kenneth Haynes (Cambridge: Cambridge University Press, 2002), 242–82. Henceforth cited as *HW*.

41. Ibid. "Lichtung des Unterschiedes kann deshalb auch nicht bedeuten, daß der Unterschied als der Unterschied erscheint" (336).

42. Marlené Zarader, *The Unthought Debt: Heidegger and the Hebraic Heritage*, trans. Bettina Bergo (Stanford: Stanford University Press, 2006), 41. Henceforth cited as *UD*.

43. Ibid., 42. In Zarader's phrasing: "Even before there is agreement between words, and as the foundation of this agreement, we should consider the vertical agreement, an agreement of that to which every word refers."

44. *UD*, 84.

45. Martin Heidegger *Phänomenologie des Religiösen Lebens* (Frankfurt: Klostermann, 1995); *The Phenomenology of Religious Life*, trans. Matthias Fritsch and Jennifer Anna-Gosetti-Ferencei (Bloomington: Indiana University Press, 2004). Henceforth cited as *GA, 60*.

46. *UD*, 152. The Pauline *kairos* is the time of the coming of the Lord, or Parousia, and Heidegger, as Marlené Zarader argues, "essentially retains the concept of *kairos*." Cf. *GA*, 60, 149–52, 154–55.

47. *UD*, 152.

48. *UD*, 152.

CHAPTER SIX

ORIGINARY INAUTHENTICITY

On Heidegger's Sein und Zeit

Simon Critchley

The past beats within me, like a second heart.

—John Banville, *The Sea*

Although its author still invites controversy and polemic, and its theses invite much misunderstanding, there is no doubting the originality and massive influence of Heidegger's *Sein und Zeit*, first published in 1927.[1] Some would argue that it is the most important work of philosophy published in the twentieth century. In this chapter, I will attempt to give a reinterpretation of Heidegger's *Sein und Zeit* through an internal commentary of the text in its own terms rather than through some sort of external and potentially reductive reading. I will do this by focusing on two phrases that provide a clue to what is going on in *Sein und Zeit*: Dasein ist geworfener Entwurf and Dasein existiert faktisch (Dasein is thrown projection and Dasein exists factically). I begin by trying to show how an interpretation of these phrases can help to clarify Heidegger's philosophical claim about what it means to be human. I then try to explain why it is that, in a couple of important passages in *Sein und Zeit*, Heidegger describes thrown projection as an *enigma*. I trace the use of enigma in *Sein und Zeit* and try to show how and why the relations between Heidegger's central conceptual pairings—state-of-mind (*Befindlich-keit*) and understanding (*Verstehen*), thrownness and projection, facticity and existentiality—are described by Heidegger as enigmatic. My thesis is that at the heart of *Sein und Zeit*, that is, at the heart of the central claim of the Dasein-analytic as to the temporal character of thrown-projective being-in-the-world, there lies an enigmatic a priori. That is to say, there is something resiliently opaque at the basis of the constitution of Dasein's being-in-the-world which both resists phenomenological description and which is that in relation to which the phenomenologist describes. In the more critical part of the chapter, I try to show with more precision how this notion of the enigmatic a priori changes the basic experience of understanding *Sein und Zeit*. I explore this in relation to three examples that are absolutely central to the argument of Division II: death, conscience, and temporality. I seek to read Heidegger's analyses of each of these concepts against the grain in order to bring into view much more resilient notions of facticity and thrownness that place in doubt the move to existentiality, projection, and authenticity. This is the perspective that I will describe as originary inauthenticity. As will become clear, this line of interpretation has significant consequences for how we might consider the political consequences of Heidegger's work, in particular—and infamously—the question of his political commitment to National Socialism in 1933.

There are two phrases that provide a clue to what is going on in *Sein und Zeit*: Dasein ist geworfener Entwurf and Dasein existiert faktisch. That is, Dasein—Heidegger's word for the person or human being—has a double, or articulated structure: it is at once thrown and the projection or throwing-off of thrownness. Yet it is a throwing *off*—which is how I hear the privative *Ent*- in *Ent-Wurf*—that remains *in* the throw. As Heidegger puts it, Dasein im Wurf bleibt (*SZ* 179). Dasein is always sucked into the turbulence of its own projection. Dasein is the name of a recoiling movement that unfolds only to fold back on itself. Its existentiality, its projective being-ahead-of-itself, is determined through and through by facticity; it is always already thrown in a world, and in a world, moreover, ontically determined in terms of fallenness: the tranquillized bustle of *das Man* ("the one" or "the they"). This movement of thrown throwing off or factical existence is the structure of *Sorge*, the care that defines the being of Dasein in *Sein und Zeit*. Heidegger summarizes the structure of care with enigmatic formulae, such as "Dasein ist befindliches Verstehen" ("Dasein is state-of-minded, or disposed understanding," SZ 260); or again, "Jedes Verstehen hat seine Stimmung.

Jede Befindlichkeit ist verstehend" (Every understanding has its mood. Every state-of-mind or disposition understands, SZ 335). The principal thesis of the published portion of *Sein und Zeit* is that the meaning of care, where meaning is defined as that upon which *(das Woraufhin SZ 324)* the thrown throwing off of Dasein takes place, is temporality *(Zeitlichkeit)*. Simply stated, the meaning of the being of Dasein is time. With the term "temporality," Heidegger seeks to capture the passage from authentic to inauthentic time and back again. That is, the masterfulness of what Heidegger calls "ecstatic" temporality, consummated in the notion of the *Augenblick* (moment of vision, or blink of the eye) always falls back into the passive awaiting *(Gewärtigen, SZ 337)* of inauthentic time. Thrown projection or factical existing is ultimately the activity of Dasein's temporalizing, its *Zeitigung*, an articulated, recoiling movement, between sinking away in the dullness of the everyday and momentarily gaining mastery over the everyday by not choosing *das Man* as one's hero.

Once this structure begins to become clear, then it can also be seen that thrown projection or factical existing defines the concept of truth. For Heidegger, truth is also a double or articulated movement of concealment and unconcealment that he finds lodged in the Greek term *aletheia*. In paragraph 44, the famous discussion of truth in *Sein und Zeit*, with an important emphasis that goes missing in the Macquarrie and Robinson translation, Heidegger writes,

> Die existenzial-ontologische Bedingung dafür, daß das In-der-Welt-sein durch "Wahrheit" und "Unwahrheit" bestimmt ist, liegt in *der* Seinsverfassung des Daseins, die wir als *geworfenen Entwurf* kennzeichneten.(SZ 223)

> The existential-ontological condition for being-in-the-world being determined through "truth" and "untruth" lies in *the* (the italics, and hence the linguistic and conceptual force of the definite article is missing in Macquarrie and Robinson) constitution of the Being of Dasein that we have designated as *thrown projection*.

That is, the condition of possibility for the play of truth and untruth in *aletheia* is the claim for Dasein as thrown projection. In his later work, however, Heidegger always wants to read *Sein und Zeit* from the perspective of what he calls "the history of being" *(Seinsgeschichte)* by claiming that the "lethic" element in truth already implies an insight into *Seinsvergessenheit*, the forgetfulness or oblivion of being. Therefore, although Heidegger will admit in his later work that *Sein und Zeit* expresses itself metaphysically, it already implies an insight into the history of being and thereby into what he calls "the overcoming of metaphysics" (die Überwindung der Metaphysik). This is how—in a manner that I always find questionable because of the complete assurance with which Heidegger feels himself able to shape and control the interpretation of his work—Heidegger continually seeks to pre-serve the unity of what he calls his Denkweg, his path of thought. To use Heidegger's own idiom from a manuscript on nihilism from the late 1940's, we might say that the basic experience (die Grunderfahrung) of Sein und Zeit is this belonging together of facticity and existence, of thrownness and projection, of fallenness and surmounting. It remains a hypothesis to be confirmed or disconfirmed by future research as to whether this is the basic experience of Heidegger's work as a whole.[2]

So, what is the being of being human for Heidegger? Or, in so far as the human being is understood as Dasein whose essence lies in Existenz, what is the nature of existence? It is care as a temporally articulated move-ment of thrown throwing off or factical existing. My concern here consists in working out why Heidegger describes this structure as an enigma and what might be the implications of this claim for an interpretation of Sein und Zeit. Once the claim for Dasein as thrown projection is introduced in paragraph 31 on Verstehen (SZ, 148), which is also where the word "enigma" makes its most significant entry into Sein und Zeit, then the rest of the book is simply the deepening or nuancing of this structure, like a leitmotif in Wagner, moving through a series of variations. Let's call them "enigma variations," to use an English rather than a German example, Elgar rather than Wagner. What fascinates me in Sein und Zeit is what I would call the spinning or oscillating movement of these variations, where Heidegger tries to capture this enigma in a series of oxymoronic formulations such as Dasein existiert faktisch, Dasein ist Geworfener Entwurf, Dasein ist befindliche Verstehen, Jedes Verstehen hat seine Stimmung, Jede Befindlichket ist verstehend, "Dasein ist in der Wahrheit" sagt gleichursprünglich . . . "Dasein ist in der Unwahrheit" (Dasein is in the truth simultaneously says . . . Dasein is in the untruth, SZ, 222). As I shall try to make clear presently, the thought which is spin-ning out or being spun out in Sein und Zeit is that of Dasein as the enigma of a temporal stretch, an almost rhythmical movement or kinesis of factical existing that is so obvious, so absolutely and completely obvious, that it is quite obscure. As Wittgenstein notes, "The aspects of things that are most important for us are hidden because of their simplicity and everydayness (Alltäglichkeit)." (One is unable to notice something—because it is always before one's eyes).[3]

The word Rätsel, enigma or riddle, kept catching my eye when reading certain key passages from Sein und Zeit, so I decided to try and follow its usage systematically. I have found at least eleven places where the words enigma (Rätsel), enigmatic (Rätselhaftig) and enigmaticity (Rätselhaftigkeit) are used in *Sein und Zeit* (*SZ*, 4, 136, 137, 148[x2], 371, 381, 387, 389, 392, 425), and I will examine these below. Enigma also appears in Heidegger's later work, in particular in his 1942 lecture course on *Der Ister*, which I discuss elsewhere.[4]

In the opening paragraph of *Sein und Zeit*, Heidegger writes that "in jedem Verhalten und Sein zu Seiendem als Seiendem a priori ein Rätsel liegt." (*SZ*, 4) That is, in every comporting oneself to beings, or intentional relation to things, there lies an a priori enigma. This claim already begins to strike a rather dissonant note with the formulation of the phenomenological notion of the a priori in the first draft of *Sein und Zeit* in the 1925 *Prolegomena zur Geschichte des Zeitbegriffs* that I discuss in detail elsewhere, where the a priori is that which shows itself in what Husserl calls "categorial intuition."[5] It would seem that the intentional comportment of the phenomenologist directs itself toward, and itself arises out of, something that eludes phenomenological manifestation. This "something" is what I call the *enigmatic a priori*.

However, the form that this enigmatic a priori takes in *Sein und Zeit* becomes much more striking in paragraphs 29 and 31, on *Stimmung, Befindlichkeit*, and *Verstehen*. Heidegger writes that *Stimmung*, mood, brings Dasein to "the That of its There" (*das Daß seines Da*) in a way that stares back at it with an inexorable enigmaticity ("*in unerbittlicher Rätselhaftigkeit entgegenstarrt*" *SZ*, 136). Let me clarify this point. Heidegger's initial claim in *Sein und Zeit* is that Dasein is the being for whom being is an issue. In Division I, chapter 5, the claim is that the being which is an issue for Dasein is the being of its "there," the disclosure of its *Da* (*SZ*, 133). Thus, Dasein is fundamentally characterized by the capacity for disclosure (*Erschlossenheit*). Or, better, Dasein itself *is* the clearing that discloses, "es selbst die Lichtung ist . . . das Dasein ist seine Erschlossenheit" (*SZ*, 133). As Tom Sheehan points out, this is what Jean Beaufret had in mind in translating Dasein as *l'ouverture*, which we might render as "the open*edness*" to convey the idea that Dasein is always already the space of its disclosure.[6] Indeed, rather than thinking of Dasein as being-there as opposed to here, we might think of being-in-the-world as an openedness which is neither here nor there, but both at once.

Heidegger's claim in paragraph 29 is that the way in which Dasein is its "there" is caught with the notion of *Befindlichkeit*, namely, that Dasein is disclosed as already having found oneself somewhere. The means of disclosure for this *Befindlichkeit* is *Stimmung*; namely, that I always find myself in some sort of mood: I am attentive, distracted, indifferent, anxious, bored, or whatever. Therefore, Dasein's primary form of disclosure is affective, and this affective disclosure reveals Dasein as *thrown* or delivered over to its existence, its "there." Therefore, what stares inexorably in the face of Dasein is the enigma of its thrownness, the fact that I am and that I am disclosed somewhere in a particular mood. This fact is like a riddle that I can see but cannot solve.

Perhaps the most thought-provoking usage of enigma in *Sein und Zeit* occurs just a little further on in the text, at the end of paragraph 31, where Heidegger summarizes the discussion of *Befindlichkeit* and *Verstehen* by introducing the idea of Dasein as thrown projection in a series of sentences that enact the very enigma that is being described,

> Befindlichkeit und Verstehen charakterisieren als Existenzialen die ursprüngliche Erschlossenheit des In-der-Welt-seins. In der Weise der Gestimmtheit "sieht" das Dasein Möglichkeiten aus denen her es ist. Im entwerfenden Erschließen solcher Möglichkeiten ist es je schon gestimmt. Der Entwurf der eigensten Seinkönnens ist dem Faktum der Geworfenheit in das Da überantwortet. Wird mit der Explikation der existenzialen Verfassung des Seins des Da im Sinne des geworfenen Entwurfs das Sein des Daseins nicht rätselfhafter? In der Tat. Wir müssen erst die volle Rätselhaftigkeit dieses Seins heraustreten lassen, wenn auch nur, um an seiner "Lösung" in echter Weise scheitern zu können und die Frage nach dem Sein des geworfenen-entwerfenden In-der-Welt-seins erneut zu stellen. (SZ, 148)

Let me closely paraphrase rather than translate this passage, as the precision of Heidegger's conceptual expression is difficult to render literally. The first sentence simply summarizes the conclusions of the opening paragraphs of chapter 5, namely, that the disclosedness of being-in-the-world is constituted through the existentials of *Befindlichkeit* and *Verstehen*—Let's call them (B) and (V). But the following three sentences enact this conclusion in the form of a series of conceptually pallindromic statements:

1. In its being-attuned in a mood (B), Dasein 'sees" possibilities (V).

2. In the projective disclosure of such possibilities (V), Dasein is already attuned in a mood (B).

3. Therefore, the projection of Dasein's ownmost potentiality-for-being (V) is delivered over to the *Faktum* of thrownness into a there (B).

Enigmatic indeed! But, Heidegger insists, the full enigmaticity (*Rätselfhaft-igkeit*) of this enigma must be allowed to emerge, even if this all comes to naught, founders, is wrecked, or shatters into smithereens, which are various connotations of the phrase "*scheitern zu können*." So although Heidegger adds that out of such a wreckage might come a new formulation ("*erneut zu stellen*") of the question of thrown-projective being-in-the-world, the disruptive force of the enigma is such as to lead to a breakdown over any phenomenological "solution" ('*Lösung*') to the riddle of Dasein.

Turning now to Division II of *Sein und Zeit*, the word "enigma" appears on the final page of chapter 4, "Temporality and Everydayness," four times in chapter 5, "Temporality and Historicality," and once in chapter 6 on time-reckoning and the genesis of our ordinary understanding of time (SZ, 389, 392, 425). I would like to look in detail at one further appearance of enigma, which occurs just after the temporal *Wiederholung* or recapitulation of the analytic of inauthenticity. Heidegger says that Dasein can for a moment—*für den Augenblick*—master the everyday, but never extinguish it (*den Alltag meistern, obzwar nie auslöschen*). He continues,

> Was in der faktischen Ausgelegtheit des Daseins *ontisch* so bekannt ist, daß wir dessen nicht einmal achten, birgt existenzial-ontologisch Rätsel über Rätsel in sich. Der "natürliche" Horizont für den ersten Ansatz der existentialen Analytik des Daseins ist *nur scheinbar selbstverständlich*. (SZ, 371)

> What is ontically so familiar in the factical interpretedness of Dasein that we never pay any heed to it, conceals enigma after enigma in itself existential-ontologically. The "natural" horizon for the first starting point of the existential analytic is *only seemingly self-evident*.

That is to say, the existential analytic renders enigmatic the everyday ontic fundament of life, what Husserl calls the natural attitude, what Plato calls the realm of *doxa*. But, and this is crucial, Heidegger does not say that the existential analytic overcomes or permanently brackets out the natural attitude of ontic life; it does not achieve some permanent breakout from the Platonic cave.[7] Rather, as Heidegger points out a few lines prior to the above-cited passage, "Die Alltäglichkeit bestimmt das Dasein auch dann, wenn es sich nicht das Man als 'Helden' gewählt hat" (SZ, 371). That is, even when I have not chosen *das Man* as my hero, when I choose to become authentically who I am, the everyday is not extinguished; it is rather rendered enigmatic or uncanny. That which is ontically so familiar hides enigma after enigma ontologically. Or, in the words of the opening paragraph of the existential analytic, "The ontically nearest and familiar is the ontologically furthest" (SZ, 43). The existential analytic of Dasein seems to return ceaselessly to the enigma from which it begins, an enigma which, in Heidegger's words, shatters the seeming self-evidence of any natural attitude from which phenomenology might begin in order to force the philosopher to formulate anew the question of being-in-the-world. That is, Heidegger transforms the beginning point of phenomenology from the self-evidence of the natural attitude to the enigma of a *Faktum*, the fact *that* one is; philosophy begins with the riddle of the completely obvious.

So, my thesis is that at the heart of *Sein und Zeit*; that is, at the heart of the central claim of the Dasein-analytic as to the temporal character of thrown-projective being-in-the-world, there lies an enigmatic a priori, a fundamental opacity that both seems to resist phenomenological description and is that in relation to which the phenomenologist describes. As such, in Kantian terms, we might say that the enigmatic a priori is not only transcendentally constitutive; it is also regulative. It is not only descriptive, or rather a limit to the activity of phenomenological description, but also normative, functioning like an imperative in the philosophical analysis of being-in-the-world. Philosophy must attempt to be equal to the enigma of our being-in-the-world, while knowing all the time that it cannot. My question will now be: what does this fact entail for our reading of *Sein und Zeit*?

Heidegger defines "phenomenon" as *was sich zeigt*, what shows itself, and the phenomena that show themselves in *Sein und Zeit* are not empirical facts, but rather the a priori structures of Dasein's being-in-the-world—the existentials (SZ, 31). However, if a phenomenon is what shows itself, then an enigma by definition is what does not show itself. It is like a mirror in which all we see is our reflection scratching its chin in perplexity. An enigma is something we see, but do not see through. We might, therefore, at the very least, wonder why the vast and sometimes cumbersome machinery of Heidegger's phenomenological apparatus should bring us face to face with an a priori enigma, with a riddle that we cannot solve. We might be even further perplexed that the riddle here is nothing particularly complex, like the final insoluble clue in a tricky crossword puzzle. On the contrary, the riddle here is that of absolute obviousness, the sheer facticity of what is under our noses, the everyday in all its palpable plainness and banality. Yet, it is this riddling quality of the obvious as the very matter or *Sache* of phenomenology that interests me here.

I began by saying that there are two formulae that provide a clue to understanding what takes place in *Sein und Zeit*: Dasein existiert faktisch and Dasein ist geworfener Entwurf. Ultimately, I would like to *modify* the way we hear the formulations, "thrown projection" or "factical existing," by placing the emphasis on the *thrown* and the *factical* rather than on projection and existence.[8] That is, on my interpretation, Dasein is fundamentally a *thrown* throwing off, a *factical* existing. It should be noted that what is continually appealed to in Heidegger, in *Sein und Zeit* and even more so in the later work, is a change in our capacity for hearing, that is, whether we *hinhören auf* or listen away to *das Man*, or whether we *hören auf* or hear the appeal that Dasein makes to itself (SZ 271—*inter alia Sein und Zeit* can be understood in musical terms, as an immense treatise on sound, hearing, and rhythm). It is my hope that a change in the way we hear these key formulae will produce an aspect change in the way we understand the project of fundamental ontology.

I will begin to spell out this aspect change presently, but why is it necessary? It is necessary to move our understanding of *Sein und Zeit* away from the heroic political pathos of authenticity, consummated in the discussions of fate and destiny in the infamous paragraph 74 on the basic constitution of historicity. As Karl Löwith was the first to learn when he met with Heidegger in Rome and Frascati in 1936, although he has subsequently been followed by other scholars, the concept of *historicity* (*Geschichtlichkeit*) is the link between fundamental ontology and Heidegger's political commitment to National Socialism in 1933.[9] Let me try to restate briefly the argument, as prima facie the connection between historicity and politics will be far from obvious for many readers.

Dasein's authentic anticipation of its death is called "fate" (*Schicksal*) by Heidegger, and this is designated as the originary historicizing or happening (*Geschehen*) of Dasein.(SZ, 384). Heidegger's claim in Division II, chapter 5, is that the condition of possibility for any authentic understanding of history lies in Dasein's historicity, which means the self-understanding of the temporal character of being human, that is, finitude. So, to repeat: the meaning of the Being of Dasein is temporality, and the meaning of temporality is finitude (SZ, 331). Dasein's authentic self-understanding of finitude is "fate," and this originary historicizing is the condition of possibility for any authentic relation to history, by which Heidegger means "world historical historicizing" (SZ, 19), or indeed for any science of history. It is clear that political events, such as revolutions, the founding of a state, or general social transformations, would qualify as world historical events for Heidegger.

Now, it was established in Division I, chapter 4, that Dasein is always already *Mitsein*. That is, the a priori condition of being-in-the-world is being together with others in that world. As is well known, the everyday, social actuality of this a priori condition of *Mitsein* is called *das Man* by Heidegger, and this is determined as inauthentic because in such everyday experience Dasein is not truly itself, but is, as it were, lived through by the customs and conventions of the existing social world. Now, returning more closely to the argument of paragraph 74, if fateful, authentic Dasein is always already *Mitsein*, then such historicizing has to be what Heidegger calls co-historicizing (*Mitgeschehen*, SZ, 384). An authentic individual life, Heidegger would seem to be suggesting, cannot be led in isolation and opposition to the shared life of the community. The question therefore arises: what is the *authentic* mode of being together with others? What is an authentic *Mitdasein* that escapes or masters the inauthenticity of *das Man*? Heideger writes, fatefully in my view, "Wenn aber das schicksalhafte Dasein als In-der-Welt-sein wesenhaft im Mitsein mit Anderen existiert, ist sein Geschehen ein Mitgeschehen und bestimmt als *Geschick*" (But if fateful Dasein as being-in-the-world essentially exists in being-with with others, its historicizing is a co-historicizing and is determined as *destiny*). So, destiny is the authentic historicizing that I share with others insofar as my individual fate is always already bound up with the collective destiny of the community to which I belong. Heidegger goes on, "Im Miteinandersein in derselben Welt und in der Entschlossenheit für bestimmte Möglichkeiten sind die Schicksale im vornhinein schon geleitet. In der Mitteilung und im Kampf wird die Macht des Geschickes erst frei" (The fates are already guided from the front in the being-with-one-another in the same world and in the resoluteness for determinate possibilities. The power of destiny first becomes free in communication and struggle. SZ, 384). So, the fates of authentic, individual Daseins are "guided from the front" by the destiny of the collective, a destiny that first becomes free for itself or self-conscious in the activity of communication and struggle. Obviously, the word "Kampf" has acquired some rather unfortunate political connotations between the period that saw the publication of *Sein und Zeit* and the present. But that is not the worst of it. Heidegger completes this run of thought with the following words, "Damit bezeichnen wir das Geschehen der Gemeinschaft, des Volkes" (In this way, we designate the historicizing of the community, of the people. SZ, 384). So, the authentic communal mode of *Mitsein* that masters the inauthenticity of *das Man* is *das Volk*, the people. In my view, it is the possible political realization of a resolute and authentic *Volk* in opposition to the inauthentic nihilism of social modernity that Heidegger identified as "the inner truth and greatness" (der inneren Wahrheit und Größe) of National Socialism just a few years later in *Einführung in die Metaphysik* in 1935. Despite the horrors of Nazi Germany, Heidegger—to the understandable consternation of the young Habermas writing on Heidegger in his first published essay—stubbornly refused to revise his judgment on "the inner truth and greatness" when the 1935 lectures were published in 1953.[10]

There is, I believe, a systematic philosophical basis to Heidegger's political commitment, which is due to the specific way in which Heidegger develops the concept of authenticity in Division II of *Sein und Zeit* and which culminates in the concept of *das Volk*. That is, the only way in which Heidegger can conceive of an authentic mode of human being-together or community, is in terms of the unity of a specific people, a particular nation, and it is the political expression of this possibility that Heidegger saw in National Socialism in 1933. In other words, as Hannah Arendt obliquely implied throughout her work, Heidegger is incapable of thinking the *plurality* of human being-together as a positive political possibility. Plurality is always determined negatively as *das Man*, as the averageness and levelling down that constitutes what Heidegger calls "publicness" (*die Öffentlichkeit. SZ,* 127). In my view, the urgent task of Heidegger interpretation—provided, of course, that one is not a Nazi and provided one is still in the business of thinking, as I do, that Heidegger is a great philosopher—is to try to defuse the systematic link between Heidegger's philosophy and his politics. As should have become clear, the key concept for establishing the link between philosophy and politics is authenticity, which is what I want to question by developing the notion of what I call *originary inauthenticity*, a possibility of interpretation that is available, if somewhat latent, in *Sein und Zeit*.[11]

Let me try to explain myself by going back to the key concept of *Befindlichkeit*: state-of-mind, attunement, or what William Richardson nicely translates as "already-having-found-oneself-there-ness." Heidegger's claim is that I always already find myself attuned in a *Stimmung*, a mood or affective disposition. Such a mood discloses me as *geworfen*, as thrown into the "there" (*Da*) of my being-in-the-world. For Heidegger, these three terms— *Befindlichkeit, Stimmung,* and *Geworfenheit*—are interconnected in bringing out the nature of facticity. As is well known, Heidegger's early work is a hermeneutics of facticity, a description of the everyday ways in which the human being exists. In being disposed in a mood, Heidegger writes that Dasein is satiated or weary (*überdrüssig*) with itself, and as such its being becomes manifest as a burden or load (*eine Last*) to be taken up. The burdensome character of one's being, the sheer weight of the that-it-is (*Das es ist*) of existence, is something that I seek to evade. Heidegger writes, "*Im Ausweichen selbst ist das Da erschlossenes*" (In evasion itself is the there disclosed. SZ, 135). This is fascinating, because Heidegger is claiming that the being of Dasein's *Da*, the there of its being-in-the-world, is disclosed in the movement that seeks to evade it. Evasion discloses that which it evades. It is precisely in the human being's turning away (*Abkehr*) from itself that the nature of existence first becomes manifest. I find myself as I flee myself, and I flee myself because I find myself. Heidegger seems to rather enjoy the paradox "*gefunden in einem Finden, das nicht so sehr einem direkten Suchen, sondern einem Fliehen entspricht*" (found in a finding that corresponds not so much to a direct seeking, but to a fleeing. SZ, 135). What is elicited in this turning away of Dasein from itself is the facticity of Dasein's being delivered over to itself (*Faktizität der Überantwortung*), and it is this that Heidegger intends by the term "thrownness," *Geworfenheit*.

The concept of *Befindlichkeit* reveals the thrown nature of Dasein in its falling movement of turning away from itself. But two paragraphs later in *Sein und Zeit*, Heidegger will contrast this movement of evasion with the concept of *Verstehen*, understood as ability-to-be, which is linked to the concepts of *Entwurf* (projection) and *Möglichkeit* (possibility). That is, Dasein is not just thrown into the world, it can throw off that thrownness in a movement of projection where it seizes hold of its possibilities-to-be, what Heidegger calls from the opening words of the existential analytic, *Seinsweisen*, ways to be. This movement of projection is the very experience of *freedom* for Heidegger. Dasein is a thrown project—but where Heidegger will place the emphasis on projection, possibility, and freedom as the essential elements in the movement towards authenticity, I would like to propose another possible trajectory of the existential analytic of *Sein und Zeit*, namely originary inauthenticity.

The thought behind the notion of originary inauthenticity is that human existence is fundamentally shaped in relation to a brute facticity or thrownness which cannot be mastered through any existential projection. Authenticity always slips back into a prior inauthenticity from which it cannot escape but which it would like to evade. As we saw above, it is in this movement of evasion, or the self's turning away from itself, that Dasein's embeddedness in factical existence is disclosed. From the perspective of originary inauthenticity, human existence is something that is first and foremost experienced as a burden, a weight, as something to which I am riveted without being able to know why or know further. Inauthentic existence has the character of an irreducible and intractable *thatness*, what Heidegger called above *das Daß seines Da*. I feel myself bound to "the that of my there," the sheer *Faktum* of my facticity, in a way that invites some sort of response.

Now, and this is where my proposed aspect change begins to kick in, the nature of this response will not, as it is in Division II of *Sein und Zeit*, be the authentic and heroic *decision* of existence that comes into the simplicity of its *Schicksal* by "shattering itself against death," as Heidegger rather dramatically puts it (SZ, 385). The response will not be the heroic mastery of the everyday in the authentic present of what Heidegger calls the *Augenblick* (the moment of vision), which produces an experience of what he calls ecstasy (*Ekstase*) and rapture (*Entrückung*) (SZ 338). On the contrary, the response to the *Faktum* of my finitude is a more passive and less heroic decision, a decision made in the face of a facticity whose demand can never be mastered and which faces me like a riddle or enigma that I cannot solve. As I try to show elsewhere, such a fact calls for comic acknowledgment rather than tragic affirmation.[12]

Dasein is, as Heidegger writes in his extraordinary pages on guilt, a thrown basis (*ein geworfene Grund*). As this basis, Dasein continually lags behind itself, "Being a basis (*Grund-seiend*), that is to say existing as thrown (*als geworfenes existierend*—another of Heidegger's enigmatic formulae), Dasein constantly lags behind its possibilities" (SZ, 284). The experience of guilt reveals the being of being human as a lack, as something wanting. In the light of these remarks, we might say that the self is not the ecstasy of a heroic leap toward authenticity energized by the experience of anxiety and being-towards-death. Such would be the reading of the existential analytic—and I do not doubt that this may well have been Heidegger's intention—that sees its goal in a form of *autarky*: self-sufficiency, self-mastery or what Heidegger calls in paragraph 64, "self-constancy" (*Die Ständigkeit des Selbst*. SZ, 323). Rather, on my view, the self's fundamental self-relation is to an unmasterable thrownness, the burden of a facticity that weighs me down without my ever being able to fully pick it up. Expressed temporally, one's self-relation is not the authentic living present of the moment of vision, but rather a delay with respect to oneself that is perhaps best expressed in the experience of fatigue or weariness. I project or throw off a thrownness that catches me in its throw and inverts the movement of possibility. As such, the present continually lags behind itself. I am always too late to meet my fate. I would like to think that Heidegger might have had this in mind at the end of *Sein und Zeit* when he writes of bringing us face to face with "the ontological enigma of the movement of historicizing in general" (SZ, 389).

It is my hope that if one follows my proposed aspect change from a heroics of authenticity to an originary inauthenticity then a good deal changes in how one views the project of *Sein und Zeit* and its political consequences. My main point is that both aspects are available to an attentive reading, and this is why the young Habermas was right in suggesting that it is necessary to think both with Heidegger and against Heidegger. However, the completion of such a reading is a considerable task whose fulfillment will have to be postponed to the future. In the remainder of this paper, I would just like to sketch how we might begin this task by briefly examining three central concepts from Division II: death, conscience, and temporality.

First, I think that the notion of originary inauthenticity places in question what Heidegger sees as the nonrelational character of the experience of finitude in the death-analysis in Division II, chapter 1 of *Sein und Zeit*. You will recall that there are four criteria in Heidegger's full existential-ontological conception of death. They are *unbezüglich, gewiß, unbestimmt*, and *unüberholbar*: nonrelational, certain, indefinite, and not to be outstripped. It is only the first of these criteria that I would take issue with, as the other three are true, if banal: (1) it is certain we are going to die; (2) the instant of our death is indefinite, since we don't know when it is going to happen; and (3) it is pretty damn important. However, if the first of the criteria falls, then the whole picture changes.

Heidegger insists on the nonrelational character of death because for him, crucially, "*der Tod ontologisch durch Jemeinigkeit und Existenz konstituiert wird*" (Death is ontologically constituted through mineness and existence.

SZ 240). Therefore, dying for an other (*sterben für*) would simply be to sacrifice oneself (*sich opfern*) for an other, or to substitute (*ersetzten*; SZ, 239) myself for another. Thus, the fundamental experience of finitude is nonrelational, and all relationality is rendered secondary because of the primacy of *Jemeinigkeit*.

Now, I just think this is wrong empirically and normatively. I would want to oppose it with the thought of the *fundamentally relational character of finitude*, namely, that death is first and foremost experienced in a relation to the death or dying of the other and others, in being-with the dying in a caring way, and in grieving after they are dead. Yet, such relationality is not a relation of understanding: the other's dying is not like placing an intuition under a concept. It is not a relation of subsumption, in Kantian terms a reflective rather than a determinate judgment. In other words, the experience of finitude opens up in relation to a brute *Faktum* that escapes my understanding or the reach of my criteria. Deliberately twisting Heidegger's example from paragraph 47, I would say that the fundamental experience of finitude is rather like being a "student of pathological anatomy" where the dead other "ist ein *lebloses* materielles Ding" (a *lifeless* material thing., SZ, 238). With all the terrible lucidity of grief, one watches the person one loves—parent, partner, or child—die and become a lifeless material thing. That is, there is a thing—a corpse—at the heart of the experience of finitude. This is why I mourn. Antigone understood this well, it seems to me, staring at the lifeless material thing of her dead brother and demanding justice. Authentic Dasein does not mourn. One might even say that authenticity is constituted by making the act of mourning secondary to Dasein's *Jemeinigkeit*. Heidegger writes, shockingly in my view, "We do not experience the death of others in a genuine sense; at most we are just 'there alongside'" (*nur 'dabei'*) (SZ, 239).

If death and finitude are fundamentally relational, that is, if they are constituted in a relation to a lifeless material thing whom I love and this thing casts a long mournful shadow across the self that undoes that self's authenticity, then this would also lead me to question a distinction that is fundamental to Heidegger's death analysis. Heidegger makes the following threefold distinction:

1. dying, *Sterben*, which is proper to Dasein; which is the very mark of Dasein's ownness and its possibility of authenticity;

2. perishing, *Verenden*, which is confined to plants and animals; and

3. demise, *Ableben*, which Heidegger calls a *Zwischenphänomen* between these two extremes, and which characterises the inauthentic death of Dasein. (SZ, 247)

Now, although one cannot be certain whether animals simply perish—"if a lion could talk, we could not understand him"—I have my doubts, particularly when one thinks of domestic pets and higher mammals. Thus, I think one should at the very least leave open the possibility that certain animals die, that they undergo *Sterben* and not just *Verenden*. I also doubt whether human beings are incapable of perishing, of dying like a dog, as Kafka's fiction and the facts of famine, war, and global poverty insistently remind us. And what of those persons who die at the end of a mentally debilitating disease or who die whilst being in what is termed "a permanently vegetative state"? Do they cease to be human on Heidegger's account? I see no other option. But, more importantly, if finitude is fundamentally relational, that is, if it is by definition a relation to the *Faktum* of an other who exceeds my powers of projection, then *the only authentic death is inauthentic*. That is, on my account, an authentic relation to death is not constituted through mineness, but rather through otherness. Death enters the world not through my own *timor mortis*, but rather through my relation to the other's dying, perhaps even through my relation to the other's fear, which I try to assuage as best I can. It is this notion of an essentially inauthentic relation to death that both Maurice Blanchot and Emmanuel Levinas have in mind when reversing Heidegger's dictum that "death is the possibility of impossibility" into "death is the impossibility of possibility" (SZ, 262). I have power over neither the other's death nor my own. Death is not a possibility of Dasein, but rather describes an empirical and normative limit to all possibility and to my fateful powers of projection. My relation to finitude limits my potentiality and my ability to be *(Seinkönnen)*. In my view, the experience of finitude impotentializes the self and disables the healthy virility of authentic Dasein.

Once this relational picture of finitude is in place, the picture of conscience would also have to change significantly. I have come to think—against some long-held prejudices about Division II—that the discussion of conscience is one of the most explosive and interesting parts of *Sein und Zeit*, and we have already had occasion to discuss certain passages above. Of course, the analysis of conscience follows on logically from the death analysis, being the concrete ontic-existentiell testimony or attestation *(Zeugnis; SZ, 267)* for the formal ontologico-existential claim about death. Death is ontological, conscience is ontic. Indeed, the word "testimony" might detain us more than it has done in reading *Sein und Zeit*. Testimony evokes both a notion of witnessing as testifying to something or someone, and also expresses a link to evidence and verification, where Heidegger is seeking in conscience the concrete ontic evidence for the formal ontological claim about death, a question which resolves itself relativistically in the key concept of "Situation" (SZ, 299–300).

My point here is simple: if death is nonrelational for Heidegger, then also *a fortiori* conscience is nonrelational. Heidegger writes, in italics, "*In conscience Dasein calls itself*" (*Das Dasein ruft im Gewissen sich selbst.*, SZ, 275). That is, although in conscience it is as though the call of conscience were an alien voice (*eine fremde Stimme*, SZ, 277) that comes *über mich*, such a call, although it is not planned, really comes *aus mir*. Its source is the self. As Heidegger insists in differentiating his concept of conscience from the 'vulgar" one, what is attested to in conscience is Dasein's ownmost or most proper ability to be (*eigensten Seinkönnen*, SZ, 295). Authentic Dasein calls to itself in conscience, and it does this not in the mode of chattering to itself, but rather in discretion (*Verschwiegenheit*) and silence (*Schweigen*). This behaviour is what Heidegger calls resoluteness (*Entschlossenheit*), which is then defined as the "*authentic Selfhood*" of Dasein.(SZ, 298) Heidegger completes this train of thought in a slightly troubling fashion by claiming that when Dasein has authentically individuated itself in conscience, ". . . it can become the 'conscience' of others (*zum "Gewissen" der Anderen werden*). Only by authentically being-their-selves in resoluteness can people authentically be with one another" (SZ, 298). Once again, the condition of possibility for collective authenticity or community is the mineness of individual conscience.

This brings me to my question: is conscience non-relational? It would seem to me that a consideration of Freud, in particular his essays on Narcissism and "Mourning and Melancholia," might throw some helpful light on Heidegger's concept of conscience.[13] The Freudian thought I would like to retain is that of conscience as the psychical imprint, interior mark, or agency, for a series of transferential relations to the other: ego ideal, paternal superego, maternal imago, or whatever. Conscience is the *Über-Ich* that stands *über mich*, it is the super-ego that stands over against me. The point is that a Freudian concept of conscience is essentially relational. Furthermore, in analytic experience it is the place of the hostile super-ego that the analyst has to occupy in order to break down the symptom that is the occasion of the patient's suffering. Conceived in this way, the appeal made by conscience would not be Dasein calling to itself or even the voice of the friend that every Dasein carries within it (SZ, 163). If that were so, then Dasein would have to be its own best friend, which is a rather solipsistic, indeed slightly sad, state of affairs. Even worse, I would want to avoid Heidegger's suggestion that the authentic self can become the conscience of others in some sort of presumptuous and potentially dominating way.

On my picture, conscience is the ontic testimony of a certain splitting or undoing of the self in relation to a *Faktum* that it cannot assimilate, the lifeless material thing of the experience of mourning and grief that the self carries within itself and which denies it from achieving self-mastery.

It is this failure of autarky that makes the self relational. The call of conscience is a voice within me whose source is not myself, but is an other's voice that calls me to respond. Pushing this slightly further, the relational experience of conscience calls me to a responsibility for the other that one might consider ethical. In other words, a relational and arguably ethical experience of conscience only becomes possible by being inauthentic, that is, in recognizing that I am not the conscience of others, but rather that it is those others who call me to have a conscience.

It would here be a question of reading Freud's concept of narcissism, as a splitting of the self into conflictual agencies (the division of ego, superego, and id in what is usually called the second topography) back into *Sein und Zeit*. If authentic Dasein cannot mourn, because its fundamental relation to finitude is a self-relation, then I think this is because, to put it in psychoanalytic terms, it has not entered into the relational experience of transference. Transference is a relation to an other whom I face, but whom I cannot completely know, whom my criteria cannot reach. Such a face-to-face relation is described by Levinas with the adjective "ethical." Of course, *Mitsein* is being-with-another, but it is standing shoulder-to-shoulder with those others in what Heidegger calls in one passage "*eigentliche Verbundenheit*" ('*authentic* alliance or being-bound-together,' SZ, 122). Such alliance might well be said to be the camaraderie that induces the political virtue of solidarity, but it is not a face-to-face relation and as such, in my view, is ethically impoverished. I sometimes think that authentic *Mitsein* is a little like being in church, it is a congregational "being-together-with-others" where we vibrate together as one body in song and prayer. Pleasant as it doubtless must be, such is not the only way of being with others.

If we begin to hear thrown projection as *thrown* projection, and factical existence as *factical* existence, then I think Heidegger's claims about temporality—the very meaning of being—would also have to be revised, away from the primacy of the future and towards the primacy of the past. To recall, Heidegger's claim in his discussion of temporality is that there are three "ecstases" of time: the future (*Zukunft*) that is revealed in the anticipation of death, the past or "having-been-ness" (*Gewesenheit*) that is opened in the notion of conscience, guilt and resoluteness, and the present or "waiting-towards" (*Gegen-wart*) that is grasped in the moment of vision (*Augenblick*), or taking action in the Situation. The claim is that Dasein *is* the movement of this temporalization, and that this movement *is* finitude: "*Die ursprüngliche Zeit ist endlich*" ('Primordial time is finite,' SZ, 331).

Now, although Heidegger insists that the structure of ecstatic temporality possesses a unity, the primary meaning of temporality is the future. (SZ, 327) As Heidegger writes, "*Zeitlichkeit zeitigt sich ursprünglich aus der Zukunft*" ('Temporality temporalizes itself primordially out of the future,'

SZ, 331). That is, it is the anticipatory experience of being-towards-death that makes possible the *Gewesenheit* of the past and the *Augenblick* of the present. For Heidegger, the *Augenblick* is the authentic present which is consummated in a vision of resolute rapture (*Entrückung*, SZ, 338), where Dasein is literally carried away (*ent-rückt*) in an experience of ecstasy. Rapture, which we encountered above in the discussion of authentic *Mitsein*, is a word that worries me, not the least because of the way in which *raptus* seems like a plundering of the past, some sort of rape of memory. If we approach *Sein und Zeit* in terms of the aspect change that I am proposing, and we emphasize the thrownness in thrown projection and the facticity in factical existence, then this would entail the primacy of the past over the future. This past is one's rather messy, indeed often opaque, personal and cultural history. In my view, it is this personal and cultural thrownness that pulls me back from any rapture of the present into a lag which I can never make up and which I can only assemble into a *fate* on the basis of a delusional and pernicious notion of historicity, and into a *destiny* on the basis of a congregational interpretation of that delusion.

On the contrary, from the perspective developed in this chapter, the unfolding future always folds back into the experience of an irredeemable past, a past that constitutes the present as always having a delay with respect to itself. Now is not the now when I say "now." My relation to the present is one where I am always trying—and failing—to catch up with myself. As such, then, I do not rise up rapturously or affirmatively into time, becoming as Nietzsche exclaimed on the verge of madness, "all the names in history." No, I wait, I await. Time passes. For Heidegger, this is the passive awaiting (*Gewärtigen*) of inauthentic time. Of course, such a passive awaiting might make the self fatigued, sleepy even. As such, in the experience of fatigue, the river of time begins to flow backwards, away from the future and the resolute rapture of the present, and toward a past that I can never make present, but which I dramatize involuntarily in the life of dreams. True, I can always interpret my dreams or, better, get another to interpret them for me. But what Freud calls the navel of the dream, its source, its facticity, always escapes me, like an enigma. In closing, let me try to identify three consequences that can be drawn from the reading of *Sein und Zeit* that I have tried to offer in this chapter.

1. The critique of authenticity, particularly with regard to social and political life, permits a revalorization of inauthentic social existence as something to be judged positively and not seen in terms of categories such as falling. Although Heidegger insists again and again—indeed, the man doth protest too much methinks—that

his concepts of falling, thrownness and inauthenticity do not and should not imply any moral critique of the modern world, there is no way around the feeling of Heidegger's lip curling as he describes the leveled down life of the "great mass,' or—in some twisted echo of Lenin or Kautsky—the "real dictatorship of the 'they.'" Such a dictatorship is evidenced in the life of leveled down "publicness," in reading "newspapers" and using "public transport," where "every Other is like the next" (SZ, 126–27). However, if we view Heidegger's descriptions from the perspective of originary inauthenticity, then a good deal changes. For example, when Heidegger writes that in the world of "the they," "Everyone is an other and no one is himself," or indeed when he says that the "who" of everyday Dasein is *Niemand*, nobody, then such phrases might be otherwise interpreted (SZ, 128). If we are, indeed, others to ourselves in social existence, if we are even nobody in particular, then this could well provide the basis for a thinking of sociality that would not be organized in terms of the goals of authenticity, autarky, or communitarian solidarity. Reading *Sein und Zeit* from the perspective of inauthenticity might allow us to see social life as constituted in relations of radical dependence on others. I am nobody in particular, and nor are you, and insofar as we are both using "public transport" to get to work, then our interactions are based on a shared dependence and even civility. I might pick up and read the "newspaper" that you leave on the seat, and we might even exchange a few courteous words about the dreadful terrorist explosion that happened the previous day (I first wrote that sentence on July 8 in central London, on the morning after the terrorist attacks). The point is that *das Man* need not be seen as an inauthentic or leveled down "publicness" that requires the authenticity of *das Volk*. We might simply abandon the latter and affirm the former. This leads to my second point.

2. On my interpretation of *Sein und Zeit*, the core of the existential analytic is not the heroic, nonrelational and constant self who achieves authentic wholeness through anticipatory resoluteness. On the contrary, sociality begins with an inauthentic self who is formed through a relational experience of finitude and conscience. This is not an autarkic and unified self that can rise up to meet its fate, but a self defined through its relations of dependence on others, a self that only *is* through its relations to others and that always arrives too late to meet its fate, it's a comic rather

than a tragic self. Indeed, such an essentially inauthentic self might not enjoy the robust health of authentic Dasein; it might be uneasy with itself, even unwell (the possibility of a sick Dasein never seems to have occurred to Heidegger). Such a self might be less an individual than a "dividual," divided against itself in the experience of conscience. In a key passage from the analysis of *Mitsein*, Heidegger writes that "because Dasein's being is being-with, in its understanding of being already lies the understanding of the Other *(das Verständnis Anderer)*" (SZ, 123). For Heidegger, the relation to the other is based on understanding, whose condition of possibility is the understanding of being. However, if we privilege the inauthentic and relational self, then this is not a self that can claim to understand the other, but is rather a self who is directed toward the other in a way that is neither based in understanding nor culminates in understanding. Perhaps the other person is simply that being that I have to acknowledge as refractory to the categories of my understanding, as exceeding my powers of projection or the reach of my criteria, but together with whom I am thrown into a social world where we can engage with each other based on relations of respect and trust. Perhaps it is such an inauthentic self that is truly ethical.

3. The temporality of such a relational self would not be primarily orientated toward the future, a future that culminates in the rapturous "moment of vision" through what I see as a redemption of the past, understood as one's "having-been-ness." On the contrary, such an inauthentic, relational self would be organized in relation to a past for which it is responsible, but which it cannot redeem, a past that constitutes the self without the self constituting or reconstituting it. It is in this way, perhaps, that we might be able to push the existential analytic towards the issue of responsibility for the past, even a guilty responsibility for a past that cannot be fully made present and for that very reason will not let go and cannot be passed over in silence.

What I hope to have done in this chapter is to begin to think about how we might approach Heidegger's existential analytic in a way that frees it from what I see as its tragic-heroic pathos of individual and collective authenticity, but in a way that is hopefully not based on a strategic or reductive external interpretation, but a possible internal reading that derives from the central theses and basic experience of *Sein und Zeit*.

NOTES

This chapter is a revision of a paper first published in 2002, "Enigma Variations: An Interpretation of Heidegger's *Sein und Zeit*," *Ratio* 15, no. 2 (June 2002), 154–75. I feel that the basic line of interpretation is still plausible, but a year of intensive Heidegger teaching at the New School for Social Research in 2005 gave me the occasion to revise my views. The chapter was presented at the American Philosophical Association Perspectives in Analytic and Continental Philosophy, Eastern section, December 2005.

1. All references to *Sein und Zeit* are to the pagination of the fifteenth edition (Tübingen: Niemeyer, 1984), which can be found in the margins of English translations of the text. Hereafter SZ.

2. In this regard, see the interesting *Beilagen* to "Das Wesen des Nihilismus," in *Metaphysik und Nihilismus*, Gesamtausgabe 67 (Frankfurt a.M.: Klostermann, 1999), 259–67. See especially 265–66, where Heidegger claims that the essence of nihilism in *Sein und Zeit* is located in the thought of *das Verfallen*, which is the condition of possibility for the surmounting (*Überstieg*) of that fallenness.

3. Wittgenstein, *Philosophical Investigations*, trans. G. E. M. Anscombe (Oxford: Blackwell, 1958), 129.

4. Heidegger, *Hölderlins Hymne "Der Ister"* (Frankfurt a.M.: Klostermann, 1984). I discuss the latter in "Enigma Variations," 158–59.

5. See "Heidegger for Beginners," *Appropriating Heidegger*, ed. J. Faulconer and M. Wrathall (Cambridge: Cambridge University Press, 2000), 101–18.

6. See Sheehan, "Kehre and Ereignis. A Prolegomenon to *Introduction to Metaphysics*," unpublished typescript, Jean Beaufret, *Entretiens avec Frédéric de Towarnicki* (Paris: PUF 1992), 17, 26, 28.

7. This phrase is Rüdiger Safranski's, which he uses to describe the undoubted Platonism of Heidegger's political commitment in 1933. See *Ein Meister aus Deutschland. Heidegger und seine Zeit* (Munich: Hanser, 1994). On the question of the enigma of the everyday in Heidegger see Michel Haar, "L'enigme de la quotidieneté," *Être et Temps de Martin Heidegger. Questions de méthode et voies de recherche*, ed. J-P Cometti and D. Janicaud (Marseille: Sud, 1989), 213–25.

8. *Modifikation* is an absolutely key concept in *Sein und Zeit*. See, for example, the claim that authentic being-one's-self is an *"existentiell modification of the 'they'—of the 'they' as an essential existentiale"* (SZ, 130). This is a claim that is simply and flatly inverted in the second section, where Heidegger amnesiacally writes, "It has been shown (but where exactly? S.C.) that proximally and for the most part Dasein is *not* itself but is lost in the they-self, which is an existentiell modification of the authentic self" (SZ, 317). Is the authentic a modification of the inauthentic, or is it the other way around? Heidegger makes noises of both sorts.

9. See Löwith's essay in *The Heidegger Controversy*, ed. R.Wolin (Cambridge: MIT, 1993). To my mind, the systematic connection between fundamental ontology and National Socialism was convincingly established by Philippe Lacoue-Labarthe in his "Transcendence Ends in Politics," *Typography* (Cambridge: Harvard University

Press, 1989) and also at greater length in his *Heidegger, Art and Politics*, trans. C. Turner (Oxford: Blackwell, 1990). The same argument has been stated much more polemically and in extraordinary scholarly detail by Johannes Fritsche in *Historical Destiny and National Socialism in Heidegger's Being and Time* (Berkeley: University of California Press, 1999). About the discussion of historicity, Fritsche claims, "Section 74 of Heidegger's *Being and Time* is as brilliant a summary of revolutionary rightist politics as one could wish for" (xii).

10. See Heidegger, *Einführung in die Metaphysik* (Tübingen: Niemeyer, 1953), 152; Habermas, "Mit Heidegger gegen Heidegger denken. Zur Veröffentlichung von Vorlesungen aus dem Jahre 1935," *Frankfurter Allgemeine Zeitung* (July 25, 1953): 67–75.

11. Let me add that I find it curious, to say the least, that certain interpretations or borrowings from Heidegger that would want to distance themselves decisively from any stain of National Socialism often deploy the concept of authenticity in an unquestioned manner. In my view, this is somewhat problematic. I am thinking in particular of the work of Charles Guignon (see *On Being Authentic* (London and New York: Routledge, 2004) and Charles Taylor (see *The Ethics of Authenticity* (Cambridge: Harvard University Press, 1992).

12. See the final chapter of my *On Humour* (London and New York: Routledge, 2002), 93–111; "Displacing the Tragic-Heroic Paradigm in Philosophy and Psychoanalysis," in *Ethics, Politics, Subjectivity* (London and New York: Verso 1999), 217–38.

13. See volume 11 of the Penguin Freud, *On Metapsychology* (Harmondsworth: Penguin, 1984).

PART III

SUBJECTIVITIES

CHAPTER SEVEN

LEVINAS AND HEIDEGGER

Ethics or Ontology?

Françoise Dastur

What is the relation of ethics to philosophy? Is ethics, as it was defined at the very beginning of philosophy, only a part of philosophy, or is it, as Spinoza suggested in giving the name "Ethica" to his entire philosophical system, what constitutes philosophy as such?

In order to try to answer this question, it is necessary first to recall the traditional definition of philosophy, as Kant does at the beginning of his preface to *Grounding for the Metaphysics of Morals,* where it is said that Greek philosophy was divided into three sciences: physics, ethics, and logic. But what has to be added to this definition, which conforms to the Aristotelian concept of philosophy, is its ground, namely, "first philosophy" or, in its modern name, "metaphysics," which in his Aristotelian definition, as "science of being as being," is nothing else than what modern philosophy calls "ontology."[1] This complete definition of philosophy was acknowledged by Descartes, who, in the preface to his *Principles of Philosophy,* declared that philosophy is like a tree, the roots of which are metaphysics, the trunk is physics, and the branches are all other sciences, namely, medicine, mechanics, and morals, this last science presupposing all the others and being the "ultimate stage of wisdom."

Is it clear from this traditional definition of philosophy that ethics, which can be considered as the aim of this "love" of wisdom that is philosophy, presupposes metaphysics, that is to say ontology, as its basis? Spinoza could consider that philosophy is in its entirety ethics only because for him there is no radical difference between God or nature and man, and therefore no necessity to follow step by step the development of the philosophical tree in order to try reaching its highest branch. Whereas philosophy, since its first beginning with Parmenides and Platon, understands itself as the *human* way to truth, a truth that remains in its entirety inaccessible, Spinoza's *Ethica* begins immediately with the source of truth, with God. For Spinoza, the human being is already in possession of truth; it is only necessary for him to become aware of it, which is possible if the human mind proceeds, as does Spinoza, *ordine geometrico*. The goal of ethics as a practical science being, as Aristotle explained, the possession of what is for the human being the highest Good, that is, happiness in conformity with virtue, Spinoza's *Ethica* can therefore be considered as the geometrical science of absolute beatitude, an absolute beatitude which can be reached by the human being in so far as he is a rational being.

Spinoza's example can help us to understand Levinas's position in relation to ethics because Levinas also proceeds to a reversal of the whole philosophical tradition, which he makes explicit when declaring at the end of *Totality and Infinity*: "Morality is not a branch of philosophy, but first philosophy."[2] However, Levinas's purpose is not only to give another definition of the human being than the traditional and philosophical one, which insists on the finitude of man, but to question in a radical manner the philosophical postulate which is still Spinoza's postulate and which defines all possible relation with being in general as a *relation of knowledge*. Already in Levinas's first book, a study published in 1930 on *The Theory of Intuition in Husserl's Phenomenology*, it is possible to find some critical remarks concerning the definition of intentionality as based, following Brentano's definition of the acts of consciousness, on the theoretical act of representation (*Vorstellung*).[3] For Levinas, this is what gives its intellectualist character to Husserl's concept of intuition in spite of the fact that for him practical and aesthetic life is also considered as belonging to the sphere of intentionality.[4] Husserl's philosophy is for Levinas marked by a strong ambivalence: on one side, it is still a form of idealism, but on the other side, it is a tentative to understand the concrete life of the subject. This explains the different inflexions of Levinas's reading of Husserl in the following years,[5] the emphasis being put either on the "downfall of representation" in Husserl's phenomenology and on its capacity to open itself to the ethical sphere of the absolute alterity of the other[6] or on the opposite on the critique of Husserl's rigorous noetico-noematical parallelism, which does not allow extracting the relation with the other from the subjective and monadic sphere, contrary to Descartes, who "leaves a door open" to the thinking of the relation with the other as an ethical relation by discovering in the subject itself the idea of an infinity that he does not constitute.[7]

Levinas, in spite of the fact that he translated in French in 1931 the first draft of Husserl's *Cartesian Meditations*, does not take into account the analysis of the "monadological intersubjectivity" of the fifth meditation, precisely because its basis is still the theoretical structure of intentionality which does not allow granting the priority to the relation with the other. But it is nevertheless the Leibnizian definition of the monad, defined as being one with oneself, which constitutes for him the starting point of his analysis of existence in *Time and the Other*, a series of lectures dating from 1946/1947: "To be is to be isolated by existing. Inasmuch as I am, I am a monad. It is by existing that I am without windows and doors, and not be some content in me that would be incommunicable."[8] The lack of communication does not come from the fact that I am a particular substance, but from the mere fact of existing as a separate being. Levinas explains that everything can be exchanged between the human beings except existing, which means that I am completely isolated as soon as I exist. "Existing resists every relationship and multiplicity. It concerns no one other than the existent. Solitude therefore appears neither as the factual isolation of a Robinson Crusoe nor as the incommunicability of a content of consciousness, but as the indissoluble unity between the existent and its work of existing. . . . Solitude lies in the very fact that there are existents."[9] Whereas for Heidegger existing means to have a relationship *with* the beings of the world, with things, with the others, and with oneself as being in the world, for Levinas, there is at first the solitude of existing, which cannot be considered, as Heidegger does, within the prior relationship with the other, so that the preposition "with" cannot for him describe the original relation with the other.[10] This means that even when I have an intentional relationship with the world, when I intend to acquire a knowledge of what is outside me, I continue to exist as a separate being: "Every enlargement of my knowledge or of my means of self-expression remains without effect on my relationship with existing, the interior relationship par excellence."[11] Levinas does not accept the idea of a possible participation to the being of the other, of an "ecstatic fusion" which could deliver us from solitude. He wants to remain at the level of the duality between the I and the other and does not accept the idea of a possible unification: "If we leave monodology we arrive at monism."[12]

The relationship of knowledge, the relation with the object, is not a way of dissolving the tie between the existent and its existing, because by going out of himself toward the object, the subject does not find something else than himself, but on the contrary finds himself again in the object.

This is what makes knowledge possible, in other words "enlightment," the process of knowledge being traditionally understood as "clarification," as a going out of the darkness of the Platonic cave: "Light is that through which something is other than myself, but already as if it came from me. The illuminated object is something one encounters, but from the very fact that it is illuminated one encounters it as if it came from us. It does not have a fundamental strangeness. Its transcendence is wrapped in immanence. The exteriority of light does not suffice for the liberation of the ego that is the self's captive."[13] Through the enlightment process, through knowledge, I may have the impression of becoming other than myself, but in fact "knowledge does not surmount solitude," on the contrary in knowledge, I experience the fact that I am "the sole and unique point of reference for everything"[14] so that for Levinas, the level of rationality is and remains the level of solipsism and not of intersubjectivity, as Husserl showed.

Levinas is here diametrically opposed to Heidegger for whom solitude is only a *deficient* mode of the being with the others, so that it is rather the proof of an originary community with the others than its negation. For Levinas, solitude is not a mode of sociality, but on the contrary, the fundamental mode of the self. Solitude does not mean the absence of the others, or the impossibility of communication; it means merely "irremissible attachment of the ego to the self," the inability of going out of oneself. That is the reason why Levinas considers solipsism in a positive way: "Solipsism is neither an aberration nor a sophism; it is the very structure of reason."[15] There is a universality of knowledge, based on "the unlimitedness of light and the impossibility for anything to be on the outside."[16] The difference between the subject and the object, between the ego and the things is not in fact a real difference, because through knowledge the subject becomes able to master the exterior world in such a manner that its objectivity becomes the extension of the subject: "The objectivity of rational knowledge removes nothing of the solitary character of reason."[17]

Consequently, the world is not for Levinas something really other than me, but a mode of existing for the I; it is all that which is not really other but remains interior to the I and constitutes the field of its self-identification. The field of being does not possess a true alterity, which means that the discourse on being is in fact a discourse on the ego: if there is really one other, it has therefore to be found *outside* being, *beyond* being. Knowledge is for Levinas only a mode of a more fundamental manner of existing which he calls identity or light, so that reason and rational knowledge are the manifestations of the identification process. But the relation of light can imply other relations than the relation of knowledge, such as the relation of need and enjoyment or the relation of power, which have the same structure as knowledge: in all these cases, the question is of appropriating something or someone in order to consolidate or extend its own identity.

We are now in the position to understand Levinas's discourse on the other. The philosophies which take as a point of departure the phenomenon of consciousness, and even of *intentional* consciousness, as Husserl does, still consider the other in the perspective of identity and light. The other can then be defined as an alter ego because he is considered as a being similar to me. But if the other is really other, he cannot be understood on the basis of a similarity with me. What Levinas wants is only to approach the other without any preconception; he wants to remain respectful of the otherness, of the alterity of the other. The other is not other than me on the basis of a common belonging to a species or to being in general. There is for Levinas no preexisting identity between him and me, but he is absolutely other, and his being consists in his absolute alterity. This comes from Levinas's definition of identity: for him identity is never given, but always results from an act of identification. This means that I am not one, but I *make* myself one, to be meaning to be one. In other words identity is not a character of being among others, but the very definition of being. There is therefore no place for any alterity in being, so the other can only be defined as a mode of existence which has nothing to do with being.

At the end of *Time and the Other*, Levinas explains his main goal in this series of lectures: he wanted to show that in order to think the other, it is necessary to overcome the Eleatic notion of being, which constitutes the very beginning of Western philosophy, because this notion reduces multiplicity to the one and cannot account for the plurality of existing. Levinas does not mention the fact that Plato refutes Parmenides in the *Sophist*, but affirms in a peremptory manner that "the Eleatic notion of being dominates Plato's philosophy."[18] This explains in his view that "beginning with Plato, the social ideal will be sought for in an ideal of fusion. It will be thought that, in its relationship with the other, the subject tends to be identified with the other, by being swallowed up in a collective representation, a common ideal."[19] Such a collectivity establishes itself around a third term, which serves as an intermediary between the subjects: in the case of Plato's *Republic*, it is the intelligible sun, the truth, which constitutes the "common" bond between the subjects. Levinas underlines that we find the same idea of community in the Heideggerian *Mitsein* and declares that "against this collectivity of the side-by-side," he himself has tried to "oppose the 'I-you' collectivity," which is not a collectivity of communion, because it does not involve the participation in a third term, but "the face to face without intermediary,"[20] where the other is as such present to the I, which remains the point of departure of all access to the alterity of the other. This explains that, paradoxically, the status of the I has to be studied first, which Levinas does in *Totality and Infinity*.

As Levinas says at the beginning of this work, to be an I is to be identical with oneself, not in a static way, in the sense of the mere tautology

"I am I," but in a dynamic way: "The I is not a being that always remains the same, but is the being whose existing consists in identifying itself, in recovering its identity throughout all that happens to it. It is the primal identity, the primordial work of identification."[21] This primal identity is in fact an *act* of identification of the I and of the world, so that "the way of the I against the 'other' of the world consists in *sojourning*, in *identifying oneself* by existing here *at home with oneself*."[22] For Levinas, "dwelling is the very mode of maintaining oneself," of remaining the same being, because dwelling means for him something quite other than what it means for Heidegger, that is, to take possession of the world and to make the same as myself what is exterior to myself: "The possibility of possessing, that is, of suspending the very alterity of what is only at first other, and other relative to me, is the *way* of the same,"[23] so there is a reversion of the alterity of the world to self-identication, and this reversion takes place first in my relation to my body, then to my home, then through labor, possession of objects, and economy in general, which constitutes the different levels of self-identification.

From there it becomes possible to understand that the act of identification of the I is neither a tautology nor a dialectical opposition to the other, because this would imply that the I and the other can constitute together a totality; it is merely the concreteness of egoism.[24] But if there is no dialectical relation with the other, how can the I enter into a relation with the other without immediately depriving him of his alterity? It can only be possible if the relation to the other is the relation to an alterity which is "prior to every initiative, to all imperialism of the same,"[25] prior to the I. The priority of the other with regard to me has to be absolute, so I can enter into a relation with the other without forming with him a community, which would mean for Levinas the nonrecognition of his alterity and his domination by the I. It is clear here that for Levinas community as such can only be unrespectful of the alterity of the other. There is therefore only one possibility left: the Other (*autrui* meaning the other human being) can only be "the absolutely other" as Levinas stresses.[26]

Does this mean that the Other is completely inaccessible? It is necessary here to differentiate accessibility from knowledge. The other cannot be an object of knowledge, since knowledge consists in identifying the unknown with what is already known. But it does not mean that the Other is inaccessible. It only means that the relation to the other is neither a relation of knowledge nor a relation of being, but a relation of another kind, which remains unknown to philosophy, as far as philosophy is the thinking of the same which cannot be open to the exteriority of the absolutely other. This is the reason why Levinas opposes here metaphysics to philosophy, metaphysics being for him "turned toward the other" because it is "a desire for the invisible."[27] Levinas sees in the metaphysical desire the true relation to the other as such, to the absolutely other, and distinguishes in a radical manner the need that can be satisfied and the desire that cannot be satisfied. What is needed can fulfill the need when it is available. But the desire is something else": it desires beyond everything that can simply complete it . . . The Desired does not fulfill it, but deepens it."[28] To have a relation of desire with the other is therefore to have access to his absolute alterity: the metaphysical desire is "a desire without satisfaction which, precisely, *understands* the remoteness, the alterity and the exteriority of the other."[29] Levinas conceives the absolute alterity of the other in terms of height and declares that "the very dimension of height is opened up by metaphysical desire," so the other is understood as higher than myself, as the most high.[30] It seems here that the other takes the place of God itself. This analogy is reinforced when Levinas insists on the fact that the I and the Other do not constitute a totality and remain in absolute separation.[31]

But there can be an absolute other only in relation to an I which is in the same manner absolutely the same. Levinas's "metaphysics of separation" implies in itself a dualistic mode of thinking which opposes in a radical manner the same and the other, the I and the other. Because the I and the other do not have anything in common, the other can only appear as an absolute stranger, a "stranger who disturbs the being at home with oneself."[32] As an absolute stranger, the other "escapes my grasp by an essential dimension, even if I have him at my disposal," because he is not wholly in my site,[33] he is not a part of my world. The only relation that I can have with him is for Levinas a relation of language, because language alone accomplishes a relation with the other which does respect his transcendance and maintains the distance between him and me. This relation of language with the other does not take place in a dialogue, but in a discourse, where the I does not renounce his egoism, but nevertheless recognizes in the other a right over his egoism and tries to justify himself. The essence of discourse is therefore not the sharing of a common meaning, as it is in dialogue, but "apology," a discourse which starts from the I, in which the I at the same time asserts itself and inclines before the transcendent Other.[34]

But this relation is nevertheless a face-to-face relation, which proceeds from me to the Other, but without reversibility, because such a reversibility would couple the I to the Other.[35] Between the I and the other, there is an absolute separation, which means that it is impossible to change places, and to consider the relation that I have with the other from the inverse point of view of the other, because it were the case, it would mean that the I and the Other still constitute a totality. As Levinas says: "The alterity, the radical heterogeneity of the other is possible only if the other is other with respect to a term whose essence is to remain at the point de departure, to serve as *entry* into the relation, to be the same not relatively but absolutely."[36] Such a term which can remain absolutely at the point of departure of relationship is and can only be an I.[37] For Levinas also, the point of departure remains the Cartesian cogito, so that as he himself underlines "alterity is only possible starting from *me*."[38]

This relation between the I and the other is for Levinas a metaphysical event, whose meaning is the "breach of totality." Levinas takes up an idea which is Franz Rosenzweig's main idea in *The Star of Redemption*, a book published in 1927, in which the author takes position against the Hegelian system of philosophy and defines Western philosophy, "from Iona to Iena," in other words from the Presocratics to Hegel's *Phenomenology of Spirit*, published in Iena in 1807, as a philosophy of totality. Levinas acknowledges in the preface of *Totality and Infinity* that he was "impressed by the opposition to the idea of totality in Franz Rosenzweig's *Stern der Erlösung*, a work he says, "too often present in this book to be cited."[39] In fact Rosenzweig's name does not appear anywhere in *Totality and Infinity*, but at the end of the section entitled "The Breach of Totality," Levinas mentions instead the name of Kierkegaard, who was the first to criticize the Hegelian systematic philosophy, because it was not able to guarantee the right of the individuals. But Kierkegaard's point of view and Levinas's point of view are not exactly the same: Kierkegaard wants to preserve the right of the I against Hegel's totalitarian way of thinking, whereas Levinas wants to preserve the transcendance of the other: "It is not the I who resist[s] the system, as Kierkegaard thought; it is the other."[40]

But if the relation to the other cannot be thought in a philosophical way, it means that this metaphysical relation has another meaning: "We propose to call 'religion' the bond that is established between the same and the other without constituting a totality."[41] What does that mean? We have already stressed the fact that for Levinas the Cartesian cogito remains the only possible point of departure. Descartes is a very important reference for Levinas, because he was able to show that the idea of infinite that I discover in myself cannot be produced by me as a finite being, but can only be introduced in myself by an infinite being, by God himself: there is "a Cartesian primacy of the idea of the perfect over the idea of the imperfect,"[42] which means that the experience of the transcendence is not a negative one; it is the experience of "a height and a nobility"[43] which is nevertheless separated from me. Levinas does not follow Descartes in so far as finding here an ontological proof of the existence of God, but maintains that the experience of the infinite that we have does not come from us, but from the transcendence of the other. It has to be stressed here that there is for Levinas an identity between metaphysics and atheism because atheism is necessary to break with "the violence of the sacred."[44] The notion of the sacred implies in itself the idea of a totality into which the sacred can manifest itself so that a relation of participation with the divine becomes possible for the human being: "Only an atheist being can relate himself to the other and already *absolve himself* from this relation. Transcendence is to be distinguished from a union with the transcendent."[45] In a paradoxical way, the monotheist faith, which is a faith "purged of myths" and "disengaged of the bonds of participation" implies "metaphysical atheism" in so far as "atheism conditions a veritable relation to a God *kath'auto*," a God who does not appear in the world, but reveals himself only through discourse.[46] God in so far as He is a personal and invisible God can only become accessible in the ethical attitude, which means that He can be approached only through the human presence: "The dimension of the divine opens forth from the human face."[47] God is not an object of knowledge; he "is" not since being means identity and not alterity: "There can be no 'knowledge' of God separated from the relationship with men. The Other is the very locus of metaphysical truth, and is indispensable for my relation with God."[48] But this does not mean that the Other plays the role of a mediator as it is the case in Christianism where God made himself human in the person of Jesus. The Other is not the sensible and mundane "incarnation" of God, but by his disincarnated face "the manifestation of the height in which God is revealed."[49] The Other can be the revelation of God because by his face he does not belong to the domain of phenomenality, to the sensible world. There is therefore a priority of the ethical relation over the theological: "It is our relations with men (. . .) that give to theological concepts the sole signification they admit of," so "everything that cannot be reduced to an interhuman relation represents not the superior form but the forever primitive form of religion."[50]

What has therefore to be opposed to the philosophical thought of totality is the metaphysical thought of infinity. Hence the title of the book: *Totality and infinity*, where the "and" has clearly the meaning of an opposition. The metaphysical experience is the experience of transcendence. As Levinas explains, "the idea of infinity is transcendence itself"[51] and in my experience of infinity, of an idea that I cannot produce, I make the experience of my separation with the transcendence of the other. For this strange relation, which is not in fact a relation, but a separation with the other (Levinas speaks in a paradoxical manner of a "relation without relation"), Levinas wants to reserve the term "religion," whose etymological meaning is often understood as coming from the latin verb *religare*, to connect. Levinas does not say that the relation to the other is a religious one in the usual meaning of this word; on the contrary, he wants to understand the "relation without relation" to the transcendence of the other under the word "religion," which is here taken in a new meaning: "Religion, where relationship subsists between the same and the other despite the impossibility of the Whole—the idea of infinity—is the ultimate structure."[52] In other words, "the face to face remains an ultimate situation," because "inevitably across my idea of the infinite the other faces me."[53]

The relation without relation with the other cannot therefore be harmonious or peaceful: no third term, no intermediary can deaden the shock of the encounter of the same with the other. As Levinas says, "The other calls into question the exercise of the same," in other words the process of identification which constitutes the I in its egoism.[54] The experience of the interruption of the work of identification is the ethical experience: "We name this calling into question of my spontaneity by the presence of the other ethics."[55] There is therefore a tight relation between metaphysics and ethics for Levinas: the metaphysical experience is the experience of transcendence, and the ethical experience is the concretization of this experience in so far as it calls into question the egoistic spontaneity of the I. Western philosophy was not able to think either metaphysics or ethics, because it has been an ontology, a reduction of the other to the same, as its main purpose was rational knowledge, knowing meaning always removing from being its alterity. From there, Levinas can define philosophy as an egology[56] and even see in modern philosophy, in phenomenology itself the domination of an "ontological imperialism"[57] and the "egoism of ontology."[58] Because what comes first is the ethical obligation to the Other, we must reverse the relation between ontology and ethics or metaphysics: the relationship with the Other commands the comprehension of being and not the other way around: "I cannot disentangle myself from society with the other, even when I consider the Being of the existent he is," so that "the relation with the other as interlocutor, this relation with an *existent*, precedes all ontology."[59] Levinas concludes therefore that "ontology presuppose[s] metaphysics."[60]

The other is the stranger, who remains in an infinite distance, but who is nevertheless experienced. The experience of the other takes place, as we have already seen, in language, in discourse. But this ethical relation to the other is also a face-to-face relation. It is the experience of the face of the other, as Levinas defines "face," the way into which the other presents itself. Because this experience is a metaphysical one, it cannot be, as it was for Husserl, an experience which is in the first place a corporeal one. It is true that I perceive the sensible corporeal face of the other, but his presence as the other cannot be experienced through the senses: "The face of the other at each moment destroys and overflows the plastic image it leaves me" which means that the visible face has to disappear in order to let appear the invisible or metaphysical face of the Other as absolute alterity.[61] Levinas points out, "It does not manifest itself by its (sensible) qualities, but

kath'auto," as what it is in itself, as absolute other. With the experience of
the face of the other, which is not disclosure, but revelation, the level of
the perceptual experience is overcome. The face is a living presence which
cannot be represented in the sensible world; it is a speaking presence: "The
face speaks. The manifestation of the face is already discourse."[62] The other
presents itself by signifying, and he signifies through his look.[63] For Levinas
there is a language of the eyes, which is the very first manifestation of the
other, a manifestation which is impossible to dissemble. The eye is not for
Levinas what it is for Plato, the medium through which light and truth
can be given to us, but the manifestation of alterity: "The eye does not
shine, it speaks."[64]

In the third part of *Totality and Infinity* entitled "Exteriority and the
Face," Levinas defines in the same manner the experience of the face of
the other as "epiphany," as the appearance of what does not belong to the
sensible realm.[65] The experience of the other is therefore not the experience of a form, a visual experience, in spite of the meaning of the French
word "visage," but a relation of language, which is a relation between separated terms, so that the transcendence of the other can only be revealed
in speech.[66] Such a relation is not established by the I; on the contrary the
ethical relation puts the I in question, and this putting in question emanates from the other.[67] This means that the face-to-face relation has here
a new meaning. It does not mean, as it is the case in knowledge, that the
consciousness brings the object in front of itself, but on the contrary that
it is the other who brings the I in front of him. Levinas stresses therefore
that "the facing position, opposition par excellence, can be only as a moral
summons. This movement proceeds from the other."[68] But such an opposition, which happens as language and discourse, is nevertheless maintained
without violence, in peace with this absolute alterity: "The first revelation of
the other, presupposed in all the other relations with him, does not consist
in grasping him in his negative resistance and in circumventing him by
ruse. I do not struggle with a faceless god, but I respond to his expression,
to his revelation."[69]

However "the face resists possession, resists my powers."[70] But precisely because the face of the other defies my powers, it is an invitation
to violence. Not to the violence of labor, which transforms the sensible
world, aims at its domination and is only a partial destruction, but to the
violence of murder, which lays claim to total destruction. Levinas explains
here that "to kill is not to dominate, but to annihilate, it is to renounce
comprehension absolutely," it is a refusal of the relation of language, so that
"murder exercises a power over what escapes power."[71] It is still a power
because the revelation of the face, although it is not a sensible experience,
happens through the sensible expression, but it is also impotency, because

the face of the other is beyond all sensible appearances. This independence of the other with regard to the sensible world is precisely what invites the desire of murder. As Levinas says, "The other is the sole being that I can wish to kill."[72]

Murder is always possible; it is the most ordinary incident in human history, but it nevertheless corresponds to an exceptional possibility, because it claims the total negation of a being, the destruction of the other as such. In the world, the other is a quasinothing, but as such he possesses an infinite transcendence. And for Levinas, this infinity is stronger than murder and already resists us in the face, is his face, his primordial expression and his first word: "You shall not commit murder." Levinas explains that "there is here a relation not with a very great resistance, but with something absolutely other: the resistance of what has no resistance: the ethical resistance" and concludes that "the epiphany of the face is ethical."[73] This is a very important conclusion, because it allows Levinas to take position against both Hegel and Sartre, who consider that the relation with the other is a relation of war, that the access to self-consciousness requires first the struggle of consciousnesses: "War presupposes peace, the antecedent and non-allergic presence of the Other; it does not represent the first event of the encounter."[74]

The encounter of the other is therefore an ethical experience: its meaning is the impossibility of the murder. There is a bond between expression and responsability, and for Levinas, it means that there is an ethical essence of language which is more originary than its ontological function. We can see here that Levinas does not understand the ethical attitude in a traditional way. In modern philosophy, morality or ethics presupposes freedom, which means the possibility of choice. But for Levinas, I cannot chose freely to respond or not to the summon of the face, because if it were the case, if my relation to the other were to be the result of my decision, the alterity of the other would be immediately denied. I would have power over him: the power to recognize or to refuse his demand. The ethical attitude cannot be for Levinas founded on a free decision, because it would mean that the other is only an occasion for the ethical act and not the very basis of it. The face has the immediate meaning of a summon and of a supplication. It interrupts my originary freedom and egoism and awakes in me responsability. The other does not impose anything to me, as if I could not resist to a superior power. As Levinas says: "The ethical presence is both other and imposes itself without violence."[75] It disarms in advance all possibility of resistance: in the face to face relation I can no longer have any power. I find myself already engaged for the other, before I could decide, and the experience of the other is nothing else than the experience of being engaged. Levinas says: "To hear his destitution which cries out for justice is not to represent an image to oneself, but is to posit oneself as responsible."[76] This means that there is an essential assymetry in the face-to-face relation. We have already seen that the other can only reveal itself in the dimension of height, as the most high. On one side, the face summons me to my obligations, and on the other side, my position as I consists in being able to respond to this essential destitution of the other. But this revelation of the transcendence of the other happens in the I itself. In other words, the I must remain what it is, if it wants to respond to the other. It means that in the experience of the other, the I discovers in itself something that is more originary than its work of self-identification, a passivity which is the true identity of the I. To be an I does not mean therefore only the capacity of self-identification, but the incapacity of escaping responsability. To respond to the other, I have to be an I, to have an identity. But this identity is not longer my doing, it is the doing and the work of the other who summons me, as the one who has to respond, and my identity comes here from the fact that nobody else can respond instead of me. It becomes clear that the ethical subject does not precede the experience of the Other, but is required by it. The Other comes first in all respects.

Ethics is therefore for Levinas a much larger domain than morality in the traditional sense of the word. This domain is in fact metaphysical and concerns the fundamental metaphysical experience of desire, which is completely different from the experience of need, and which implies a passivity which is not a sensible phenomenon, a passivity which has nothing to do with sensibility. The domain of ethics involves also the dimension of signification and language. The face speaks, summons, appeals, and I have to respond. This constitutes the originary ethical essence of language. In other words, I do not speak because I have something to say about the world that I want to communicate to the other. It is the other way around: I have something to say because I first speak to the other. My discourse is not the communication of a meaning, but an address (une adresse) to the Other.

Levinas's definition of ethics raises many questions. But the first and the most important one concerns Levinas's belonging to the phenomenological movement. Does Levinas remain a phenomenologist when he defines the relation to the Other as a metaphysical and ethical relation? When Levinas declares in an explicit manner that "the metaphysical relation—the idea of infinity—connects with the noumenon,"[77] this implies that the Other can by no means belong to the domain of phenomenology. It has here to be recalled that the Kantian distinction between phenomenon and noumenon as well as between two different kinds of intuition, one derived and human, the other originary and divine, is for Husserl meaningless. In Ideas pertaining to a pure phenomenology, he explains that believing that human sensible perception does not reach the thing itself which could be known only by

God is a "fundamental error," because this would mean that the perceived thing is only an image or a sign, which cannot be the case because between perception on one side and symbolic representation and imagination on the other side, there is "an unbridgeable eidetic différence."[78] There is therefore no possibility to enter in relationship with anything that exists without having as basis a sensible perception. In the sixth *Logical Investigation*, Husserl explains that besides sensible intuition, there is also a categorial intuition, in other words an intuition of the intelligible, and that the categorial act of ideation needs to be founded in a sensible perception, which implies the absurdity of the idea of an intellect as independent from sensibility. It is true (as Levinas says not only of phenomenology but of Western philosophy in general) that for Husserl the theory of transcendental subject, egology, includes in itself the theory of being, ontology,[79] but this implies a quite new kind of idealism which is more radical than Kant's transcendental idealism in the sense that there is for Husserl no absolute reality which could limit in a negative manner the phenomenal domain of knowledge. There is therefore nothing "behind" or "beyond" phenomena neither for Husserl nor for Heidegger, who differentiates clearly the phenomenon of phenomenology from the Kantian *Erscheinung* or appearance, precisely because "Essentially, nothing else stands 'behind' the phenomena of phenomenology."[80] Even if Husserl could declare that "in itself ontology is not phenomenology"[81] in the sense that there is no possibility of a radical intelligibility of what is ontic and includes in itself contingency, he admits nevertheless, even if such an ideal remains indefinitely remote, that "a completely and systematically developed phenomenology would be *eo ipso* the true and authentic universal ontology."[82]

As for Heidegger, he defines the phenomenological concept of phenomenon as that which needs to be explicitly thematized and does not show itself initially, being concealed in contrast to what initially and for the most part shows itself, but belongs nevertheless *essentially* to it as its meaning and ground. That which is therefore by essence the theme of phenomenology is what is concealed and can even be forgotten, that is—in a paradoxical way in respect to the traditional concept of Being—Being itself, because "the being of beings can least of all be something" behind which "something else stands, something that "does not appear."[83] The phenomenon of phenomenology being identical with the being of beings, the result is that "ontology is possible only as phenomenology."[84] Under the word "ontology," Heidegger does not mean any preexisting philosophical discipline and stresses that he uses this term in the broad and formal meaning of a discipline that has to be constituted on the basis of a questioning starting from "the things themselves," that is to say on the basis of phenomenology. Heidegger's ontology is therefore as different from traditional ontology as Levinas's metaphysics is from traditional metaphysics. Levinas insists on the identity of atheism and metaphysics, which gives to his concept of infinity a meaning that could be characterized as "anthropocentric" in so far as what is "beyond" the sensible is the "human" as such.[85] In the same manner, Heidegger wants to show that what Western philosophy since its beginning has named "being" has a temporal meaning. *Ousia* is the fundamental term that, for Plato and Aristotle, designates the being of beings understood as beingness, as what is common to all beings. In the Greek language this term means a dwelling place, an estate or property that is what is constantly available and present. Heidegger's analysis of the Greek concept of being, *ousia*, could to some extent be in agreement with Levinas's understanding of ontology as philosophy of power and possession.[86] But it is precisely the privilege granted to presence and based on the temporal meaning of being, which runs throughout the entire history of philosophy, that has to be brought to light in what Heidegger calls "destruction of the history of ontology."

As Heidegger himself suggests, such a deconstruction of the traditional concept of being requires a questioning going "beyond" being itself, in the direction of what Plato designates in the allegory of the sun in *The Republic* as the *epekeina tes ousias*, which has the function of light for all unveiling of beings.[87] This passage of *The Republic* which places the idea of the Good beyond being is considered by Levinas as "the most profound teaching" of philosophy,[88] which is in itself questionable in so far as the Good is here symbolized by the sun and identified to light, which is for Levinas a mere means of knowledge and appropriation. Furthermore, the mere fact of translating the Greek *to agathon* by "the Good" deprives it from the ethical meaning that Levinas intends to give to it, insofar as good as well as *gut* in German, *bonum* in Latin, or *bien* in French have the originary meaning of "possession." Heidegger, when commenting this same passage in 1940 in *Platons Lehre von der Wahrheit*, was more cautious, when he stressed that *to agathon* when it is thought in the Greek way has no moral value and does not mean something like prosperity or welfare, but "what makes something suitable for something." Therefore, the *idea tou agathou* is what makes possible the appearance of all things in the visibility of their respective ideas. As such it is what appears in the supreme manner, as Plato himself says, and this definition of the supreme cause of everything as *idea*, as a visible, implies for Heidegger the domination of vision and knowledge upon *aletheia*—truth as belonging to being itself, truth as unconcealment—the beginning at the same time of metaphysics and of humanism.[89]

All this makes it difficult to accept Levinas's peremptory judgments on Heidegger's thinking of Being. Saying, as Heidegger does, that "Being is inseparable from the comprehension of Being" in other words thinking a *finite* transcendence of Being,[90] does not mean that "Being is already an appeal to subjectivity,"[91] since Dasein can by no means be identified with that which modern philosophy names "subject." Levinas insists on the fact that the ego and the Other do not "form a number" and are not "individuals of a commun concept."[92] In the same manner Dasein is not for Heidegger the name of the species "man," but has to be understood in the light of the *distributive* structure of *Jemeinigkeit*, of "each time being my own being," as the "essence" of Dasein lies in its existence[93] which means that there is no general essence of Dasein. But this implies nevertheless a plurality of Dasein, and "the dispersion of Dasein as such, i.e. *Mitsein*, Being-with in général."[94] For Heidegger Being-with is a structure of existence, an existential, and does not require the actual presence of the other. This explains why *Jemeingkeit* and Being-with are not at all incompatible, because solitude, in the extreme form it takes in Being-toward-death, is precisely that which finally gives to Dasein his own self, so that this individuation process "individualizes in such a manner that it makes all individuals alike."[95] The belonging to the "same" is based here on alterity, alterity being fundamentally understood as *temporal* alterity in so far as each existence is a quite unexchangeable portion of time, or a *moira*, a destiny, as the ancient Greeks said. This is therefore precisely what separates each existent from all the others which can be shared by all of them. This is what opposes diametrically Heidegger's thinking as an ontology of participation to Levinas's metaphysics of separation.

There is therefore on Levinas's side absolute separation and impossibility of sharing or communion; on Heidegger's side temporal separation and sharing of differences, on the basis of something common. But the "same" is here nothing else than time, that has no "essence," being a pure process of differentiation or maturation, a pure *Zeitigung*. It is time, this *hen diapheron eautô*, this "One that differs from itself," expression that Hölderlin learned from Plato's reading of Heraclitus,[96] which can be the ground of all possible thinking, whereas the "One that remains in itself" which in the form of the Ab-solute is that which has no relation with anything else, is still at the bottom of Levinas's "metaphysics." In a kind of reply to Heidegger's temporal ontology, Levinas tried in *Time and the Other* to see in time "a mode of the beyond being," a relationship to that which is "unassimilable, absolutely other," to "the Wholly Other, the Transcendent, the Infinite," "a relation or religion that is not structured like knowing—that is, an intentionality, "so that the main thesis of the essay consists in thinking time as diachrony, noncoincidence and inadequation, time signifying" this always of noncoincidence, but also the always of Relationship."[97] The question is here not only in general of the *effective* possibility of this "relation without relation" with the Absolute, with what is absolutely separated, complete in itself and forming a perfect totality—these are the meanings of the Latin word *ab-solutus*—and of the necessity of thinking at least some "partial coincidence" with it, if not this identity of nature between the organ of knowledge and what is known, between the eye and the sun, that was precisely at the basis of Plato's "metaphysics of light"; the question is rather of the structure of thought in Heidegger, which is precisely not "intentionality," not a relation of knowledge.

As he declares in *Being and Time*: "Knowing neither first creates a *commercium* of the subject with the world, nor does this commercium *originate* from an effect of the world on the subject. Knowing is a mode of Dasein which is founded in being-in-the-world."[98] Heidegger's fundamental idea is that the relation of knowledge, the theoretical relation, is not the primary relationship, precisely because this primary relationship is not a relationship with an object, but with the world. The world is neither purely subjective nor purely objective; it is the horizon which is projected as soon as Dasein exists and inside which alone there can be an intentional relationship between subject and object. This is what Heidegger explains in the essay he dedicated to Husserl in 1928 under the title "Of the Essence of Ground." For him, the "transcendent" is not, as it is for Husserl, the object, but Dasein, to which the structure of *epekeina*, of "going beyond" belongs originarily. There is not therefore at first a subject which could "transcend" itself toward the objects, but there is originarily a movement of transcendence on the basis of which a "self" can be constituted. Transcendence is always a going beyond the totality of objects in direction of the world, which belongs to the structure of Dasein. This explains, as Heidegger stresses, that intentionality, that is, a relationship with an object, can only be possible on the basis of transcendence, which is the projection of the worldly horizon. Levinas could still object that the relation with the other, object or person in the world, "is here accomplished only through a third term which I find in myself."[99] But this third term, the world as the common soil between subject and object, is not the result of the self, but precedes it and does not consist in a theoretical act, but depends on what is traditionally named "affectivity." It is the fact to "find itself" in a certain attunement in the world—which corresponds to this existential that Heidegger names *Befindlichkeit*, disposition—that allows the encounter of the different kinds of beings. In order to have a relationship with a being, this being must be manifest as *a* being, which implies that it has to be manifest in the context of the world. In *Being and Time*, Heidegger stresses that "the attunement of disposition constitutes existentially the openness to world of Dasein"[100] and shows that it is in the fundamental disposition of Angst that "the world as such" opens itself for the first time.[101] There is therefore a privilege of attunement, which, in opposition to pure intellect, has the power to open ourselves to the entirety of being, to the reign of the world, which can never be understood as the totality of beings, but only as *das Grundgeschehen*, the fundamental event of Dasein.

Levinas has always wanted to be read as a philosopher and not as a Jewish thinker only and made a strict distinction between his philosophical works and the texts he dedicated to the study of Talmud. But such a strict division of his thought cannot be maintained as he has clearly intended to shake the entire philosophical and ontological tradition by invoking another tradition, which is precisely the Jewish one, in which ethics is the basis of all thought. This explains the violence of Levinas's judgment on ontology, especially on Heidegger's ontology which in his view leads to "imperialist domination, to tyranny," of which origin "lies back in the pagan moods, in the enrootedness in the earth, in the adoration that enslaved men can devote to their masters."[102] Here it is clearly the Jewish thinker who is speaking, since paganism is not a "philosophical" concept—all antic philosophers, including Plato, are "pagans"!—but a "religious" designation, which can be used only in a monotheistic perspective. Levinas expresses himself in a similar manner in the "engaged" and polemical articles he wrote for various reviews, when he speaks of the "eternal seduction of paganism" and declares that Judaism is perhaps only the negation of the "sacred filtering through the world," "the mystery of things being the source of all cruaulty toward human beings."[103] He goes even further in quite a disturbing manner in one of his Talmudic readings where he characterizes the victory of Persia over Rome as the victory of "animal energy" and "biological forces" and the antic Greece as "the work of young animals," its culture without morality having been only "a pretence, a fragile and deceitful superstructure, mystification and camouflage."[104] The conviction of the superiority of monotheism drives him to the limits of ethnocentrism, when he defines paganism as "nationalism in its crual and pityless character 'and sees in a pagan humanity' a forest-humanity, a pre-human humanity."[105] Such an ethnocentrism takes the form of an exemplarism, of a specificity which has the status of a norm and becomes the basis of a pseudouniversalism. Thus Levinas explains that the position of Israel apart of the nations is "a particularism that conditions universality,"[106] which allows him to declare that "what is authentically human is the being-Jewish in all men."[107]

This explains why Levinas refuses to take into account the experience of the primitive man, who, as Levy-Bruhl showed, "through participation not only sees the other, but is the other" and affirms that the solitude of existing characterizes the "modern consciousness" that has a knowledge of its solitude and is therefore only to be considered.[108] There seems to be for him two different kinds of humanity: a "prehuman" humanity, including all kinds of humanities except the monotheistic and Jewish one, and the "authentically human" one, the monotheistic and Jewish one, which is the only one taken into account in all Levinas's ethical analyses. Heidegger's point of view is completely opposed to such a difference of level in "humanity." He declares on the contrary that Dasein is a structure of existence that can be applied to all human beings and not only to modern men, so there is indeed a "primitive" Dasein, and that orienting the analysis of Dasein toward the life of so called primitive peoples can even have a positive methodical significance since primitive Dasein speaks out of a more primordial absorption in "phenomena."[109] And, as we know, he has shown a great interest, after the beginning of the thirties, in archaic and mythic Greece, precisely because it is the dawn of Western history and not, as Levinas says, because he finds "in Presocratism thought as obedience to the truth of Being 'that' would be accomplished in existing as builder and cultivator," which testifies that "Heidegger, with the whole of western history, takes the relation with the Other as enacted in the destiny of sedentary peoples, the possessors and builders of the earth."[110] Are such massive assertions still "philosophical"? For, leaving aside the anthropological question of the possibility for humanity in general to be nomadic and not sedentary, considering all the benefits in terms of culture and development brought by sedentarity, it has to be strongly underlined that such a definition of the human being as enrooted in the earth is nowhere to be found in Heidegger, who saw precisely in man—in agreement with the "nomadic" nature of man—"the shepherd of Being" and not "the lord of beings."[111] On the contrary, Heidegger defines the fundamental manner for Dasein to be a *Da*, a "there," as angst, which involves a breach with the familiarity of the everyday being-in-the-world and reveals a more primordial phenomenon which is precisely the not-being-at-home of Dasein.[112] It is precisely before the *Unheimlichkeit*, the uncanniness of his own being, that in *Verfallenheit* Dasein takes his flight toward the familiarity of the everyday. The same thematic of the fundamental not-being-at-home of Dasein is further developed in Heidegger's 1935 lecture course Introduction to Metaphysics on the basis of his commentary of Sophocles' choir in Antigone where man is defined as *to deinotaton*, the most violent being on earth. Heidegger insists in translating the Greek word *deinon*, which means at the same time terrifying and marvelous, by *unheimlich*, in the sense of what throws the human being outside of what is *heimisch*, familiar, and prevents him from remaining in his element. Saying that man is what is the most *unheimlich* means that he is at the same time the most "uncanny" and the most devoid of home of all beings. But this is precisely in Heidegger's view "the true *Greek* definition of the human being,"[113] such a "pagan" definition being not opposed to the Jewish one, contrary to Levinas's opinion.

To be "at home" is never something already given, but on the contrary it has always to be conquered. This is what Heidegger learned during the thirties from Hölderlin, who wrote in 1801 to his friend Böhlendorff that "what is familiar must be learned as well as what is alien," so "the free use of what is one's own is the most difficult."[114] In his 1942 lecture course on Hölderlins Hymne "Der Ister," Heidegger explains that the poet's only concern was to succeed in feeling himself at home, which implied that he had to first explain what is foreign.[115] In the same manner, Heidegger explains that a historical people is never by itself at home in its own language and exists only out of a dialogue between its language and foreign languages, so that what is one's own and what is foreign remain tightly connected.[116] There is therefore a negative relation to the home which cannot be eliminated nor overcome, but has to be endured, as Hölderlin understood, because only the one who is without home can have a true relation to it. In the same period, Heidegger begins to see in *Heimatlosigkeit,* a homelessness which is "the symptom of the oblivion of Being," "the destiny of the world" as he writes in 1946 to Jean Beaufret.[117] For, as he says in a text dealing with nihilism and dating from the same year, it is precisely because in modernity, in the period of nihilism, the human being is more than ever deprived of home that he tries to find in the organized conquest of the earth and his expansion in cosmic space a compensation to his homelessness.[118] It is in the light of this homelessness of the modern man that it is possible to understand what could be authentic dwelling, *ethos,* as Heidegger recalls in the *Letter on Humanism.*[119] As he explains in his commentary of Heraclitus' saying *ethos anthropoi daimon,* dwelling does not mean a being familiar with the *Umwelt,* a mere being at home in the tranquility and enjoyment of a firm possession, but on the contrary the being opened to the strangeness of the being in the world and to the woes of *Geworfenheit,* of the being-thrown into existence. That is the reason why ethics, understood as dwelling, does not consist simply in enjoying life and finding pleasure in the familiarity of its home, as Levinas wanted, but in exposing oneself to the strangeness and the pains that are at the bottom of all familiarity and enjoyment. Dwelling requires the capacity of seeing the unfamiliar in the familiar, the *daimon* in the *anthropon,* in other terms, God in the human being. Dwelling in the proper sense of the word can therefore only mean the capacity to maintain distance in proximity and to open one's own home to the foreign. This is what Heraclitus wants to indicate, when, in the story told by Heidegger, he declares to the curious crowd that has come to see him and that found him shivering near a fire, like any other human being trying to find a shelter: "einai gar kai entautha theous" (here also the Gods are present), at the level of ordinary life, of the most elementary needs which are common to all human beings. What constitutes human life is precisely the fact that the sphere of the most elementary needs is not separated from the upper sphere of the most sublime aspirations, so no human being can ever be satisfied of simply being alive, but wants more than mere life, wants to ek-sist, to be opened to the strangeness of the other, to the extraordinary which is already present for him into the ordinary.

Levinas's purpose was to invert the hierarchy established in the Aristotelian definition of philosophy between ontology and ethics. Heidegger, by returning to the earlier period of the Presocratic thought, brings to light the fact that such a definition of philosophy is already a matter for school and academic pursuits which comes from the characterization of thinking as *theoria* in order to make from it a technical tool in service of doing and making.[120] Previous to this, there was no distinction between *theoria* and *praxis* nor between different philosophical disciplines, because for the Presocratics "thinking acts insofar as it thinks."[121] This explains why to Beaufret's question concerning the relation of ontology to ethics, Heidegger gives the following answer: "If the name 'ethics,' in keeping the basic meaning of the word *ethos*, should now say that 'ethics' ponders the abode of man, then that thinking which thinks the truth of Being as the primordial element of man, as one who ek-ists, is in itself the original ethics."[122] In Heidegger's view there is no separate ethical domain. As he showed in his 1946 commentary of Anaximander's saying, remaining in this respect in a great proximity to the Nietzschean identification of morality and metaphysics, it is often the case that in the ethical point of view, *das Gerächte*, the revenged, constitutes *das Gerechte*, the just,[123] so it becomes impossible to think the domain of what is called "right" or "justice" without reference to the idea of revenge, payment, and penance. And following what Nietzsche said in his *Zarathoustra*, revenge is nothing else than the *ressentiment* against time which depreciates all what is transitory,[124] thas is, in the Heideggerian view of the nondifference between Becoming and Being, a lack of *tisis*, of estimation and care for Being itself, for the *finity* of Being which there is only as long as *Dasein* is. There can be a separate ethical domain and separate moral and juridical representations only on the ground of such a spirit of revenge against Being and Time, a "spirit" which does not want to let Being be *at the same time* accord and discord, to let Being be *finite*. For such a finity means at the same time the belonging of man to Being and the possibility of his turning against it. What has to be respected in man can therefore not only be his irreducible singularity or otherness, his "share" of time, but the *freedom* which makes him able or not able to *affirm* Being and to see yes to time—for what can be the "object" of a "yes" and of an affirmation if not what *already is as what will be*, that is, Being in his nondifference to Becoming? That is the reason why Heidegger declared in the *Letter on Humanism* that the thinking of the truth of Being, as fundamental ontology, that is, as ontology of *Dasein*, is already in itself the originary ethics.[125]

NOTES

1. It has to be emphasized that neither the word "ontology" nor the word "metaphysics" can be found in Greek philosophy. "Ontology" was coined by the German theologian and philosopher Johannes Clauberg in 1664 in his *Elementa philosophiae sive Ontosophia* and became a main philosophical term with the publication in 1730 by Wolff of a treatise entitled "Ontologia." As Heidegger explains in *Kant und das Problem der Metaphysik* (Frankfurt aM: Klostermann, 1973), 6, the expression "meta ta physica" was first used by Aristotle's disciples as a name for the treatises following his *Physics*, *meta* meaning here merely "after," and only much later to designate the contents of these books, "beyond."

2. *Totality and Infinity: An Essay on Exteriority*, trans. A. Lingis (Pittsburgh: Duquesne University Press, 1969), 304.

3. E. Levinas, *La théorie de l'intuition dans la phénoménologie de Husserl* (Paris: Vrin, 1984), 86.

4. Ibid., 141.

5. On Levinas's reading of Husserl see F. Dastur, "Intentionnalité et métaphysique," *Emmanuel Lévinas, Positivité et transcendance* (Paris: PUF, 2000), 125–42.

6. See E. Levinas, "La ruine de la représentation" (1959), *En découvrant l'existence avec Husserl et Heidegger* (Paris: Vrin 1967), 135; *Totality and Infinity*, 28.

7. See E. Levinas, *Totalité et infini* (Paris: Le livre de Poche, 2003); "Préface à l'édition allemande (Janvier 1987)," iv (not reproduced in the English translation); *Totality and Infinity*, 210–11.

8. E. Levinas, *Time and the Other*, trans. R. A. Cohen (Pittsburgh: Duquesne University Press, 1997), 42.

9. Ibid., 43.

10. Ibid., 40.

11. Ibid., 42.

12. Ibid., 43.

13. Ibid., 64–65.

14. Ibid., 65.

15. Ibid.

16. Ibid.

17. Ibid.

18. Ibid., 92.

19. Ibid., 93.

20. Ibid., 94.

21. *Totality and Infinity*, 36.

22. Ibid., 37.

23. Ibid., 38.

24. Ibid.

25. Ibid., 38–39

26. Ibid., 39. *Autrui* (from the latin *alteri*), which is translated with a capital O, is in French a collective name for the others.

27. Ibid., 33.

28. Ibid., 34.

29. Ibid.

30. Ibid., 35.

31. Ibid.

32. Ibid., 39. There is here a strong similarity with Sartre's description of the encounter of the Other in *Being and Nothingness*, where the appearance of the other is the experience of the decentralization of the world: "Thus suddenly an object has appeared which has stolen the world from me" (*Being and Nothingness*, trans. H. E. Barnes (New York: Washington Square, 1956), 343. The subject is experiencing the loss of his universe, which means that the experience that he has now of himself is the passive experience of being seen by the Other: "Being-seen by the other is the truth of seing the other" so that "the other is on principle the one who looks at me" (*Being and Nothingness*, 345–46).

33. Ibid.

34. Ibid., 40.

35. Ibid., 35.

36. Ibid., 36.

37. Ibid,

38. Ibid., 40.

39. Ibid., 28.

40. Ibid., 40.

41. Ibid.

42. Ibid., 41.

43. Ibid.

44. Ibid., 77.

45. Ibid.

46. Ibid.

47. Ibid., 78.

48. Ibid.

49. Ibid., 79.

50. Ibid.

51. Ibid., 80.

52. Ibid.

53. Ibid., 81.

54. Ibid., 43.

55. Ibid.

56. Ibid., 35.

57. Ibid., 44.

58. Ibid., 46.

59. Ibid., 47–48.

60. Ibid., 48.

61. Ibid., 51.

62. Ibid., 66.

63. There is here again a strong similarity with Sartre's analysis of the look in *Being and Nothingness*, where Sartre explains that the look is not necessarily connected with the appearance of a sensible form in our perceptive field and that the experience of being looked at is not an empirical experience: "far from perceiving

the look *on* the objects which manifest it, my apprehension of a look turned towards me appears on the ground of the destruction of the eyes which 'look at me'" (*Being and Nothingness*, 346). Sartre remarks that when we apprehend the look, we cease to perceive the eyes so that it is impossible to notice the color of the eyes that are looking at you, because the other's look seems to hide his eyes. I cannot at the same time see the eyes of the other and see his look. This means that for me it is impossible to situation the source of the look in the world, because if I try to do it, I become for myself a look, and I can find only objects of the world and no longer the look of other subjects. The experience of the look can therefore only be the experience of my being looked at.

64. Ibid., 66.
65. Ibid., 199.
66. Ibid., 193. The French word "visage," which comes from the verb *voir*, can be translated as "face" which can be seen of the other. But paradoxically enough, for Levinas the visage (like the Platonic *eidos* that has the same meaning) cannot be seen, since it belongs to the invisible.
67. Ibid., 195.
68. Ibid., 196.
69. Ibid., 197.
70. Ibid.
71. Ibid., 198.
72. Ibid.
73. Ibid., 199.
74. Ibid.
75. Ibid., 219.
76. Ibid., 215.
77. Ibid., 77.
78. E. Husserl, *Ideas Pertaining to a Pure Phenomenology and to a Phenomenological Philosophy*, First Book, modified trans. F. Kersten (The Hague: Nijhoff, 1983), 92–93.
79. See E. Husserl, *Cartesianische Meditationen*, Husserliana 1 (Den Haag: Nijhoff, 1950), § 41, where it is said that "all either immanent or transcendent sense and being that can be conceived, belong to the domain of transcendental subjectivity as what constitutes all sense and being."
80. M. Heidegger, *Being and Time*, trans. J. Stambaugh (Albany: State University of New York Press, 1996), 31 [36].
81. E. Husserl, *Ideen III* (Nijhoff: den Haag, 1952), Beilage1, § 6.
82. *Cartesianische Meditationen*, § 64.
83. *Being and Time*, § 7, 31 [35].
84. Ibid., § 7, 31 [36].
85. Cf. *Totality and Infinity*, 59 where Levinas, taking up again Protagoras' famous saying, declares that man is the "measure of all things, that is, measured by nothing, comparing all things but incomparable."
86. *Totality and Infinity*, 46.
87. M. Heidegger, *Die Grundprobleme der Phänomenologie* (Frankfurt aM: Klostermann, 1975), GA Band 24, §20 (b), 404.

88. *Totality and Infinity*, 103.
89. See M. Heidegger, *Wegmarken* (Frankfurt aM: Klostermann, 1967), 132–33 and 139–42.
90. See M. Heidegger, "What Is Metaphysics ?," *Basic Writings*, ed. D. F. Krell (San Franscisco: Harper, 1992), 108: "Being itself is essentially finite and reveals itself only in the transcendence of Dasein."
91. *Totality and Infinity*, 45.
92. Ibid., 39.
93. *Being and Time*, § 9, p. 40 [42]. The translation of *Jemeinigkeit* by each time being my own being is here prefered to "always being my own being" in order to stress the distributive meaning of the German adverb "je" which means "at a time." It has to be recalled that Heidegger spoke at first (in 1924) of "Jeweiligkeit," that is, of the momentary character of Dasein. See *Der Begriff der Zeit*, GA Band 64 (Frankfurt aM: Klostermann), 115.
94. See M. Heidegger, *Metaphysische Anfangsgründe der Logik* (1928), GA, Band 26 (Frankfurt a M: Klostermann, 1978), § 10, 175.
95. Ibid., 124.
96. See Plato, *Symposium*, 187a; Hölderlin, *Hyperion* (Frankfurt aM: Insel Verlag, 1969), 367.
97. *Time and the Other*, 31–32.
98. *Being and Time*, § 13, 58 [62].
99. *Totality and Infinity*, 45.
100. *Being and Time*, § 29, 129 [137] (modified translation).
101. Ibid., § 40, 175 [187]
102. *Totality and Infinity*, 47.
103. E. Levinas, "Heidegger, Gagarine et nous" (*Information juive*,1961), *Difficile Liberté, Essais sur le judaïsme* (Paris: Albin Michel, Livre de Poche, 1963), 325.
104. E. Levinas, *L'au-delà du verset* (Paris: E. de Minuit, 1982), 75, 80.
105. "Simone Weil contre la Bible" (*Evidences*, 1952), *Difficile Liberté*, 325.
106. "Une religion d'adultes" (1957), *Difficile Liberté*, 39.
107. E. Levinas, *A l'heure des nations* (Paris: Minuit, 1988), 192.
108. *Time and the Other*, 43.
109. *Being and Time,*§ 11, 47 [51].
110. *Totality and Infinity*, 46.
111. "Letter on Humanism," *Basic Writings*, 245.
112. *Being and Time*, § 40, 177 [189].
113. M. Heidegger, *Einführung in die Metaphysik*, GA Band 40 (Frankfurt am Main: Klostermann 1983), 160. See F. Dastur," La question de l'être de l'homme dans l'*Introduction à la métaphysique*," *L'Introduction à la métaphysique de Heidegger*, ed. J.-Fr. Courtine (Pari: Vrin, 2007), 213–33.
114. F. Hölderlin, *Essays and Letters on Theory*, tr. and ed. Th. Fau (Albany: State University of New York Press, 1988), 150.
115. M. Heidegger, *Hölderlins Hymne" Der Ister*," GA Band 53 (Frankfurt aM: Klostermann, 1984), 67.
116. Ibid., 80.
117. "Letter on humanism," *Basic Writings*, 242, 243.

118. M. Heidegger, *Nietzsche* (Neske, Pfullingen: Zweiter Band, 1961), 395.

119. Ibid., 256.

120. *Letter on Humanism,.* 218.

121. Ibid., 217.

122. Ibid., 258.

123. M. Heidegger, "Der Spruch des Anaximander," *Holzwege* (Frankfurt aM: Klostermann, 1963), 328. See F. Dastur, "Anaximander and Heidegger: Being and Justice," *Interrogating the Tradition, Hermeneutics and the History of Philosophy*, ed. C. E. Scott and J. Sallis (Albany: State University of New York Press, 2000), 179–90.

124. See M. Heidegger, *Vorträge und Aufsätze* (Neske: Pfullingen, 1954), 115.

125. *Letter on Humanism*, 258.

CHAPTER EIGHT

USELESS SACRIFICE

Robert Bernasconi

Levinas was among Heidegger's best early readers and was recognized as such by his contemporaries, but as he developed his own philosophy, his readings of Heidegger became increasingly idiosyncratic. They were conducted less according to the rules of scholarship than what Heidegger himself called "the dialogue between thinkers," which, as he said, had its own rules.[1] Nevertheless, in the late essay "Dying for . . . ," Levinas's interpretation became once again rigorous, and that makes it an appropriate place to start, an examination of Levinas's highly conflicted relation to his former teacher.[2]

"Dying for . . ." represents the culmination of Levinas's confrontation with Heidegger's analysis of Dasein's "being towards death." He delivered the lecture in March 1987 at a conference of Heidegger scholars—including Jacques Derrida—at the College International de Philosophie in Paris. The conclusion of the lecture was that Heidegger could not find a place for sacrifice "in an order divided between the authentic and the unauthentic."[3] In the course of developing that objection Levinas employed the Bataillan phrase "an ethics of sacrifice." What did Levinas mean by "an ethics of sacrifice"? Does it provide a good way for him to encapsulate his own philosophy? Can it be used to differentiate his philosophy from that of Heidegger?

If by "an ethics of sacrifice," Levinas meant an ethics in which only those actions that one performed without regard to any possible gain to oneself could be deemed ethical, then it would seem that the now familiar Derridean paradoxes would be generated with the result that his thought would quickly be transformed beyond recognition. Jacques Derrida at the end of *The Gift of Death* explored what he called the economy of sacrifice, which suspends the strict circular economy of exchange by promoting a giving without any hope of return, even the token reward of simple gratitude.[4] That such giving could not even be aware of itself because of the sense of self-satisfaction that might follow from an awareness of being good is self-defeating because it seems, at least at first sight, that one cannot give without knowingly transferring ownership. Similarly, giving one's life—or one's death—is a sacrifice only, it would seem, if one knows what one is doing. Did Derrida succeed in involving Levinas in these problems and paradoxes without any expectation of escape? The fact that, at the beginning of *The Gift of Death*, Derrida referenced Levinas's argument that Heidegger cannot account for sacrifice, even while questioning the power of that objection against Heidegger, suggests that this was Derrida's intention (DM, 46; GD, 42), just as Derrida in *Given Time* implicitly embroils Levinas in his account of the paradox of the gift.[5] Furthermore, in his essays on hospitality Derrida draws Levinas's remarks on this topic into a similar paradox where the conditions of its possibility prove to be the conditions of its impossibility as one tries to unite the Other into one's home, giving the Other the run of one's home, even without asking his or her name.[6]

The materials from which Derrida weaves the paradoxes have a long heritage. At least one prominent strand of Christian thinking seems to advocate sacrifice, but in so far as one's sacrifices here on earth allow one to store up rewards in heaven, one has not escaped the system of exchange. When Derrida, referencing Kant, suggests that "in order to conduct oneself in a moral manner, one must act as though God did not exist or no longer concerned himself with our salvation," he is raising precisely this problem that a reward, even—perhaps especially—one postponed to another world, compromises the ethicality of the act.[7] Nevertheless, the need to keep one's eyes off the prize is highlighted not only by Christ's injunctions to give in secret, but also by the condition of goodness that the left hand not know what the right hand is doing (Matthew 6:1–4). In other words, one cannot be in on one's own secret, which complicates greatly and perhaps renders impossible altogether any self-conscious attempt to do good, let alone be good.

In the background of any rereading of Levinasian ethics today and particularly when referencing the "ethics of sacrifice" that Levinas evokes at the same time that he attempts to move beyond Heidegger, there is always today the question as to whether Derrida's questions redirect Levinas's ethical thought somewhere else than he himself wanted to take it. I will return to this question at the end of this chapter, because it is unavoidable today, but I will do so only after exploring in some detail the nature of Levinas's objections against Heidegger's analysis of being toward death, which is my main topic.

So far as I am aware, Levinas used the phrase "an ethics of sacrifice" only once in print. The phrase appeared in "Dying for . . ." as part of what the scholastics would have called a *videtur quod non*, an "it seems that not." Levinas refers to section 47 of *Being and Time*, where Heidegger explained that, although someone can always die in someone else's place in the sense of sacrificing him- or herself for the Other "in some definite affair," this does not take death away from the Other because the Other will still die some time.[8] The fact that Heidegger explicitly acknowledged sacrifice in this passage is what enables Levinas to ventriloquize on behalf of the Heideggerian who could well respond to Levinas by saying, "The ethics of sacrifice does not succeed in shaking the rigor of being and the ontology of the authentic" (*EN* 229; *ENT*, 216). The phrase "ethics of sacrifice" is thus employed by Levinas in his attempt to anticipate the Heideggerian response to his own view. Is it significant that he puts it into the mouth of those on Heidegger's side in the debate? Does that mean that, far from underwriting the idea, he is, contrary to expectation, attributing it to Heidegger?

To attempt to answer that question, it is necessary to ask how Levinas addresses the suggestion that Heidegger had already in *Being and Time* allowed for an ethics of sacrifice. Somewhat characteristically, Levinas follows the point about the ethics of sacrifice with a rhetorical question, thereby leaving his readers to wonder how he meant it. He asks whether "the relationship to the other in sacrifice" indicates a responsibility for the other on the part of a "me (*moi*)" that is neither a subject nor an authentic Dasein (*EN*, 229; *ENT*, 217). In developing this question, Levinas finds two ways to make the same point. First, he locates this relationship to the other in sacrifice beyond or prior to ontology, even while it would determine any such ontology. Second, he specifies that the responsible one is the self through the uniqueness of election: "This would be the I (*le moi*) of the one who is chosen to answer for his fellowman and is *thus* identical to itself (*soi*) and *thus* the self (*le soi-même*)" (*EN*, 229; *ENT*, 217). Both formulations, and particularly the second one, evoke the complex framework that Levinas developed over a fifty-year period to make the point that if the philosopher starts the analysis at the level of the human subject, or even Dasein, the philosopher starts too late. Levinas, in an apparently traditional gesture, moves back before or behind what others take to be the starting point so as to find what one could only with appropriate reservations call the conditions of that starting point.

So at this late point in the essay "Dying for . . ." Levinas, somewhat surprisingly given his record of opposing Heidegger, produces no knock-down argument against him. He simply refers the reader to what he has said elsewhere. The suggestion is that although Heidegger talks about sacrifice as if he had accounted for it, he had not in fact done so. But if Levinas discounts

Heidegger's acknowledgment of the possibility of sacrifice as insufficient, what would one need to say in order to find a place for it?

Levinas's polemic against Heidegger's account of being toward death had begun over forty years before the publication of "Dying for . . . ," in 1946 in *Time and the Other*, if not earlier. Levinas already draws there what he calls the byzantine distinction between Heidegger's conception of being toward death as the assumption of the possibility of impossibility and his own conception of it as the impossibility of possibility.[9] The point is that in Heidegger authentic being toward death underlies freedom as the making possible of all other possibilities, whereas Levinas sees in death the limits of the possible in the form of the impossibility of having a project. The relation to death leaves the subject "enchained, overwhelmed, and in some way passive" (*TA*, 57–58; *TO*, 70–71). Whereas Heidegger allegedly presents authentic being toward death as a supreme lucidity and thus as a virility, Levinas himself regards death as a mystery and as "the limit of the subject's virility" (*TA*, 52, 62; *TO*, 70, 74). That is to say, the relation to death does not open one to mastery, as in Heidegger, but to passivity (*TA*, 62; *TO*, 74). Levinas rehearses the same point over ten years later in *Totality and Infinity*: "My death comes from an instant upon which I can in no way exercise my power."[10]

Levinas proceeds in *Time and the Other* to question whether from this perspective death could still be said to be "*my* death," whether death does not crush solitude and subjectivity (*TA*, 65; *TO*, 77). The question, introduced abruptly at the end of the discussion, is not the afterthought it might appear to be. It is at the heart of his polemic against Heidegger. Levinas is not questioning whether one dies alone, although it is tempting to think that that is the issue, and at times Levinas has used phrases, such as the reference to solitude in *Time and the Other* that suggest this. However, in "Nameless" (*Sans Nom*) he is clear: "One always dies alone."[11] Nevertheless, Levinas does not mean thereby that there is in death "a dissolution of all relations with the other" (*EN*, 226; *ENT*, 214) which was Heidegger's view of authentic being toward death. Heidegger writes: "When it stands before itself in this way, all its relations to any other Dasein have been undone" (*SZ*, 250; *BT*, 294). On this basis Levinas attributes to Heidegger the belief that "everyone dies for himself" (*EN*, 229; *ENT*, 216), albeit Heidegger does not exactly say that. This leads Levinas to the conclusion that there is no place for sacrifice in Heidegger.

Levinas repeatedly returns to this theme throughout the 1960s and 1970s, albeit with frequent changes of emphasis, as he comes to a better understanding of the place of the analysis of being toward death in *Being and Time*. In *God, Death, and Time*, lectures from 1975–1976, Levinas readily acknowledges that one dies one's own death. His support of the idea is underlined by the fact that he attributes it to Jankélévitch rather than Heidegger.[12] Nevertheless, Levinas again does not locate the starting-point of a consideration of death in one's own death (DMT 22; GDT 13) but rather in my emotional relation to the death of another (DMT, 25; GDT, 16).

This is just one example of how Levinas treated Heidegger's discussion of death in isolation, but as time went on he refined his critique and began to phrase it in ways that show a richer appreciation of the structure of *Being and Time*. Heidegger introduced being toward death in an attempt to include the whole of Dasein. Death had to be included both because death comes at the end and in the expectation that it would clarify the nature of authenticity, the discussion of which had been largely excluded from the preceding sections. It was with an eye toward authenticity that as a prelude to his discussion of being towards death, Heidegger says of death what he has already said of existence: it is in each case mine (SZ, 41, 240; BT, 67, 284). This is the basis for Heidegger's point that death is not alien or other, but a possibility-of-Being which belongs to Dasein's being (SZ, 239; BT, 283). Heidegger seeks confirmation of this in the fact that "No one can take the Other's dying away from him" (SZ, 240; BT, 284). That is the context for Heidegger's comment that one can sacrifice oneself for someone in some definite affair, but that the person will still die eventually at some point or another (SZ, 240; BT, 284). The emphasis is on the argument that because one cannot save anybody from death in the long run, one must concede that each person's death belongs to them alone. That is why it seems open to a Heideggerian to respond to Levinas that it is only because my death is mine and mine alone that I can die for another in an act of personal sacrifice. Indeed, Derrida makes this point on Heidegger's behalf in *The Gift of Death* when he submits that one's irreplaceability in the face of death is the condition of possibility of sacrifice, and not of its impossibility. Derrida argues that "the fundamental and founding possibility of sacrifice" was as important to Heidegger as it was to Levinas (DM, 46; GD, 42).

However, none of this seems to intimidate Levinas who creatively rewrites Heidegger's sentence from section 9 of *Being and Time* that Dasein is the being who is concerned with Being, the being for which Being is an issue (DMT, 35; GDT, 25). In "Dying for . . ." authenticity is glossed by Levinas in this way: "Primordial importance is attached to *one's own being*" (EN, 224; ENT, 211). Levinas thereby locates the *conatus essendi* at the heart of Heidegger's account of human being.[13]

Levinas, it should be remembered, is not against the *conatus essendi*, although it sometimes sounds as if he is. He is merely saying that not everything can be reduced to it. Nevertheless, having recognized the prominence of the *conatus essendi* in Western thought in general and having seen it as culminating in Social Darwinism and in Heidegger, as he reads

him, Levinas attempts to undo the *conatus essendi* by reference to the gratuitousness of ethics (*DMT*, 39; *GDT*, 29). Sacrifice, dying for the other,
as Levinas understands it, would be a surpassing of the *conatus essendi* (*EN*,
228; *ENT*, 215). He explores this further in a Talmudic reading from 1988,
"Beyond the State in the State." Once again he takes life beyond the egoism of biological reality, "beyond the 'at all costs' of the *conatus essendi*,"
to a love that is "already self sacrifice going in its essential intention right
up to dying for another." Sacrifice renders living possible.[14] But would this
amount to an ethics of sacrifice?

Levinas's initial complaints in *Time and the Other* against Heidegger's
death analysis are not drawn from ethics. This largely still holds for *Totality and Infinity* where the contrast is also made in terms of the difference
between Heidegger's account of anguish or fear of nothingness and Levinas's
account of fear of the Other, as a fear of violence against oneself (*TeI*,
212; *TI*, 235). Even where the theme of death is introduced in a specifically ethical context, which he does first in the 1951 essay "Is Ontology
Fundamental?," it is simply to make the point that, although I can kill, and
although the other is the only being I want to kill, I cannot kill the other,
who as other, always escapes me (*EN*, 22; *ENT*, 9–10). Levinas's subsequent
objections against Heidegger's account of being-toward-death can be made
to sound like ethical objections, but that is not how they were initially
formulated. That is why one needs to be careful not to attribute to Levinas's
appeals to sacrifice a significance they do not have. To be sure, death on
Levinas's account does not find a place within ontology, even fundamental
ontology, which is defined for him in this regard by the opposition it imposes
on death between being and nothingness (*DMT*, 16; *GDT*, 8). But that does
not mean that it is immediately located within ethics. As we saw, death is
approached by Levinas in terms of mystery: "[T]he subject is in relationship
with what does not come from itself" (*TA*, 56; *TO*, 70. See also *TeI*, 211;
TI, 235). That is to say, it is a relation of transcendence. And that is why
death "approaches without being able to be assumed" (*TeI*, 211; *TI*, 235),
which excludes Heideggerian authenticity as Levinas understands it.

Although fictional examples can often be misleading, it may be helpful to introduce one here to illustrate the difference between Heidegger's
and Levinas's accounts. It might seem that when one reads at the end of
Charles Dickens' *A Tale of Two Cities*, Sydney Corton goes to the guillotine
in the place of Darnay, one is witnessing the quintessential substitution
of one person for another. It might seem that this is what Levinas had in
mind except that the "prophetic" speech Corton would have uttered as he
went to his death, had he had the opportunity, was too lucid in its fixation
on himself. Thirteen sentences begin "I see" even if what he sees is the
lives for which he lays down his life. Is this not the voice of virility or of

authentic resoluteness rather than passivity? This seems to be confirmed by the final famous sentence: "It is a far, far better thing that I do, than I have ever done; it is a far, far better rest that I go to than I have ever known."[15] Corton's final thought is of himself. Of course, he is a fictional character, and the speech tells us more about Dickens' sense of himself as a preacher than anything else, but the example illustrates how what might look from the outside like the embodiment of Levinasian ethics can, with access to the mind if one going to his or her death emerges as its Heideggerian antithesis.

However, it would be a mistake to suppose that ethical considerations alone are decisive in making the difference. Levinas's interest in the theme of sacrifice arises from a concern with transcendence, rather than ethics. That ethics is first philosophy is not Levinas's starting point in the sense of an assumption which he brings to philosophy. It is a conclusion which he draws only slowly as a result of his conviction that philosophy is fundamentally concerned with transcendence. His point is that philosophers have hitherto been largely mistaken in their efforts to characterize the formal structure of transcendence, and this has led them in turn to misidentify the concretizations of this formal structure. That is to say Levinas focuses on ethics because of his concern for transcendence rather than the other way around.[16] Levinas's discussions of sacrifice confirm this. So, for example, in 1965 in "Enigma and Phenomenon," Levinas says that sacrifice is "without calculation" and that it is by sacrificing oneself that one can go beyond death to the infinite.[17]

It is true that Levinas's insistence on the "priority" of dying for the other has an ethical form in "Dying for . . ." (*EN*, 230; *ENT*, 217): Heidegger has either overlooked or given insufficient warrant to nonindifference. Levinas had elsewhere already established that nonindifference to the other has its basis in indifference to one's own death. It is to be open to a "time without me . . . in an eschatology without hope for oneself."[18] Levinas's point is that Heidegger (among others) cannot account for the gratuitousness of sacrifice. Levinas by this argument is seeking to take the focus away from my own death to the death of the Other. He is, one might say, proposing a paradigm shift, albeit one that he already finds exemplified in the utopian Marxist philosophy of Ernst Bloch, which is said by him to have "an ethical structure" because he effectively subordinates being and the world to human liberation (*DMT*, 114; *GDT*, 98).[19]

Levinas clarified his objection against Heidegger in his Talmudic reading, "Temptation of the Temptation," delivered in October 1964. Levinas announced there that the impossibility of escaping from God lies not only in the possibility of death, understood in Heideggerian fashion as the possibility of impossibility, but also—and primarily—as the possibility of sacrifice: being able to die is subordinated to knowing how to sacrifice oneself.[20] The fact that these few lines are repeated eight years later in a revised form in the 1968 essay "Substitution," from where they were subsequently taken up for inclusion into *Otherwise than Being or Beyond Essence* is an indication of the importance Levinas attributes to what he says there.[21] The conclusion Levinas draws is that it is because I know how to sacrifice myself that I cannot escape God. This confirms that Levinas was even in these analyses striving to offer an account of transcendence that avoids the path of mysticism.

Levinas insists that one needs to *know* how to sacrifice oneself because this sacrifice, for all its passivity, must still be mine in some sense. The impossibility of escaping God is the ultimate passivity of an impossibility of possibility as we have seen, remains a form of mastery. It goes beyond the possibility of impossibility. To know how to sacrifice oneself is to know how to embrace what Levinas calls this passivity more passive than passivity and do so as a relation of transcendence. Furthermore, in sacrificing one's life, one goes beyond all egoistical calculation. The very possibility of sacrifice shows that egoism at best represents only one mode of existence. Egoism leaves much unaccounted for, and if sacrifice is possible, the claims of an all-encompassing egoism are refuted. But why could sacrifice not be understood as a mode of existence for Heidegger, who always seems to have a place in his ontology for both deficient and preeminent modes?

The claim that Heidegger cannot account for one person sacrificing him- or herself for another is not just a subtheme in Levinas's polemic against Heidegger. It is the most clearly developed case of a more general argument that lies at the very heart of Levinas's mature philosophy, according to which philosophy as conventionally conducted cannot account for the ethical acts that nevertheless do happen. The attempt to account for it is what leads Levinas to the notion of substitution. The heart of the idea is revealed in Levinas's formulation: "the passage of the identical to the other in substitution, which makes possible sacrifice" (S, 500; BPW, 90. See also AE, 146; OB, 115).[22]

The idea of substitution is that the I is an other in the sense that it is already substituted for the other.[23] Substitution, as he means it, is not something I bring about by going to someone else's death in place of her, although perhaps this usage played a role in his adoption of the word. An actual case of sacrifice is the concretization of substitution. Levinas seems in this way to anticipate Derrida's portrayal of an economy of sacrifice that disrupts the general economy of the real (EN, 234; ENT, 157). A sacred universe threatens always to compromise the excessiveness of sacrifice, drawing it back into an economy of sacrifice. Levinas invites us to think of a sacrifice beyond or without the sacred. It is for this reason that Levinas associates the excessiveness or unboundlessness (*démesure*) of sacrifice not with the sacred, as is usually the case, but with the holy, sacrifice without the sacred (*EN*, 230; *ENT*, 217).[24] We must consider the possibility, contrary to expectations, that Levinas was not promoting an ethics of sacrifice but objecting to the possibility. Is it possible that, even while making sacrifice a central notion in his thought, Levinas rejected the promotion of sacrifice as an ethical act?

Levinas's main preoccupation in his discussion of responsibility is how ethical discourse, modeled as it often has been on legal discourse, is preoccupied with showing the limits of one's accountability, what one can get away with. Levinas's conception of responsibility rules out those kinds of excuses from the outset: I am responsible for everything. But Levinas is concerned with my own excuses to myself. He is not pointing the finger at others and saying that they are also responsible in this same sense. It would not least be for him a form of abrogation of the very responsibility he had just claimed for himself. The discourse of Levinasian ethics (as distinct from Levinasian politics, albeit they are not always as easily separable as one might think) resists universalization, and by the same token it resists preaching. It does not want to explain or justify the ways of God to man. For this reason it renounces theodicy on the grounds that this would be impossible after Auschwitz. This is the tenor of the essay "Useless Suffering." We must renounce attempts to show that suffering makes sense in some longer plan. Suffering is an outrage, a scandal. There is no advantage to be had from it. It is useless. One should say of sacrifice what Levinas says of suffering: "meaningful in me, useless in the Other" (*EN*, 118; *ENT*, 100). To be sure, Heidegger did not think of sacrifice as measured by utility either.[25] The difference is that Levinas rejects the idea that one can make sense of the suffering of another, by construing it as redemptive, and the same is true of the other's sacrifices. Whatever Levinas means when he asks what makes sacrifice possible, it does not mean finding a general justification for it.

Accounting for the possibility of sacrifice would not mean making sense of sacrifice so that it came to be understood as the most natural thing in the world. Sacrifice is always "excessive" (*EN*, 230; *ENT*, 217). The argument is that for a modern individualist philosophy that has abandoned all remnants of the religious consciousness which believes in rewards after death, sacrifice seems to be senseless. By contrast, Levinas presents sacrifice as the source of sense, but without making it a possible source of calculation. Does this mean that Levinas proposed that all sacrifice is good whatever its result? A sentence from "Enigma and Phenomenon" could be read this way. Following the statement that "I approach the infinite by sacrificing myself," he adds: "Sacrifice is the norm and the criterion of the approach" (*DEHH*, 215; *BPW*, 76). "The norm and the criterion" is a unique formulation in Levinas. The sentence could be read as promoting sacrifice in the way that Heidegger seems to do in "The Origin of the Work of Art."

Levinas and most other commentators on this topic fail to examine Heidegger's extensive remarks on sacrifice. Soon after writing *Being and Time*, Heidegger clearly embraced the language of sacrifice. According to "The Origin of the Work of Art," "the essential sacrifice is one of the ways in which truth establishes itself in beings, alongside the founding of a political state, the thinking of Being, and, of course, the work of art."[26] In the postscript to "What Is Metaphysics?" (1943), Heidegger gave a very abstract account of sacrifice as answering the need for the preservation of the truth of being by the human essence expending itself.[27] However, prior to both these texts, in the Winter semester 1934–35, in lectures on Hölderlin's poems "Germanien" and "Der Rhein," Heidegger took a concrete approach to sacrifice: he described how for individual soldiers on the front line the nearness of death and the readiness to sacrifice create the space for community.[28] Sacrifice thus plays a foundational role for Heidegger's account of a people (*Volk*) as opposed to a mere conglomeration, as "the they" (*das Man*) is. This is all the more striking given that Heidegger in the previous semester, summer 1934, had given a rich account of the *Volk* in terms of the existentials of *Being and Time*. It would need a great deal more argument than Levinas supplies to establish that Heidegger could not account for sacrifice. Furthermore, Heidegger does not limit himself to describing the role of sacrifice in shaping a people. He actively promoted it. In a speech Heidegger delivered to the students at the beginning of the same semester, he called for the courage to sacrifice in the cause of the state: "In you there must unceasingly develop the courage of your sacrifice for the salvation (*Rettung*) of the essence of our people (*Volk*) within their state (*Staat*) and for the elevation of its innermost force."[29]

In order to weigh the significance of Heidegger's remarks embracing sacrifice, it is necessary to restore them to their historical context. According to Adolf Hitler, in *Mein Kampf*, the Aryan might not have been the cleverest type, but the Aryan was most strongly developed in terms of the capacity for self-sacrifice even to the point of giving up his or her life for others. Needless to say, Hitler singled out the Jews as deficient in this regard (MK, 330–31; MKT, 301–02). On Hitler's account self-preservation and sacrifice are aligned (MK, 166; MKT, 151).[30] One should not therefore be surprised to find that Heidegger also combines the *conatus essendi* and a call to sacrifice, albeit, in texts that were not available to Levinas, at a certain point he specifically renounced all attempts to promote the preservation of the *Volk* as a goal.[31]

Is it enough ethically speaking that one die for another or for others, such as one's family or one's nation, and it makes no difference whether one's cause was just? There is a way of reading Levinas that separates ethics so radically from politics that encourages that conclusion. The ethics of intention might also side with that same view, that it is enough so long as one *thought* that one's cause was just. However, one can reasonably suspect that Levinas more than anyone would have written his philosophy in such a way as to guard against such a conclusion that could make a Nazi into a hero.

Is it the case then that Heidegger promotes a practice of sacrifice that in fact he cannot account for? Heidegger's account seems to show that in so far as one identifies with a people, one can sacrifice oneself for others. Although it seems that in *Being and Time* it would be inauthentic to identify with another, he subsequently has no hesitation in suggesting that in the case of a people this might be an authentic possibility. Nor, once that is conceded, does it seem to make sense to limit this possibility to a people, when it would seem that it could equally apply to a class, a race, and members of a religion or any other group. Indeed, going to one's death comes to be presented by Heidegger as a happening of truth. He had in mind sacrifices on the part of authentic individuals that would contribute to the Germans becoming an authentic people (e.g., H, 66; OBT, 55–56). Seen in this light, Levinas's focus on Dasein's virility becomes more compelling than it might initially have seemed to be. In "Dying for . . ." Levinas recycled his early objections in *Time and the Other* to Heideggerian virility, inflating them so as to attribute to present this authenticity as "the virility of a free ability-to-be, like a will of race and sword" (EN, 219; ENT, 207). But what does this mean for the attempt to differentiate Heidegger's virile sacrifice from Levinas's gratuitous sacrifice without calculation? Was Levinas wrong to claim that Heidegger could not account for sacrifice? It would seem that Levinas's objection would still stand only if what was at stake was a more rarefied notion of sacrifice than Heidegger envisaged.

That this is the case is confirmed by the fact that Levinas persistently claims that it is not just Heidegger, but the whole tradition, that promotes conceptions of the self that make it impossible to think how sacrifice is possible. Levinas believes that Heidegger promotes under the name "sacrifice" what is not worthy of the name. One way in which one could understand Levinas as refining the notion of self-sacrifice so that Heidegger's account of sacrifice ceased to meet it would be by highlighting the notion of alterity in the phrase "dying for others." However, this seems to lead Levinas down the Derridean path. It would only be to the extent that the one for whom one dies is a total stranger, even to the point of being anonymous that the act is gratuitous, whereas it would have to be considered compromised by a level of self-interest to the extent that one is already implicated in the lives of those for whom one dies, as a child is for his or her parents, parents for their children, citizens for their country, a believer for his or her religion. In contrast to Hitler's view, sacrifice and all forms of self-preservation must be separated. But even though this excludes thinking of dying for one's nation as entirely gratuitous, there are still problems. One might well grant that it is more altruistic to die in the place of a total stranger than in the place of one's own child, but that does not mean that, when faced with a situation where one had to choose between giving up one's life for one's child or for a stranger, one is ethically obliged to choose to die in the place of the stranger simply because this choice is more excessive, that is to say, more distant from egoism. Perhaps it would be more in keeping with Levinasian philosophy to suppose that the sacrifice is not so much for someone who is anonymous in the sense that they did not give their name, but for someone who is anonymous because they are regarded as socially insignificant: the poor, the widow, the orphan, the one in relation to whom I am someone, the one who—at least if we follow Hegel—cannot give me the recognition I seek, but the same problem would arise.[32]

Another way of being led to the same conclusion is to consider the question whether one truly sacrifices oneself for another if one identifies with them as might be the case if one sacrifices oneself for one's friends, one's family, one's religion, or one's country. Would this not mean sacrificing one's self in a narrow sense simply for this larger sense of self? However, there is a way of understanding Levinas's claim that "I is an other" as his account of what makes sacrifice possible that has been lacking from the tradition, even though it sounds like other such attempts to explain or promote sacrifice: he sacrifices himself for his country, his children, or whomever. This helps to explain why Levinas must go to such lengths to insist on the fact that the Other for whom I sacrifice myself lacks identity. I cannot know who this other is because I must not be able to identify with him or her. This is an aspect of the nature of alterity with which Derrida has so much fun.

One sees this in Derrida's account of hospitality: one cannot know for whom one was opening the door or introduce conditions during their stay. The very unconditionality makes it seemingly impossible for the conditions to be met, so the conditions of possibility become the conditions of impossibility. For Levinas, by contrast, what makes hospitality toward the Other possible is its very mundanity. More precisely, it would be impossible for him, if it was happening at the level of an individual subject, if it was me showing hospitality. But Levinas locates it at the level of the self (*le soi*).

In contrast with Derrida, Levinas closely associates the fact that in the ethical relation the Other is without identity with his sense that in sacrifice I too am without identity, a point he sometimes makes by saying that sacrifice takes place at the level of the self (*le soi*) and not of the me (*le moi*).[33] That is to say, Levinas's account of my own anonymity to myself, which is in addition to the anonymity of the Other for whom the sacrifice is made, helps differentiate his position from that of Derrida, even though Derrida's language and themes sound superficially much like Levinas's. Otherwise said, however demanding Levinas's talk of infinite responsibility might be, it is not demanding in the precise way that Derrida is about what constitutes an ethical act. Derrida would acknowledge that sacrifice happens, but his focus would fall on how the conditions of its possibility are the conditions of its impossibility, whereas Levinas wants to take our understanding of sacrifice—and indeed ethics generally—to the point where it is ordinary and that it is the unethical that is extraordinary.

Whereas an ethics of sacrifice organized by the opposition between the authentic and the inauthentic remained in Levinas's eyes under the auspices of a form of virile egoism, sacrifice, as he understood it, does not know itself as such. The only sacrifice Levinas would want to promote is the one that I would be able to call my own were it not for the fact that it is so much dominated by the Other that I would never know it as mine. Self-sacrifice is not only the essential intention, but "the unavowed intention" (NTR, 61, 93). Levinas's thought comes to be oriented by ethics, but even so all ideas of an ethics of sacrifice must for this reason be sacrificed.[34] What counts is transcendence, and in sacrifice death, which challenges our ordinary sense of self and from which there is no escape, meets up with an inescapable obligation that transcends death. And yet for all this talk of transcendence, sacrifice remains in Levinas's thought something very ordinary, even mundane. It is mundane precisely in so far as it is ethical or, more precisely, because the meaning of sacrifice, albeit not its justification, is ethical. The meaning of sacrifice does not lie in its utility, and the sacrifices that are made in collusion with evil are not useless, but worse than useless. But this also points to the fact that the reason why Heidegger's thought on sacrifice can never be brought into harmony with Levinas's account of sacrifice is the methodological reason that Levinas provides in Totality and Infinity: for him the meaning of the formal structure lies not at the formal level but in its concretization (TeI, 148; TI, 173). In the final analysis, this is what enables Levinas to use the phrase "ethics of sacrifice" to encapsulate the crucial point of difference between Heidegger's philosophy and his own, but once it is understood that Heidegger is the one who promotes the ethics of sacrifice.

NOTES

I am grateful to the members of the Department of Philosophy at Sussex University for their comments on an earlier draft of this chapter in June 2008, in particular Rickie Damman, Michael Morris, Tanja Stähler, and especially Paul Davies.

1. Martin Heidegger, Kant und das Problem der Metaphysik, Gesamtausgabe 3 (Frankfurt: Klostermann, 1991), xvii; trans. Richard Taft, Kant and the Problem of Metaphysics (Bloomington: Indiana University Press, 1990), xviii.

2. Two anecdotes when taken together capture Levinas's ambivalence toward Heidegger. The first time I met Levinas when I told him I was teaching his

philosophy to my students at Essex University his response was simply: "But they must read Heidegger." However, Michel Haar told me that Levinas once asked him if he was still reading Heidegger. Levinas's response to the news that Haar was reading Heidegger was simply: "Remember to wash your hands afterwards."

3. Emmanuel Levinas, "Mourir pour . . . ," *Entre nous* (Paris: Bernard Grasset, 1991), 229; trans. Michael B. Smith and Barbara Harshav, *Entre Nous* (New York: Columbia University Press, 1998), 217. Henceforth *EN* and *ENT*, respectively. The proceedings of the conference was published under the title *Heidegger. Questions Ouvertes* (Paris: Osiris, 1988).

4. Jacques Derrida, "Donner la mort," in *L'Éthique du don*, ed. Jean-Michel Rabaté and Michael Wetzel (Pairs: Métailié-Transition, 1992), 95; trans. David Wills, *The Gift of Death* (Chicago: University of Chicago Press, 1995), 101. Henceforth *DM* and *GD*, respectively.

5. Jacques Derrida, *Donner le temps* (Paris: Galilée, 1991); trans. Peggy Kanuf, *Given Time* (Chicago: University of Chicago Press, 1992). On the connection with Levinas, see Robert Bernasconi, "'What Goes Around Comes Around: Derrida and Levinas on the Economy of the Gift and the Gift of Genealogy," in *The Logic of the Gift*, ed. Alan D. Schrift (New York: Routledge, 1997), 256–73.

6. See, for example, Jacques Derrida, *De l'hospitalité* (Paris: Calmann-Levy, 1997); trans. Rachel Bowlby, *Of Hospitality* (Stanford: Stanford University Press, 2000).

7. Jacques Derrida, "Foi et savoir," in *La Religion*, ed. Jacques Derrida and Gianni Vattimo (Paris: Seuil, 1996, 10); trans. Samuel Weber, "Faith and Knowledge," in *Religion*, ed. Jacques Derrida and Gianni Vattimo (Stanford: Stanford University Press, 1998), 11.

8. Martin Heidegger, *Sein und Zeit* (Tübingen: Max Niemeyer, 1949), 240; trans. John Macquarrie and Edward Robinson, *Being and Time* (Oxford: Basil Blackwell, 1967), 284. Henceforth *SZ* and *BT*, respectively.

9. Emmanuel Levinas, *Le temps et l'autre* (Montpellier: Fata Morgana, 1979), 62–63; trans. Richard A. Cohen, *Time and the Other* (Pittsburgh: Duquesne University Press, 1987), 74. Henceforth *TA* and *TO*, respectively. Levinas explains his understanding of Heidegger's phrase most clearly in a discussion held after a talk by Jean Wahl. See Jean Wahl, *Esquissse poure une histoire de "l'existentialisme"* (Paris: L'Arche, 1949, 97–100); trans. Forrest Williams and Stanley Maron, *A Short History of Existentialism* (New York: Philosophical Library, 1949), 50–53.

10. Emmanuel Levinas, *Totalité et Infini* (The Hague: Martinus Nijhoff, 1961), 211; trans. Alphonso Lingis, *Totality and Infinity* (Pittsburgh: Duquesne University Press, 1969), 234. Henceforth *TeI* and *TI*, respectively.

11. Emmanuel Levinas, "Sans nom," *Noms Propres* (Montpellier: Fata Morgana, 1976), 177; trans. Michael B. Smith, "Nameless," *Proper Names* (Stanford: Stanford University Press, 1996), 119.

12. Emmanuel Levinas, *Dieu, la mort et le temps* (Paris: Grasset, 1993), 16; trans. Bettina Bergo, *God, Death, and Time* (Stanford: Stanford University Press, 2000), 8. Henceforth *DMT* and *GDT*, respectively.

13. This is a more complex issue than can be indicated here. I treat it at more length in "Levinas and the Struggle for Existence," in Eric Sean Nelson, Antje

Kapust, and Kent Still, eds., *Addressing Levinas* (Evanston: Northwestern University Press, 2005), 170–84.

14. Emmanuel Levinas, "Au-dela de l'etat dans l'etat," *Nouvelles Lectures Talmudiques* (Paris: Minuit, 1996), 61; trans. Richard A. Cohen, *New Talmudic Readings* (Pittsburgh: Duquesne University Press, 1999), 93.

15. Charles Dickens, *A Tale of Two Cities* (Oxford: Oxford University Press, 1988), 466.

16. For a more thorough discussion of this crucial issue, see Robert Bernasconi, "No Exit: Levinas's Aporetic Account of Transcendence," *Research in Phenomenology* 35 (2005): 101–17.

17. Emmanuel Levinas, "Enigme et phénomène," *En découvrant l'existence avec Husserl et Heidegger* (Paris: Vrin: 1974), 215; trans. Alphonso Lingis, "Phenomenon and Enigma," *Basic Philosophical Writings*, ed. Adriaan Peperzak, Simon Critchley, and Robert Bernasconi (Bloomington: Indiana University Press, 1996), 76. Henceforth *DEHH* and *BPW*, respectively.

18. Emmanuel Levinas, *Humanism de l'autre homme* (Montpelier: Fata Morgana, 1987), 42; trans. Alphonso Lingis, "Phenomenon and Enigma," *Collected Philosophical Papers* (Dordrecht: Martinus Nijhoff, 1987), 92.

19. I have discussed this aspect of Levinas's thought in "A Love That Is Stronger than Death," *Angelaki* 7, no. 2 (August 2002): 9–16.

20. Emmanuel Levinas, "La tentation de la tentation," *Quatre lectures talmudiques* (Paris: Minuit, 1968), 109; trans. Annette Aronowicz, "The Temptation of Temptation," *Nine Talmudic Readings* (Bloomington: Indiana University Press, 1990), 50.

21. Emmanuel Levinas, "La substitution," *Revue Philosophique de Louvain* 64 (1968): 527–28; trans. Peter Atterton, Simon Critchley, and Graham Noctor, "Substitution," in *Basic Philosophical Writings*, ed. Adriaan T. Peperzak, Simon Critchley, and Robert Bernasconi (Bloomington: Indiana University Press, 1996), 95; *Autrement qu'être ou au-dela de l'essence* (The Hague: Martinus Nijhoff, 1974), 165; trans. Alphonso Lingis, *Otherwise than Being or beyond Essence* (The Hague: Martinus Nijhoff, 1981), 128. Henceforth S, *BPW*, *AE*, and *OB*, respectively.

22. For more on this argument see Robert Bernasconi, "To What Question Is Substitution the Answer?" in *The Cambridge Companion to Levinas*, ed. Simon Critchley and Robert Bernasconi (Cambridge: Cambridge University Press, 2002), 234–51.

23. Levinas adopts the phrase "je est un autre" from Arthur Rimbaud's letter to George Izambard, May 13, 1871. *Oeuvres complètes*, ed. Rolland de Renéville and Jules Mouquet (Paris: Gallimard, 1963), 268.

24. On this important distinction, see *Du sacré au saint* (Paris: Minuit, 1977), 88–90; trans. *Nine Talmudic Writings*, 140–41. For Levinas desacrilization is the condition of the reception of the holy.

25. Heidegger questions Hitler for promoting utility in this sense. Martin Heidegger, *Besinnung*, Gesamtausgabe 60 (Frankfurt: Klostermann, 1997), 122–31; trans. Parvis Enad and Thomas Kalary, *Mindfulness* (London: Continuum, 2006), 102–03.

26. Martin Heidegger, "Der Ursprung des Kunstwerkes" *Holzwege*, Gesamtausgabe 5 (Frankfurt: Klostermann, 1977), 49; trans. Julian Young and Kenneth Haynes,

"The Origin of the Work of Art," *Off the Beaten Track* (Cambridge: Cambridge University Press, 2002), 37. Henceforth *H* and *OBT*, respectively.

27. Martin Heidegger, " 'Nachwort' zu 'Was ist Metaphysik?,' " *Wegmarken*, Gesamtausgabe 9 (Frankfurt: Klostermann, 1976), 105; trans. William McNeill, *Pathmarks* (Cambridge: Cambridge University Press, 1998), 236.

28. Martin Heidegger, *Hölderlins "Germanien" und "Der Rhein,"* Gesamtausgabe 39 (Frankfurt: Klostermann, 1980), 72–73.

29. Martin Heidegger, *Reden und an der Zeugnisse eines Lebensweges*, Gesamtausgabe 16 (Frankfurt: Klostermann, 2000), 184. Farias cited in full Heidegger's address to the students at the beginning of the winter semester 1933–34, which contained the sentence referred to in Victor Farias, *Heidegger et le nazisme* (Paris: Verdier, 1987), 129–30; trans. Paul Burrell, *Heidegger and Nazism* (Philadelphia: Temple University Press, 1989), 118.

30. Adolf Hitler, *Mein Kampf* (Munich: Franz Eher, 1942), 325–26; trans. Ralph Manheim, *Mein Kampf* (Boston: Houghton Mifflin, 1971), 297. Henceforth *MK* and *MKT*, respectively.

31. Martin Heidegger, *Beiträge zur Philosophie*, Gesamtausgabe 65 (Frankfurt: Klostermann, 1989), 319; trans. Parvis Enad and Kenneth Maly, *Contributions to a Philosophy* (Bloomington: Indiana University Press, 1999), 224.

32. I develop this interpretation in Robert Bernasconi, "The Third Party," *Journal of the British Society for Phenomenology* 30, no. 1 (January 1999): 76–87.

33. On questions of identity, see Robert Bernasconi, "The Defection of Identity," *Subject Matters* 3, no. 1 (2006): 57–62.

34. See Dennis King Keenan, *The Question of Sacrifice* (Bloomington: Indiana University Press, 2005), 74–88.

CHAPTER NINE

THE QUESTION OF RESPONSIBILITY
BETWEEN LEVINAS AND HEIDEGGER

François Raffoul

LEVINAS'S EXPROPRIATION OF
EGOLOGICAL RESPONSIBILITY

Levinas's entire itinerary of thought has been structured by the effort to escape the closure of philosophies of totality, to exceed the horizon as such, to move beyond ontology, a movement toward exteriority or toward the other that has taken with it and redefined the very concept of responsibility. Levinas's corpus presents an extraordinary revolution in the thought of responsibility, a peculiar "reversal," to use his terms, of the concept of responsibility: far from assigning responsibility to the actions of an agent, on the basis of the freedom of the subject, following an entire tradition, Levinas reconceptualizes responsibility as a being "for-the-other," no longer a responsibility for oneself, or for one's actions, but a responsibility for the other and for the sake of the other. In fact, for Levinas, the other "is above all the one I am responsible for."[1] Levinas approaches responsibility as that which could not have begun from me, going so far as to write that responsibility "is not mine,"[2] a responsibility "of the other," anticipating what Derrida would write on a responsibility and a decision "of the other." As he explains in The Gift of Death, "Levinas wants to remind us that responsibility is not at first responsibility of myself for myself, that the sameness of myself is derived from the other, as if it were second to the other, coming to itself

175

as responsible and mortal from the position of my responsibility before the other, for the other's death and in the face of it."[3] Such a "for-the-other" expresses the very structure of subjectivity as "*the other in the same*" (*AE*, 46) and is so radical that Levinas would give it the meaning of a being-hostage to the other. This sense of responsibility for the other expropriates the subject.

In thinking the question of responsibility between Levinas and Heidegger, it is this movement of expropriation toward the other, always more radicalized in Levinas's thinking, which I seek to question in its assumptions and implications. How does Levinas conceive of such an exit or escape? What is implied in the very notion of an *exit* toward the other? In particular, should the self be assumed to be alone and separated, as self-same, as Levinas does, in order to then have no other option to find the other than an exit out of the self into exteriority? Does this manner of performing it allow for a genuine overcoming of the egological tradition, of giving thought to responsibility as such? We will see how Levinas's thinking of responsibility arises out of a peculiar reversal of the modern Cartesian tradition in philosophy, from Descartes to Husserl, that is, a reversal of the primacy of egology and the predominance of the will, which Levinas seeks to overturn. However, it may well be the case that reversing a tradition is not sufficient to freeing oneself from it and that Levinas's revolution owes perhaps more that it would like to admit to the egological tradition that it seeks to reverse, *precisely insofar as it determines itself in symmetrical opposition to it and as its reversal*. The question becomes: does Levinas's expropriation of the subject, his radicalization of the opposition between the Cartesian tradition and a thinking "of the other," allow one to take into view being-responsible as such, a being-responsible that would amount neither to the closure of the horizon of egology nor to its simple reversal? Is the experience of alterity to be thought of in terms of an overturning of egology, in terms of an exit toward an exteriority? Indeed, is alterity to be thought of as exteriority? Can the other only be said to lie beyond being, if being, as Heidegger would show, is itself the beyond, the transcendent pure and simple? Far from any opposition between egology and heterology, shouldn't the very structure of selfhood involve an openness to the other? If the gesture toward a "beyond being" is rendered problematic, if not untenable, one should seek to inquire into the ontological senses of responsibility. Heidegger's thought of being entails a profound philosophy of responsibility. Indeed Heidegger claims that Dasein means a responsibility for being. However, since Dasein is not the self-enclosed ego of the Cartesian tradition but an ecstatic opening, he also stresses that Dasein is responsible for the other entity, whether the entity that is Dasein-like (that is the mode of *Fürsorge* or care for the other) or the entity that is intraworldly (that is the mode of concern). Being-responsible—responsibility for being—would thus not be exclusive of an openness to the other, with these differences with Levinas that such otherness is not exteriority and that responsibility is not rooted in the subject: Levinas posits that responsibility for the other represents the essence of *subjectivity*. However, does responsibility as openness to the other not require a nonsubjective experience? And if for Heidegger, as we will see, one is ultimately responsible for an inappropriable, secret or mystery, doesn't this secret of being represent a sense of otherness that is not reduced, as in Levinas, to the "other *man*,"[4] that is, within a subjectivist, anthropocentric *horizon*? These are some of the questions that I would like to follow in reengaging the question of responsibility between Levinas and Heidegger.

The Escape from Ontology

Levinas's thought of ethics and responsibility developed out of a movement of exit out of ontology. As Levinas recounted in several autobiographical texts or interviews,[5] he began his philosophical career as a commentator of Husserl's phenomenology and Heidegger's fundamental ontology, indeed introduced Husserl and Heidegger in France.[6] These were references from which he broke decisively as he began to develop his own *ethical* thought. One of the key features of such a departure, in addition to the rupture with the paradigm of totality, was the break with ontology as such (and with a certain phenomenology of intentionality and consciousness). For Levinas, the access to ethics (which for him should be raised to first philosophy) and *to responsibility* takes place in such a rupture with ontology, that is, in a rupture with Heidegger. Far from being included within the horizon of being, ethics is situated in the relationship to the other person, in the "intersubjective," a relation which for Levinas takes place beyond being: "A responsibility beyond being," as he writes in *Otherwise than Being* (AE, 31). The intersubjective relation is the original experience. Thus Levinas insists that the origin of meaning is not Dasein's relation to being, not the understanding of being displayed by Dasein, but arises first in the intersubjective relation. He writes, "My main point in saying that [the face of the other is perhaps the very beginning of philosophy] was that the order of meaning, which seems to me primary, is precisely what comes to us from the inter-human relation, so that the face . . . is the beginning of intelligibility" (EN, 103). The relation to the other is thus the origin of meaning. This claim already places the ethical—the relation to the other—as prior to the order of knowledge, outside of the element of being, and situates Levinas in opposition to traditional ontology and the privilege of knowledge in Western philosophy. This privileging reduces the other to a principle of identity, or "the Same," a reduction that is always an act of violence, a murder of the other, as Levinas claims that "with regard to beings, understanding carries out an act of violence and of negation" (*EN*, 9). Levinas aims at reversing the traditional hierarchy in which ethics is reduced to being a branch of ontology and epistemology. Ethical responsibility will take place for Levinas beyond being and knowledge.

This move beyond being and toward the other (the other human) constitutes the core of Levinas's thought, and he indeed characterized this movement in a late interview as "the kernel of all I would say later" (*Is It Righteous to be?*, 46). One could in fact approach Levinas'ss thought as a whole from this effort to escape, exit, or go beyond, toward an other that does not return to a same, that does not come back, and in that sense is in-finite. His decisive early essay *On Escape*[7] thematizes and articulates a need to break with the "suffocating" horizon of being, the "there is" and with the isolation or solitude of existence. *Time and the Other*, he explained in a late interview, was also a book that represented for him an attempt to escape "from this isolation of existing, as the preceding book [*Existence and Existents*] signified an attempt to escape from the 'there is'" (*EI*, 57). Ultimately, it was a matter of "escaping *from being*" (*EI*, 59), an escape that takes place in my devotion to the other, that is to say, in my *responsibility* to the other. Levinas clarifies that "the true exit from the *there is* is in obligation" (*Is It Righteous?*, 45), in responsibility for the other in the sense of being concerned, not for one's own self, but for the other: "Leaving oneself, that is, being occupied with the other," he writes in a striking formulation (*Is It Righteous?*, 46). This is why it is also a matter of escaping *from oneself*. Indeed, for Levinas, anxiety is not about death as possibility, but rather about *being* as inescapable, "the horror of the *there is*, of existence. It is not the fear of death; it is the 'too much' of oneself" (*Is It Righteous?*, 46). It is as if there was a circle between being and the self (Dasein is the concern for being and for oneself), a circle from which Levinas seeks to escape. "The horror of the *there is* is close to disgust for oneself, close to the weariness of oneself" (*Is It Righteous?*, 46) and being encumbered with being is being encumbered with one's own being, with oneself: "Escape is the need to get out of oneself, that is, to break that most radical and unalterably binding of chains, the fact that the I [*moi*] is oneself [*soi-même*]" (*OE*, 55). The self is detestable, writes Levinas (*EN*, 130), echoing Pascal's famous saying. How does one escape from being, from oneself? By going beyond oneself toward the other. The exit from both the "there is" (impersonal being) and oneself (egology) is opening onto the other. In the end, for Levinas, the true exit out of being, out of the ego, lies in responsibility for the other (to the point, as we will see, of dying for the other).

This need to escape the horizon of being and the enclosure of the self accounts for Levinas's critique of totality and totalizing philosophies, although one should note that for him "it is in fact the whole trend of Western philosophy," culminating with Hegel, that has "this nostalgia for totality" and that seeks a "panoramic vision of the real" (EI, 76). He understands that quest as "an attempt at universal synthesis, a reduction of all experience, of all that is reasonable, to a totality wherein consciousness embraces the world, leaves nothing other outside itself, and thus becomes absolute thought" (EI, 75). Levinas found the sources of his critique of totality first in Frank Rosenzweig's critique of Hegel (but also in those moments in the history of philosophy such as Plato's Good beyond being, Descartes' "Third Meditation," and the idea of God as infinite), and he conceives of it in terms of the inappropriability—or, as he terms it, exteriority and infinity—of the other. The encounter with such inappropriable other is the original experience: before knowledge, since knowledge presupposes such an encounter, and before ontology, since being as such presupposes the encounter with the specific being. Such encounter is the original meaning of ethics as what cannot be totalized. "The irreducible and ultimate experience of relationship appears to me in fact to be . . . not in synthesis, but in the face to face of humans, in sociality, in its moral signification . . . First philosophy is an ethics" (EI, 77). Ethics breaks totality, opening onto an irreducible exteriority, and inappropriability. The face to face is transcendence, and "the face breaks the system" (EN, 34). There is for Levinas a nonsynthesizable, and that is the face to face ("The relationship between man is certainly the non-synthesizable par excellence," EI, 77). There is simply no context (being, the world, and horizon) that would include the face to face with the other, as the face "originally signifies or commands outside the context of the world" (EN, 167). The true relation to the other is not a being-together in a shared world, but lies in an encounter in a face to face without intermediary, without mediation and outside of concept, in what Levinas would call the "insurmountable duality of beings" (EI, 67). There is no third unifying term that could provide a reduction of that relationship. Even the notion of the third in Levinas confirms the irreducibility of the face to face, as it is defined from the perspective and original fact of the face to face, a face to face that is the irreducible and ultimate experience.

The Death of the Other as Origin of Responsibility

Levinas describes the original ethical experience as the face to face with the other, in which I am faced with the destitute and vulnerable nature of the other. Faced with such vulnerability (ultimately, the mortality or irremediable exposure to death of the other), I am called to responsibility for the other. This is why Levinas challenges Heideggerian egoistic solipsistic death and opposes to it a death that would be more primordial, the death of the other. The death of the other, he asserts, is the first death. Reversing the

Heideggerian mineness of death, Levinas claims that I would be concerned for the other's death before my own death. In his effort to give thought to an experience of alterity that cannot to be reduced to the Same, Levinas rejects the Heideggerian primacy of mineness based on death. It is a matter of leaving "the *Jemeinigkeit* of the *cogito* and its immanence construed as authenticity" (*EN*, 221). He explains, in "Dying for . . ." that for him it is a matter of a genuine "alternative between, on the one hand, the identical in its authenticity, in its *own right* or its unalterable *mine* of the human, in its *Eigentlichkeit*, independence and freedom, and on the other hand being as human devotion to the other" (*EN*, 211; my emphasis). Levinas opposes to "solitary mineness" a being-for-the-other that would be more authentic, a being-for-the-other *that is defined in terms of responsibility*. This will be achieved by another conception of the self, no longer a subject or even a Dasein, but a hostage to the other. This being-hostage, that is, a nonchosen responsibility for the other ("Condition of hostage—not chosen," *AE*, 214) testifies, as Derrida shows in his *Adieu à Emmanuel Levinas*,[8] to the radical dispossession or expropriation of the subject in Levinas'ss work. The figure of this expropriation is what Levinas calls the face.

What does Levinas mean by the face (visage)? In one word: vulnerability; more precisely, he means a *human* vulnerability or vulnerability itself as the humanity of man.[9] Even more precisely, the face signifies the vulnerability of the other human, as for Levinas humanity is the humanity of the other human. This vulnerability opens the following alternative: violence or nonviolence, respect or defacing, ethics or its negation. In *Ethics and Infinity*, Levinas begins by noting that the face is not an object of perception, a perceptual phenomenon, indeed perhaps not even a phenomenon, if a phenomenon is what appears and becomes present. The face, seen as it were from *beyond the visible*, has a proximity, but it is not a present phenomenon. In *Otherwise than Being*, Levinas specifies in this respect that the face escapes presentation and representation and that it is indeed "the very defection of phenomenality" (*AE*, 141). The face exceeds presentation, not because it would be too much as an appearance, but on the contrary due to its poverty, its weakness: "a non-phenomenon because 'less' than the phenomenon" (*AE*, 141). Phenomenology is here exceeded, and Levinas does state in *Otherwise than Being* that his work exceeds the confines of appearance in being (*l'apparoir de l'être*), and therefore "ventures beyond phenomenology" (*AE*, 281). One should stress here that Levinas may not move beyond phenomenology as such as gesture in this excess toward what Heidegger has called a "phenomenology of the inapparent"[10] or toward an excess that a Jean-Luc Marion has designated as a phenomenology of the saturated phenomenon.[11] Despite what some would like to claim with respect to a theological nature of Levinas's discourse, Levinas has stressed that his vocabulary, even if at times borrowing from a religious discourse, takes on a phenomenological meaning. For instance: "The terminology I use sounds religious: I speak of the uniqueness of the I on the basis of a *chosenness* that it would be difficult for it to escape, for it constitutes it; of a debt of the I, older than any loan. This way of approaching an idea by asserting the concreteness of a situation in which it originally assumes meaning seems to me essential to phenomenology. It is presupposed in everything I have said" (*EN*, 227). Even the absolute of which Levinas speaks, the absoluteness of the other, is to be taken in its phenomenological sense: "The absolute—an abusive word—could probably take place concretely and *have meaning only* in the phenomenology, or in the rupture of the phenomenology, to which the face of the other gives rise" (*EN*, 167; my emphasis). The interruption of phenomenology of which Levinas speaks remains an interruption affecting and displacing phenomenology, an interruption that phenomenology undergoes. Interrupted by this in-visibility of the face, phenomenology itself is transformed from a phenomenology of the present being, of perception, to a phenomenology assigned to the givenness of the otherness of the other in the face.

It is in this sense that Levinas states that "one can say that the face is not 'seen'" (*EI*, 86), not the object of a thematic gaze. Levinas removes the face from the domain of vision and perception, and rejects "the notion of vision to describe the authentic relationship to the Other" (*EI*, 87–88). What is being seen in the face is its own invisibility, that is, its absolute alterity, what Derrida would call the secret of the other. This break with a phenomenology of perception is apparent when Levinas states that the best way of encountering the face "is not even to notice the color of his eyes" (*EI*, 85). In fact, this way of looking at the face would be a kind of defacement, and the face seen in this perceptual way would then be "defaced," as in the French *devisagé*. To *de-visager* or scrutinize someone is tantamount to a defacing. This is why Levinas specifies that "Defacement occurs also as a way of looking, a way of knowing, for example, what color your eyes are. No, the face is not this" (*Is It Righteous?*, 144–45). The face does not *present* a countenance or a form but exposes a nakedness and a passivity: "The disclosure of the face is nudity—non-form—abandon of oneself, aging, dying; more naked than nakedness: poverty, wrinkled skin" (*AE*, 141). Levinas describes further the moral aspect of the face, in his analysis of the skin (*la peau* and not the flesh, *la chair*).[12] The skin of the face, he tells us, "is the most naked" (*EI*, 86), a nakedness that is described in its moral dimension. To this extent, the access to the face is not perceptual but *ethical* ("I think rather that access to the face is straightaway ethical" [*EI*, 85]). In what sense? For Levinas, the face displays a *droiture*, a kind of uprightness or straightfulness (*droiture*, in French, designates both the

physical characteristics of being straight or upright and a moral signification. Someone who is *"droit"* is someone who is direct, honest, a "straight
arrow," as we say in English. This straightfulness and frankness is also the
naked exposure of a vulnerability, an exposure without defense; "there is
first the very uprightness of the face, its upright exposure, without defense"
(*EI*, 86). *That exposure is an originary honesty*, not an intentional honesty,
but an honesty of exposure. It is straight because exposed and vulnerable
because exposed.

The face is thus exposure, an exposure to injury, that is, already, to
death. *The face is above all exposure to death.* This radical exposure of the
face is radically stripped of protection, defenseless: the face is defenselessness
itself. The other's vulnerability, ultimately, reveals his or her mortality. For,
if the face is what can be outraged, defaced, done violence to, if it can be
injured, it is because the other is mortal, already exposed to death. What
is an injury is not the announcement of death? Levinas speaks of the exposure of the face to death, to "an invisible death and mysterious forsaking"
(*EN*, 145). What is laid bare in the face? The answer is: death. The face
expresses the death of the other, behind all the masks and defenses: "Face
of the other—*underlying* all the particular forms of expression in which he
or she, already right 'in character,' plays a role—is no less *pure expression*,
extradition with neither defense nor cover, precisely the extreme rectitude
of a *facing*, which in this nakedness *is an exposure unto death*: nakedness,
destitution, passivity, and pure vulnerability. *Face as the very mortality of the
human being*" (*EN*, 167; my emphasis).

Levinas writes that the rectitude of the face indicates a movement
forward, "as if it were exposed to some threat at point blank range, as if
it presented itself wholly delivered up to death" (*Is It Righteous?*, 126–27),
extreme exposure, beyond or before all human intending, "as to a shot at
'point blank,'" *à bout portant!* (*EN*, 145). Yet—this is what is most peculiar
and paradoxical—that same vulnerability inviting violence is *at the same time*
a call to the suspension of violence, nonviolence. Levinas writes, "The face
is exposed, menaced, as if inviting us to an act of violence. *At the same time*,
the face is what forbids us to kill" (*EI*, 86; my emphasis). Thou shalt not
kill is a command that Levinas significantly specifies as a "Thou Shalt not
leave me alone in my dying!" *At the same time*: in a dangerous proximity,
threatening its very purity, if not possibility, ethics is rooted in an experience
that also constitutes the possibility of violence. The separation between ethics and violence is here almost undecidable. There is for instance a violence
of ethics or done *in the name* of ethics that Levinas seems to recognize and
accept when confronted with the problem of the executioner's face: in this
case, he specifies, the executioner "is the one who threatens my neighbor
and, in this sense, *calls for violence* and no longer has a face (*EN*, 105; my

emphasis). Conversely, violence "can involve justice" and "one cannot say that there is no legitimate violence" (*EN*, 106). Most decisively, ethics is *defined* in relation to violence: "[T]he face is what forbids us to kill." Ethics is thus the interruption of violence, its suspension; violence, in turn, is also defined in terms of ethics, as the negation of the face, which supposes that the face in its inviolability, has already given itself. Violence supposes the face, and thus ethics. Paradoxically, it is that inviolable character of the other that can give rise to the desire to kill, as the "other is the only being I can want to kill" (*EN*, 9). That desire is doomed to fail for Levinas, and there is an inherent aporia in murder: one can only want to kill that which cannot be killed; Levinas speaking of "the temptation *and impossibility* of murder" (*EN*, 11; my emphasis). Levinas makes that point: "The face is what one cannot kill, or at least it is that whose *meaning* consists in saying: 'thou shalt not kill'" (*EI*, 87). The prohibition against killing "does not render murder impossible," because the ethical command not to kill is "not an ontological necessity" (*EI*, 87). Killing is ontologically *impossible*, ethically *forbidden*, all the while happening everyday, incited by the other's face, and through a desire arising out of the very inviolability of the other. This impure origin of ethics, the intertwining between ethics and violence (ethics is the suspension of violence; violence is the negation of ethics) will always represent a continual threat to the integrity of ethics. In the final analysis, Levinas tends to sever that knot by a priority to ethics over violence. As he puts it, "I even think that the good is older than evil" (*Is It Righteous?*, 55). Violence is not strictly speaking the absence of ethics, but its negation: it thus requires the ethical dimension being opened in its very possibility. This is why Levinas would stress that war supposes a prior ethical peace: "War supposes peace, the prior and non-allergic presence of the other; war does not constitute the first event of the encounter" (*TI*, 218).

The face is invisible, but it speaks. Its speech is a command. The face is like a "master" to us, "as if a master spoke to me," from above. However, the height of obligation, of that categorical imperative of the face, does not express a power. That vertical command emanates from someone who is destitute: "[I]t is the poor for whom I can do all and to whom I owe all" (*EI*, 89). Levinas breaks here decisively with the Kantian formulation of respect and universality, for, as he explains, "To respect is to bow down not before the law, but before a being who commands a work from me" (*EN*, 35). One has to answer for someone, "not by appealing to the abstraction of some anonymous law, some juridical entity" (*EN*, 144). Levinas distinguishes his approach from Kantian universalism: "My manner of approaching the question is, in effect, different. It takes off from the idea that ethics arises in the relation to the other and not straightaway by a reference to the universality of a law" (*Is It Righteous?*, 114). Ethics is not a relation to a universal but to the unique, the other as unique. "When I speak of uniqueness, I am also expressing the otherness of the other" (*EN*, 205).

What is responsibility? It is *fearing for the other*: I fear for the death of the other. That is *my* fear, although it is not, Levinas clarifies, a fear *for oneself*. "Fear for the other, fear for the death of the other man is my fear, but it is in no way a fear for *oneself*," *EN*, 146. Rather, it is *my* fear *for another*, following the structure of subjectivity as "for-the-other." This fear is the origin of responsibility (and recalls Hans Jonas's notion of a "heuristic of fear" in his thinking of responsibility.)[13] I fear for the other's suffering, but also for my own potential violence as a being-in-the-world who can establish a home expulsing and excluding all others in some third (or fourth!) world, in other words, a fear "for all the violence and murder my existing . . . can bring about" (*EN*, 144). Levinas goes so far as to raise this suffering of the other to the level of the "supreme principle of ethics" (*EN*, 94)! Ethics is not grounded on the universal moral law but on the suffering of the other person. It is thus a suffering, a poverty, and a vulnerability that command and call me. And who am I? "I am he who finds the resources to respond to the call" (*EN*, 94).

Responsibility for the Other as Expropriation of the Subject

The encounter with the face of the other assigns me as responsible for him/her. As soon as "the other looks at me, I am responsible for him" (*EI*, 96). That responsibility for the other leads to, indeed arises out, of my deposing as masterful ego, my expropriation as subject. Levinas'ss radicalization of this responsibility for another follows and registers the expropriation of the subject. The being of the subject is no longer for-itself but for-the-other. The self is emptied in such for-the-other. "For the other" is not a responsibility ensuing from my deed, not a responsibility based on my accountability for my actions. Levinas severs the traditional relation between responsibility and the action of a free subject: I have not done anything, yet I am responsible. I am assigned to the other before any engagement on my part, a relationship before the act, which Levinas calls "obsession": obsession signifies that the other had a hold on me before I could reseize myself in an act of freedom. I am obsessed because I am not free to respond to the other but have to; I am obsessed by the other without any possibility of reappropriating oneself from such a pre-originary hold of the other on my being in responsibility: (The) I belong(s) to the other: obsession. I am obligated before any vow, "before being present to myself or returning to self" (*EN*, 149): radical expropriation of the self that is at once an obligation to the other! Obligation is not preceded by a free decision but is placed on me by the other's claim, following here the structure of subjectivity as a "for-the-other" reversing and expropriating the "for-itself." Levinas describes this expropriation as a kind of defeat, a "defection from the unity of transcendental apperception, just as there is here a defeat of the originary intentionality in every act."[14] The other has not done anything, and I am responsible for him/her. I do not even *take* a responsibility for the other, as "his responsibility is incumbent on me. It is responsibility that goes beyond what I do" (*EI*, 96). It goes beyond what I do because such responsibility occurs before action, before a free acting, because my responsibility expresses an originary one-for-the-other: "Usually, one is responsible for what one does oneself. I say, in *Otherwise than Being or beyond Essence*, that responsibility is initially *a for the other*" (*EI*, 96). This is what Levinas calls "persecution": I have done nothing and yet I have always been accused, thus persecuted. No longer assigned to the interests of the ego, no longer about oneself, I am now responsible for what is foreign to me, for "what does not even matter to me" (*EI*, 95). I am concerned for what does not matter to me, because as such, as a matter of the other, it matters to me. Such is Levinas's conception of responsibility, a caring for what does not matter to me as a self, a mattering to me as other, in the experience of the face.

This responsibility for the other is nonreciprocal, dissymmetrical or asymmetrical, infinite, and nonchosen; it is the experience of being "hostage" to the other. All concerns for reciprocity, contracts, and agreements with others are inadequate to capture my original responsibility to the other as preoriginary passivity before the infinite obligation to the other (equivalent to being "hostage of the other") and ultimately for Levinas are examples of (egoistic) calculative thinking. It is a pure concern for the other, an asymmetrical concern oblivious of reciprocity. Against Buber, Levinas rejects the symmetry and reciprocity of the I-Thou. What the other does for me is *his or her business*. Levinas would speak of the "exceptional position of the I as the only one having to respond for the other" (*Is It Righteous?*, 230). I am responsible, more than the others, Levinas repeats like a leitmotif, thereby expressing this "originary constitution" of the I or the unique, "in a responsibility for the neighbor or the other, and the impossibility of escaping responsibility or of being replaced" (*Is It Righteous?*, 229). This is not the human condition, but the *human incondition* (*l'incondition humaine*), as Levinas stresses the destitute insubstantiality of the expropriated I hostage of the other. Because subjectivity is from the outset such a being-for-the-other, "heteronomy is somehow stronger than autonomy" (*EN*, 111), leading to the radical deposing of the ego: "The conversion of the for-itself into the for-the-other of responsibility could not be played again within an autonomous *for-itself*, even in the guise of a simple discovery made by the 'I think,' inflexible but still reflecting on itself" (*EN*, 152; tr. modified).

It is indeed an expropriation that is at the basis of the deposing of the I. "Is the human I first? Is it not he who, in place of being posed, ought to be de-posed?" (*Is It Righteous?*, 97). Levinas's thought of responsibility represents a destitution of the subject. It is "a matter of saying the very identity of the human I starting from responsibility, that is, starting from this position or deposition of the sovereign I in self-consciousness, a deposition which is precisely its responsibility for the other" (*EI*, 100–01). This logic of expropriation allows us to account for Levinas's fundamental categories. The notions of "hostage," of as subject as subjected, of obsession, persecution, accusation, of the "other as infinite" can be traced back to a logic of expropriation that reveals the radical *dispossession* and *destitution* of the subject, the *ex-propriation* of any sense of "home," of "ownership," of ego-hood. This reveals the true radicality of Levinas's claim that the "subject" is to be understood in ethical terms. This radical expropriation of any proper self occurs in the experience of responsibility for the other. Responsibility registers for Levinas the expropriation of the subject, expropriated toward the other for whom it is now responsible.

OVERCOMING EGOLOGY?

A few assumptions governing—and perhaps limiting—Levinas's discourse on responsibility need at this point to be examined. I will briefly mention four motifs: (1) the opposition of being and the other in Levinas's understanding of ethics; (2) his conception of otherness; (3) the role of death in responsibility; (4) the place of subjectivity in his thought of responsibility.

First, as we saw, the access to the ethical takes place for Levinas in a break with ontology. One may ask, should the question of ethics be raised according to this alternative: the other or being? Should being be identified with what Levinas calls "the Same"? Should one oppose ethics to ontology, the thought of the other to the thought of being?[15] Can the question of the other and therefore—for Levinas—of ethics only be raised "beyond being," beyond ontology? How are we to conceive of the relation between being and the other? Does ontology necessarily represent the obliteration of ethical concern? Is there a possibility, despite Levinas's claims, of developing an *ontological* sense of ethics and responsibility?

In fact, one could stress the practical dimension of Heideggerian ontology,[16] and its ethical scope. Instead of attempting to enframe Heidegger's thought of ethics in preestablished schemas, it would be an issue of understanding how he specifically approached the question of ethics in his thinking of being. The first gesture by Heidegger is to no longer separate ethics from existence, as if they constituted separate independent spheres. Thought from the perspective of the question on the truth of being, ethics cannot be approached except in terms of the event of being. There is thus no need to "add" an ethics to an ontology that would have been presupposed as unethical. In a sense, for Heidegger, ethics is ontology itself. That ethicality of being reveals existence as openness and a relation to the other, to the other Dasein-like, to the other than Dasein, and to the otherness of Dasein (as will appear in the call of conscience). Being is the openness of a relation to otherness, itself a *relation to* an alterity. Is being not thought in Heidegger as transcendence, on the basis of the ek-static, that is to say as a boundless expropriating exposure to the other? On this account, what of Levinas's attempt to go "beyond" being if being *is* already the beyond? To Levinas, who asks us not to think "being otherwise, but otherwise than being" (*AE*, 13), one could reply: not otherwise *than* being, but otherwise *as* being, the otherness *of* being. Being is openness to otherness, which explains why Heidegger states that being-with is a fundamental constitution of Dasein. Levinas claims that for Heidegger the other is only a "possible case" of the relation to beings, that being with-one-another—*Miteinandersein*—depends on the ontological relation. Yet, being is from the outset defined as a relation to an alterity, from the outset a *being-with. Sein* is constitutively *Mit-Sein,* and Heidegger stresses that being-with is not an accidental phenomenon but an irreducible feature and existential of Dasein. The "with" is coextensive with being *so that the ethical is co-extensive with the ontological.* The other, far from being opposed to being, becomes the very problem of being, or as Jean-Luc Nancy would write, "*the most proper problem of Being*"[17]

Second, it is indeed around this question of otherness that one could raise another set of questions. Should otherness be raised to the level of a metacategory, capitalized by Levinas as in the Other, and oppose such category to the other metacategory of the Same? One could question here Levinas's conceptualizing of otherness, his transforming it into a supracategory, running the risk, as Dastur notes judiciously, of "otherness suppressing itself in becoming the same as itself" (*HPP*, 88). Further, should the other be opposed as exteriority to the ego as self-same? The phenomenon of the call of conscience will reveal the being-called as exposition to alterity, both the alterity of the self and the alterity of the other. More precisely, the alterity of the other is revealed in the alterity of conscience and takes place in the alteration of the self. Instead of opposing a self-identical ego to an external other, it would be a matter of determining the self as openness to an alterity. In that case, alterity can no longer be understood as exteriority and the relation to the other as a separation. As Jean-Luc Nancy stressed, the other is neither exteriority nor separation but intertwining or interlacement (*entrelacement*): "The intertwining of the limit and of the continuity between the several *theres* must determine proximity not as pure juxtaposition but as *composition* in a precise sense, which must rest on a rigorous construction of the *com-*. This is nothing other than what is made necessary by Heidegger's insistence on the character of a *with* that cannot be reduced to an exteriority." This implies that there is a permeability between self and others: "For the *being-with-the-there* there must be contact, thus also contagion and encroachment, however minimal, and even an infinitesimal derivation of the tangent between the openings in question."[18] The emphasis would thus shift, from the transcendent and infinite other to the finite structure of receptivity of the self; from the escape to the infinity of transcendence to phenomenology as a thought of finitude; from a fleeing beyond being to a return to being-with. In that case, alterity is not that absolute exteriority of which Levinas speaks, but the event of an encounter and of an encounter intertwining intimately the self and the other. This last motif also raises questions on Levinas's opposition between a solipsistic death and the death of the other in his thinking of responsibility.

Third, as we saw, Levinas opposes to the dying for oneself in Heidegger a dying for the other that would be more primordial. As he states in a lecture course from January 9, 1976, "The death of the other: therein lies the first death" (*God, Death, and Time*, 48). The motif of death as it operates in *Being and Time* is for Levinas the indication of a solipsism of Heidegger's thought. According to Levinas, "the fundamental relation of Being, in Heidegger, is not the relation with the other, but with death, where everything inauthentic in the relation with the other is denounced, since one dies alone" (*EI*, 51). Levinas challenges that privilege of a dying for oneself in Heidegger, its priority over the concern for the other's death (which Heidegger dismisses from the analysis of death), and he attempts to imagine a dying—namely, a dying *of the other*—that would "concern me before and more that my own death" (*EN*, 240). Ultimately for Levinas, this concern would indicate "a beyond ontology" (*EN*, 214). With respect to the charge of a solipsistic death, it is a fact that Heidegger himself stated that in the authentic relation to my death, "[A]ll relations to other Dasein are dissolved."[19] Death, as mine alone, is for Heidegger the ground for responsibility, as Jacques Derrida recalled: in *Being and Time*, responsibility is tied to the singularity of my own dying, since it is "from the site of death as the place of my irreplaceability, that is, of my singularity, that I feel called to responsibility. In this sense, only a mortal can be responsible" (*GD*, 41). Indeed, it could be argued that in order to be able to sacrifice oneself for the other, to die for the other, I must already be able to die, *myself*. Death must already be, as Heidegger defines it, a possibility of *my* being. I must already be a mortal, that is, be capable of death. As Dastur argues, to state that the death of the other is the "first death," is "to give oneself in advance what it is precisely a matter of establishing. One can only be moved (*s'émouvoir*) about the death of the other if one is *already* a self, if that structure of receptivity that selfhood is, the self, is already present, and it can only be present as a relation to one's own having-to-die."[20]

Furthermore, dying *for* the other cannot mean dying *in place* of the other, if one understands this expression to mean to "die the other's death." I cannot take away the other's death, at most just delay it, and Derrida is right when he writes that I can give the other everything "except immortality," that I can die for the other "in a situation where my death gives him a little longer to live, I can save someone by throwing myself in the water or fire in order to temporally snatch him from the jaws of death, I can give her my heart in the literal or figurative sense in order to assure her of a certain longevity. But I cannot die in her place, I cannot give her my life in exchange for her death. Only a mortal can give" (GD, 43). Significantly, as we noted, when Levinas describes one's responsibility for the death of the other, he always characterizes it as a "not leaving the other [to] die alone," as if to suggest that the closest I can be to the other's death is in accompaniment to a death that remains to his or her.

Such a solitude of dying is in any case not exclusive of the relation to the other. In the first place, solitude or the absence of others, far from being opposed to being-with others, actually presupposes it. The experience of mourning shows this: the other is never more present than when she is gone: her absence makes her present, as other. To be alone is in a sense experiencing the presence of the other, in her very absence. The mineness of existence is thus in no way incompatible with our being-with others. Mineness is in fact the basis of being-with, "since what I share with others is precisely this untransferable character of existence which separates me abysmally from him or her" (HQA, 21).

Fourth, and finally, perhaps the most determinative assumption in Levinas's discourse is his paradoxical reliance on the motif of subjectivity. We recall how Levinas rejected the neutrality and impersonality of being, of the "there is," to return to the subjective. The origin of meaning, he claimed, lies in the intersubjective. Responsibility for the other, he insisted, is the very structure of subjectivity. Therein also lies Levinas's undeconstructed, indeed assumed and proclaimed, humanism, a humanism of the other man, and Levinas states: "I advocate, as in the title of one of my books, the humanism of the other man" (EN, 112). Responsibility is for the other, more precisely, the other *human* (*l'autre homme*): "To me," he clarifies without ambiguity, "*Autrui* is the other human being" (EN, 110; tr. modified). Levinas is not interested in deconstructing humanism, and in fact he is critical of the contemporary critiques of humanism and of the subject. He takes issue, for instance, with structuralist thought, with its appeals to impersonal principles ("what they want is a principle of intelligibility that is no longer enveloped by the human"; EN, 112), but also with the later Heidegger who places Dasein at the service of a neutral and impersonal power ("What *scares me* a little is also the development of a discourse in which the human becomes an articulation of an anonymous or neutral intelligibility," he writes, *Entre nous*, 116; my emphasis). He goes on to criticize the Merleau-Pontian touching-touched chiasm as example of a thought where "man is only an aspect" (*EN*, 112) of a nonhuman reflexive structure ("it is as if space were touching itself through man"), and he interprets the contemporary mistrust of humanism in the following way: "What they want is a principle of intelligibility that is no longer enveloped by the human; they want the subject to appeal to a principle that would not be enveloped by concern for human fate" (*EN*, 112).

It should therefore not come as a surprise if Levinas actually declares, in *Totality and Infinity*, that his work is "a defense of subjectivity" (*TI*, 11)! It is a *defense* of subjectivity, even as it takes the paradoxical form of a subjection of the subject to the other: but precisely *as* destitute, expropriated, the subject is maintained and becomes what Levinas calls the elected or chosen one. Levinas goes so far as to designate this destitute, expropriated ego as the true *subjectum*. As he explains in *Of God Who Comes to Mind*: "The ego is no longer taken as a particular case of the Ego in general, it is the unique point which supports the universe ('supports' in both senses of bearing the unbearable, as suffering for, and supporting it)."[21] Subjectivity, the *subjectum*—indeed, that which is thrown underneath—means for Levinas such a being subjected, "as subjection to all, as a supporting all (*un tout supporter*) and supporting of the whole (*un supporter le tout*)" (*AE*, 255). To be a subject means to be subjected, and to be subjected is paradoxically the establishing of a *subjectum*. For to state that the subject is subjected, that it is always in the accusative position, and never in the nominative, to substitute the "I think" with the accusative "*Me voici*," "here I am," to state that the subject is "the called one," the "persecuted one," does this not precisely posit the subject as the true and irreducible *subjectum*? Levinas thus reinforces the position of ground of the *subjectum*, now rethought in terms of the accusation and passivity of the subject, as persecuted subject of responsibility.

Ultimately, this maintaining of the motif of the subject, of the *subjectum*, testifies to the Cartesian-Husserlian point of departure assumed by Levinas. The analysis begins with the I, with the ego (as we recall, for Levinas the origin of meaning is the intersubjective relation, "the original experience," therefore within the horizon of subjectivity), which Levinas *then* attempts to exceed toward the other. We know that Levinas understands the other as *exteriority*.[22] Exteriority to what, if not to the ego, the self-enclosed ego of the Cartesian tradition? It is in fact from a Cartesian perspective of the self-enclosure of the ego that the other can be taken as exteriority (to that ego). Levinas's thought could be characterized as an exploration of the *underpinnings* of the egological tradition, which he reverses. Indeed, this accounts for the excess proper to Levinas's thinking and vocabulary: Paul Ricœur in this regard argues that the very vocabulary of Levinas's philosophy, in its very desire for rupture, in its exasperation as it were, still attests to the egological tradition secretly determining its itinerary. In *Oneself as Another* among other places,[23] Paul Ricœur argues that Levinas's thought is a *reactive* thought, a thought "of rupture," of "excess," of "hyperbole" leading to the "paroxistic" formulations of *Otherwise than Being or Beyond Essence*, a kind of symmetrical reversal of the Cartesian and Husserlian tradition in philosophy, opposing it but never really questioning its foundations. Indeed, it is one thing to reverse this tradition, and quite another to no longer use it as a point of departure. In particularly revealing passages of *Otherwise than Being or Beyond Essence*, Levinas betrays this reactive dimension of his thought. He writes that the responsibility for the other "*goes against the grain (à rebours)* of intentionality and the will" (*AE*, 221) or that the persecution of the subject "goes against the grain (à *rebours*) of intentionality" (*AE*, 177). Responsibility is defined in relation to such a tradition, as it is said to be "irreducible to intentionality . . . and will" (*AE*, 176). Levinas also characterizes his thinking of the passivity of the subject as an "'inversion' of intentionality . . . the abandonment of sovereign and active subjectivity" (*AE*, 81). The subject "thus is not to be described from the intentionality of the representational activity, of objectivation, of freedom and will. [The subject] is to be described from the passivity of time" (*AE*, 90). He often characterizes his thought in such an oppositional way. For instance in "Dialogue on Thinking-of-the-Other," he writes of the "human inversion of the in-itself and the for-itself (of 'everyman for himself') into an ethical self, into a priority of the for-the-other," or of the "replacement of the for-itself of ontological persistence by an I henceforth unique . . . because of its chosenness for a responsibility for the other man" (*EN*, 202). Levinas explicitly presents his understanding of subjectivity as a reversal of the traditional subject. For instance: "Subjectivity as hostage. This notion *reverses (renverse)* the position from which the presence of the ego to itself appears as the beginning or the accomplishment of philosophy" (*AE*, 202; my emphasis). Among many instances of this reversal of the modern tradition in philosophy, let us mention but the following list: first, the subject is not a for-itself, but a for-the-other; second, the subject is not a freedom, but a passivity; third, the subject does not posit or constitute the meaning of the other, but is "affected" by the other. The I is not a nominative, but an accusative; the subject does not initiate, but can only respond. The subject is not a spontaneity, but a receptivity. Responsibility no longer designates an activity of the subject, but is reversed into a symmetrical passivity. The subject does not thematize, but is exposed to the transcendence of the infinite. The subject, finally, is precisely not an

active subject, a spontaneity, but is subjected, as a hostage, to the other.
Responsibility for the other is "the defeat of the I think," the defeat of "the
originary *activity* of all *acting*, source of the *spontaneity of the subject*, or of
the subject as spontaneity" (AE, 220). As one can see, all the features of
the Levinasian concept of responsibility as subjection of the subject to the
other amount to a peculiar reversal of its traditional sense as accountability
of the free acting spontaneous subject. Ultimately this hermeneutical situation—which provides both the radicality as well as the limits of Levinas'ss
thinking—reveals, still, paradoxically, the Cartesian-Husserlian heritage of
Levinas. Levinas's critique of Heidegger paradoxically arises out of a site that
Heidegger had already deconstructed, that of subjectivity and humanism. As
Françoise Dastur notes, "just as in the case of Sartre . . . in the last analysis,
it was also a Cartesian motif that Levinas opposed to Heidegger's thought."²⁴

   We may ask: Does responsibility need to be tied to the figure of the
subject? Does it in fact not require a nonsubjective experience? Reversing egological responsibility still leaves the question of the *being-responsible*
still open: for only a being who *can* be responsible at all, that is to say,
is capable of answering to and answering for, can answer for the other.
Levinas assumes what needs to be first established, namely, the very possibility of *being* responsible. Through such a neglect, he is falling back on
the traditional and inappropriate motifs of subjectivity and will, which as
we saw he only reverses. If the gesture toward a "beyond being" is rendered
problematic, if not untenable, the question becomes: what are the ontological senses of responsibility? In Heidegger's understanding of the *ontological*
sources of responsibility, one will note how responsibility is tied to a nonsubjective experience of being, is revealed as an openness to otherness (in
a way distinct from Levinas's conceptualization of the other as exteriority),
and ultimately as exposure to a secret, an inappropriable.

HEIDEGGER AND ORIGINARY RESPONSIBILITY

Of a NonSubjective Responsibility

Heidegger's corpus, it is perhaps not stressed enough, entails a major thought
of responsibility. Being is an event for which each Dasein is responsible,
responding and corresponding to the call of being. This is why, while Heidegger deconstructed any notion of accountability of the subject, he also
consistently maintained that Dasein is to be thought in terms of responsibility in at least three respects: responsibility defines the essence of Dasein
as a concern for being, or care; Dasein comes to itself in a responsiveness
to a call; responsibility names humans' relationship to being, that is, the
cobelonging of being and humans. The very concept of Dasein means to

be a responsibility of being, as Dasein designates that being in which being is at issue, called by being to respond and correspond to its givenness. Being gives itself to an originary responsiveness and co-respondence and is given in such a way that I have to take it over and be responsible for it. Being is mine to be. One recalls this well-known passage from *Being and Time* where Heidegger writes, "The question of the meaning of Being is the most universal and the emptiest of questions, *but at the same time it is possible to individualize it very precisely for any particular Dasein*" (SZ, 39). This passage reveals that being itself, as Heidegger already established in the very first paragraph of *Being and Time*, is not a generic universality but has a singularizing reach. Heidegger names this phenomenon the "offensive" or "challenging" character of the question of being, its "strike-power,"[25] reaching the singular being thus "touched" by being. Being happens to Dasein. In its very givenness, being is singularized by engaging Dasein in its event. In this sense, being cannot be distinguished from the singular event of an existence which is in each case delivered over to itself, and which is to that very extent responsible for itself. Dasein is a being that never "is" what it is (as a present-at-hand being), but is to be taken over. This determination from the outset defines Dasein as a responsibility for being. This is what the expression of Care (*Sorge*) seeks to express, namely, the primordial responsibility that Dasein, as *Zu-sein*, is. Dasein is that entity that does not "simply occur among other being"; rather, Dasein "is concerned *about* its very being" (SZ, 12).

After *Being and Time*, Dasein will be referred to more and more as the "called one," *der Gerufene*, having to answer for the very openness and givenness of being and be its "guardian." To be responsible here means to have been struck, always already, by the event of being. Responsibility refers to that event by which being "enowns" humans and designates human beings' very belonging to being as well as their essence as humans. Heidegger speaks of being's "need" of humans for its givenness, refers to humans' guarding and taking on of the essence and truth of being, and of the "correspondence" of being and humans. In the *Zollikon Seminars*, Heidegger clarifies the sense of that correspondence, explaining, "The expression 'to correspond' means to answer the claim, to comport oneself in response to it. Re-spond [*Ent-*sprechen] → to answer to [*Ant-*worten]."[26] The response is not external to the call but belongs intimately to it, does not follow the call but is simultaneous with it. As Françoise Dastur notes, Heidegger seeks to develop a "thinking of the encounter of being and man as "simultaneity of the call and response" (in HPP, 90). We are responsible in so far as we are claimed by being, which in turn needs us for its givenness. This is how Heidegger further describes this phenomenon in the *Zollikon Seminars*: "Being, the manifestness of being, is only given through the presence of beings. In order that beings can come to presence, and, therefore, that being, the manifestness of being, can be given at all, what is needed is the [ecstatic] standing-in [*Innestehen*] of the human being in the *Da* [there], in the clearing, in the clearedness [*Gelichtetheit*] of being as which the human being exists. Therefore, there cannot be the being of beings at *without* the human being."[27] Through this belonging, man has always already been appropriated by the event of being, in a correspondence that constitutes an original responsibility. In such original responsibility, the notion of the human being as subject is abandoned.

Original responsibility is indeed not simply the reversal of accountability. Rather, Heidegger situates the question of responsibility outside of a problematic of the ego, outside of the accountability of the free acting subject, and arising out of the very openness of being where the human being dwells as Dasein. Heidegger's thinking of Dasein breaks decisively with the tradition of subjectivity.[28] We saw how the radical individuation of Dasein is no longer related to some subjective or individual ego-pole, but to being itself (the self being singularized only through being). It attests to the radical nonsubjectivism of Heidegger's thinking of Dasein. Heidegger does not think the human being in terms of subject, nor does he conceive of the self as an ego. This is the import of his thinking of Dasein: it is a matter of seizing the human being no longer as subject but in terms of the openness of being, and solely in terms of such relationship to being. This is why the term "Dasein," in later writings, is often hyphenated as Da-sein, in order to stress the sheer relatedness to being, a relatedness that is not posited or initiated by us. Heidegger's thought of responsibility thus needs to be approached, from the outset, in terms of what he called, in the "Letter on Humanism," an "originary ethics" (*ursprüngliche Ethik*).[29] The most significant feature of such an expression is that it seeks to capture the thinking of being itself as an originary ethics. This already indicates that Heidegger's understanding of ethics and responsibility will develop in terms of being itself, and no longer in terms of subjectivity, will, or agency. This is the first decisive difference with Levinas: responsibility is not about the subject, even as subjected. Responsibility is about being.

Heidegger's thinking increasingly turned toward the truth of be-ing as such (and no longer beingness), as it inquired into the truth of be-ing "out of be-ing *itself*."[30] This turning in his thought led to a desubjectivizing of thought yet did not amount to an abandonment of the reference to the human being, but rather, to its transformation: indeed, in the attempt to think the truth of be-ing at issue is the "transformation of man himself" (*Contributions*, 58). The shift from a questioning of the meaning of being to one out of the truth of be-ing itself means that there is a sort of dis-placing (*Verrückung*) of man into a dimension, which Heidegger calls the "between," from which he becomes for the first time *himself*. "In the history of the truth of being Dasein is the essential *case of the between* (*Zwischenfall*), that is, the case of falling-into that "between" (*Zwischen*) into which man must be displaced (*ver-rückt*), in order above all to be *himself*" (*Contributions*, 223). In paragraph 227, Heidegger speaks of the displacing of man into Dasein and how through this displacing *out of* the desolation of the abandonment of be-ing, man will come to stand in enowning and find "his abode in the truth of be-ing." (*Contributions*, 19). The origin of Dasein is thus the happening of be-ing itself, and the shift from fundamental ontology to be-ing-historical thinking implies a revolution of the site of the human being, and of what is meant by "ethics." How does Heidegger explain the shift from "meaning of being" to "truth of be-ing" in his thinking? In terms of a *turning* of the question of being, a turning that would have to part from a certain subjectivism and anthropocentrism still dangerously threatening to affect the analyses of *Being and Time*. Heidegger himself admits it plainly: "In *Being and Time* Da-sein still stands in the shadow of the 'anthropologi-cal,' the 'subjectivistic,' and the individualistic,' etc." (*Contributions*, 208). Heidegger gives examples of such a "turning in thinking," when, for instance in paragraph 41 of the *Contributions*, he explains that the word "decision" can be taken first as an anthropological human act, "until it suddenly means the essential sway of be-ing" (*Contributions*, 58). Thinking "from enowning" will thus involve that "man [be] put back into the essential sway of be-ing and cut of from the fetters of 'anthropology'" (*Contributions*, 58). Decision is here desubjectified, and the realm of ethical responsibility will have to be severed from the predominance of subjectivity.

The treatment of decision as it intervenes in Heidegger's later thought indeed indicates a radically nonsubjectivistic approach to ethical respon-sibility, as decision is removed from the horizon of subjectivity. We see that break with subjectivity and anthropology in the thinking of decision already expressed in *Introduction to Metaphysics*, where Heidegger stresses that "de-cision (*Ent-scheidung*) here does not mean the judgment and choice of human beings but rather a division (*Scheidung*) in the . . . togetherness of Being, unconcealment, seeming and not-Being."[31] The measure of decision, of responsibility, is no longer the subject as decision is said to pertain to being itself. This break is further developed in the *Contributions to Philoso-phy*. In paragraph 43, Heidegger states clearly that ordinarily, when "we speak here of de-cision (*Ent-scheidung*), we think of an activity of man, of an enactment, of a process." However, decision for Heidegger is not a power or a faculty of man: "But here neither the human character in an activity nor the process-dimension is essential" (*Contributions*, 60).[32] This is why he clarifies, "Decision [is] related to the truth of being, not only related but determined only from within it" (*Contributions*, 69). Decision is then no longer about the subject, about the power of a subject, and is

displaced from a subject-based thinking to a thinking which is concerned
with what the decision is about, the "decisive," that is, being. The decisive is not the subject who decides, and Heidegger separates the freedom
of decision (decision, he writes, is "the necessary enactment of freedom";
Contributions, 71) from its subjectivist understanding in terms of causality
of the will as a faculty of the subject ("this is how we think 'causally' and
take freedom to be a faculty"). At the risk of tautology, one should say
that what matters in decision is "the matter" of the decision itself. This
is why Heidegger says that decision is about decision, "about deciding or
not-deciding" (*Contributions*, 70)! For Heidegger, decision is not to be taken
in its "morally-anthropologically" sense, but as pertaining to being itself in
its decidedness. Being is a matter of a decision, of a responsible decision.
Decidedness is the site of being itself.

We can even wonder whether such an original responsibility can be
characterized at all as a *human* responsibility, following Heidegger's claim
that "in the determination of the humanity of man as ek-sistence what is
essential is not man but Being" (*BW*, 237). In fact, for Heidegger responsibility is not a human characteristic, but instead is a phenomenon that
belongs to being itself (insofar as humans are called by being). Decision and
responsibility are approached outside of the anthropological or humanistic
enclosure. In his thinking of responsibility, Heidegger breaks with a subject-
based thinking, breaks from the tradition of autonomous subject, and breaks
with an anthropological way of thinking. The task is to think ethics, and
responsibility, away from any anthropological account. The entirety of ethics is to be recast in terms of being itself, responsibility instead naming the
cobelonging of being and Dasein (a cobelonging not posited by man but
rather one in which man is thrown).

Responsibility is no longer attached to the subject, but to the event
or enactment of being. Such an enactment is not the act of a subjectivity,
because, as Heidegger says of project or projection (*Entwurf*), it is always
thrown (*Geworfen*), and therefore it is an event that happens, so to speak,
before the subject. Being is always already under way, always already in
motion, "before" the will and before the subject. The "act" or "enactment"
of being refers to such a motion, *which we are*, but not as its authors. Rather,
we are "en-owned" by it: "*This* throw is *thrown* in the resonance of en-own-
ment," Heidegger writes in a very compact sentence (*Contributions*, 320).
Freedom, the "free throw," thus "never succeeds by mere human impetus
[*Antrieb*] and human make up" (*Contributions*, 320). Humans do not initiate the free throw; they are the ones who, as Heidegger puts it, "always
return from the free throw" (*Contributions*, 320). Any projecting-open is thus
thrown, and in the *Contributions*, thrownness is understood as belongingness
to be-ing (that is, *not* as the project of the subject!), so to be thrown now

means being en-owned. Thrownness will be experienced above all from within the truth of be-ing. Heidegger stresses that "the projecting-open of the essential sway of be-ing is merely a response to the call" (GA, 65, 56; *Contributions*, 39), and one sees here how the realm of responsibility—of originary responsibility—is located in the space of a certain call, a call to which a response always corresponds.

The Otherness of Responsibility

The phenomenon of the call of conscience in *Being and Time* reveals a singular inscription of otherness within the selfhood of Dasein. As we saw, the very concept of Dasein is a responsibility for being, as being is given in such a way that I have to take it over and be responsible for it. Dasein is delivered over to its being, "entrusted" with being, or charged with the responsibility for its being (SZ, 41–42). Care, concern, solicitude, anxiety, authenticity, and being-guilty all are different names for such originary responsibility. Dasein is concerned about its own being, or about being as each time its own. However, this "own" is not the sphere of ownness of an ego. Responsibility is the taking on of such an "own" in a way that reveals an otherness at its heart. It is often claimed that the call of conscience manifests an egological enclosure, as conscience *calls* Dasein to its ownmost potentiality-of-being-a-self. Heidegger indeed writes, "Conscience, in its basis and its essence, is *each time mine*" (SZ, 278). It is my ownmost being-a-self that is called, and "the call comes from that being which I am each time" (SZ, 278). It would even seem that Dasein is at once the origin and destination of the call, for Heidegger writes that *"Dasein calls itself in conscience"* (SZ, 275), and, "Dasein is *at the same time* both the caller and the one summoned (*Das Dasein ist der Rufer und der Angerufene zumal*)" (SZ, 275).

It might therefore be concluded from such passages that in the call of conscience Dasein is closed upon itself in a solipsistic way, in a kind of "soliloquy" that would reproduce within the sphere of ownness of the self the Platonic "dialogue of the soul with itself." However, before we are to speak of an "auto-affection," "auto-interpellation," or "auto-nomy" in the call of conscience, we ought to note that Heidegger does not say simply that the call comes "from me." Rather, the call is said to come from the being "which I am each time." Now, as we know, I am this being only in the mode of a *zu-sein*, a having-to-be, that is, in the manner of a possibility to be. I have to assume this being, whether authentically or inauthentically. It does not therefore "belong to me," if what is meant by this is projected by me. When Heidegger writes that Dasein "calls itself," it does not mean that the "I," as author, is the origin of the call (as we will see, he on the contrary insists that there is *no author* of the call), or even that there is a strict identity

between the caller and the called one. In the context of the passage, this
statement intervenes when Heidegger is attempting to stress that the call
does come from an entity other than Dasein, whether an ontic other or
a transcendent theological other. Heidegger rejects the theological notion
of a call coming from God, *and, in fact, from any entity.* The theological
representation of the call is an ontic representation of the call. Rather, to
"call oneself" means that the call resonates in the dimension of selfhood,
not projected by a self-identical subject, but to take on and respond to.
One already notes here the presence of an otherness in the phenomenon,
which Heidegger approaches in terms of the "uncanniness" of the call of
conscience. There is no ontic origin of the call, and there is also no pre-
given subject or prior self-identity on the basis of which the call would be
initiated. There is no self at the basis of the call, because *the self itself arises
out of the call.* It is the very movement of the call that brings a self-to-come,
the impersonal or prepersonal event of being that precedes and exceeds the
one who will have to assume it as its own. The fact that the I arises out
of a nonsubjective call allows us to understand why the "author" of the
call, in a certain sense, escapes all attempts at identification (SZ, 274–75).
The caller remains "in a striking indefiniteness"; it "fails to answer questions about name, status, origin, and repute" (SZ, 274). The author of the
call remains *other, foreign,* and "absolutely distances any kind of becoming
familiar" (SZ, 275). The "caller" evades any attempt at identification simply
because there is no "author" of the call. This agent is "other" as uncanny.
The "caller" in fact is identified with the calling itself: *the caller is the calling.*

Heidegger thus clarifies that it is not sufficient to state that Dasein is
at the same time the caller and the called one. For this "at the same time"
is misleading: it is not synonymous with an identity of Dasein with itself.
Dasein is not *simply* itself. Most often, Dasein "fails to hear (*überhört*) its
own self" (SZ, 271). In fact, a dissymmetry and otherness within the self is
becoming apparent: "When Dasein is summoned, *is* it not 'there' in another
way from that in which it does the calling?" asks Heidegger (SZ, 275). We
should therefore qualify Heidegger's statements, "Dasein calls itself" or "the
call certainly from the being that I am each time," and Heidegger himself
speaks of the "formal" character of this formulation ("The statement that
Da-sein is at the same time the caller and the one summoned has now lost
its empty formal character"; SZ, 277). The call comes from the being that I
am (that is, *not* from another entity, an ontic other), but as something that
falls upon me, thus in a sense, *as something that does not come from me.* This
is why Heidegger clearly states that the "call is precisely something that *we
ourselves* have neither planned nor prepared for nor willfully brought about"
(SZ, 275). The call sur-prises me: " 'It' calls, against our expectations and
even against our will" (SZ, 275). Nonetheless, it calls *me* ("*es ruft micht,*"

writes Heidegger, SZ, 277), as if the self arose from the impersonal event of the call. The "caller" is an "it" because it cannot be referred to any entity, be it divine, as it is the event and advent of presence itself. It happens, before me, without me, but nonetheless "it" happens only to me, because it calls me: *Es ruft mich*. There lies what we could call the verticality of the call, calling me from a height that is nonetheless not foreign to the self. Paul Ricoeur makes this point in *Oneself as Another*. With respect to the alterity of the voice of conscience, he marks the dissymmetry of the call of conscience, a dissymmetry that interrupts any autonomous self-relation, and introduces heteronomy in auto-nomy: "Unlike the dialogue of the soul with itself, of which Plato speaks, this affection by another voice presents a remarkable dissymmetry, one that can be called vertical, between the agency that calls and the self called upon."[33] These are the very terms that Heidegger uses: "The call comes *from* me and yet from *above and beyond* me (*Der Ruf kommt aus mir und doch über mich*)" (SZ, 275). In Derrida's words, "it falls *upon* it *from inside*" (DM, 49). Conscience is indeed, as Dastur suggested, "the most intimate alterity."

One thus needs to recognize in conscience a certain dissymmetry, a gap within identity, a transcendence within the self, allowing for the call to be heard. As Dastur remarks, this "interior knowledge [of conscience] thus supposes in some way that one makes oneself witness to oneself . . . But the witnessing of oneself demands that this Being-with-oneself be experienced in a rigorous dissymmetry, and this is brought forth by the call of the voice of conscience" (HPP, 92). This verticality, or dissymmetry, prevents all autonomous closure of the self and in fact represents the irruption or the "breach" of otherness within Dasein itself. Auto-nomy is hetero-nomy, and the call of conscience is a hetero-affection, manifesting the otherness at the heart of Dasein's selfhood. This is what Françoise Dastur emphasizes, when she writes, "What is here essential for the verticality of the call (which constitutes the self as self)—that is, within the self-affection through which selfhood occurs, in the immanence of the self—is a breach of transcendence (i.e., the dimension of hetero-affection)" (HPP, 92). Because of this inscription of otherness in the coming to itself of the self, responsibility can no longer be for Heidegger a responsibility for oneself, if that means the responsibility of a self-enclosed ego for itself. As we saw, Levinas opposes a responsibility for the other to self-responsibility. However, unlike Levinas, who situates the other outside of the ego (as exteriority), Heidegger inscribes otherness in the structure of the self as hetero-affection, *rendering the opposition between a responsibility to the other and a responsibility-to-self moot*. This is what the determination of being-with as an existential of Dasein makes clear: the other is inscribed in the structure of selfhood. It is on the basis of this primordial openness of Dasein that a relation to others can occur. For as Heidegger puts it, hearing the call, the very capacity to hear the call "is Dasein's existential way of Being-open as Being-with for Others" (SZ, 163).

It is thus incorrect to claim that Heidegger privileged the "pole" of the self over the other or that he conceives of responsibility as being primarily for oneself, existence unfolding (an)ethically as an infamous "struggle for existence." Heidegger explicitly rejected this social Darwinism, as early as a 1921–22 course, where he explained, "Caring is not a factually occurring *struggle for existence*, understood as elapsing and 'taking place' within so-called Objective unities of life."[34] On the contrary, care includes a care for others because of the hetero-affection of Dasein and due to the fundamental constitution of Dasein as being-with. Heidegger consistently stressed the constitutive openness to the other of Dasein, from his early courses all the way to his last seminars, as this passage from the *Zollikon Seminars* reveals. Answering a question by Medard Boss, regarding the signification of that proposition from *Being and Time*, "Dasein is that being for which, in its being, that being is an issue," Heidegger clarifies: "Da-sein must always be seen as being-in-the-world, as concern for things, and as caring for other [Da-seins], as the being-with the human beings it encounters, and never as a self-contained subject."[35] To that extent, responsibility will always include a responsibility for others.

Care (*Sorge*) is thus always already "care for" others, solicitude (*Fürsorge*). This care or responsibility for others, which is an existential of Dasein, includes even those deficient modes that are "inconsiderateness" (*Rücksichtlosigkeit*) and "indifference" (*Naschsehen*). As deficient modes, these actually confirm Dasein's care for others. Heidegger distinguishes two fundamental modalities, or "extreme possibilities," of this caring-for-others: one kind of solicitude will consist in taking over the care of the other upon by substituting oneself to him: it consists in leaping in (*Einspringen*) for him, that is, in taking his responsibility of being *away* from him. That solicitude is inauthentic: first, because it treats the other Dasein as something ready-to-hand, a *zuhandenes*, as Heidegger notes (SZ, 122); second, because it consists in taking the place of the other, taking "the other's 'care' away from him" (SZ, 122), such a substitution representing for Heidegger an inauthentic relation to others. I can never be the other, I cannot take her responsibility away from her, though, in turn, I can never be without the other. I can at most *accompany* (*Mitgehen*) the other, and this is how Dasein is *with* others. No substitution, then, but accompaniment of the other's solitude (we recall how Levinas spoke of an accompaniment of the other—not "letting the other die alone"—in his or her dying as primordial responsibility for the other). Third, and most importantly, such leaping in is inauthentic because it *disburdens* the other Dasein of his care and responsibility. Now the latter is for Heidegger inauthenticity par excellence, if it is the case that inauthenticity consists in a fleeing of Dasein in the face of its own existence and of its weight: in other words, in being irresponsible. Inauthenticity thus means for Heidegger irresponsibility as a fleeing before the weight of responsibility. What weighs in the weight of responsibility is a certain inappropriability remaining other to Dasein. Responsibility, once understood apart from the tradition of egology, signifies an essential exposure to the other, and cannot simply be reduced to the responsibility of the "self-contained subject" of which the *Zollikon Seminars* spoke. Now, insofar as an otherness is inscribed at the heart of responsibility, there will always be an inappropriable in the motion of our responsible being. This is why Heidegger understands responsibility as exposure to an inappropriable, to a "secret."

Responsibility to a Secret

For what, in the end, does the call of conscience, later renamed call of being, reveal? An inappropriable. *Schuldigsein* or *Nichtigkeit* in *Being and Time*, withdrawal of being in later writings, in each case Heidegger shows that an inappropriable inhabits the motion of responsible being, indeed, that such an inappropriable is the very possibility of responsibility. Derrida has stressed the aporetic structure of responsibility, situating an impossible at its heart.[36] Far from being identified to the position of a good conscience, "the concepts of responsibility, of decision, or of duty, are condemned a priori to paradox, scandal, and aporia" (GD, 68). Responsibility becomes less about the establishment of a sphere of control and power, less about the establishment of a sovereign subject, and more about an exposure to an inappropriable event that does not come from us and yet calls us. The call of conscience brings Dasein back from its disburdened, irresponsible existence in the everyday back to its own being-guilty. Existing authentically, far from overcoming such being-guilty, is projecting oneself resolutely toward it. It means taking over or making oneself responsible for this "not." Heidegger states this quite clearly: by choosing itself, Dasein chooses its being-guilty and its finitude: "in so choosing, Dasein makes possible its ownmost being-guilty" (SZ, 288). Being-guilty, the call of conscience, thrownness, the taking on of the inappropriable, all these motifs point to *facticity* as the site of ontological responsibility. Responsibility is to be thought in terms of such facticity, as Heidegger suggests when he forges the expression of Faktizität der Überantwortung, the "facticity of responsibility" (SZ, 135). Facticity is not what faces the position of a consciousness, but the "throw" of an existence that is called from such a throw to appropriate what will always remain inappropriable for it: responsibility to a "not."

This negativity or "nullity" lies in the fact of *not* being the basis of one's own being, of being *thrown* into existence; the "guilt" lies in the fact that I must make myself the origin or basis of this existence of which *I am not* the origin. Dasein exists as thrown; that is to say, it did not bring *itself* into existence by first projecting itself on the basis of a preexisting self. There lies the fundamental and irreducible impotence or powerlessness of Dasein. *Dasein can never overcome the finitude of thrownness.* Heidegger would speak of such powerlessness in the course entitled Introduction to Philosophy (Einleitung in die Philosophie), claiming that *"Dasein exists always in an essential exposure to the darkness and impotence of its origin, even if only in the prevailing form of a habitual deep forgetting in the face of this essential determination of its facticity."*[37] This thrownness constitutes the "nullity" of Dasein, as well as its paradox: Dasein at once belongs to itself and yet did not give itself to itself. The dispossession or expropriation that comes to light in my incapacity to make myself the author or master of my existence is precisely what opens this existence to itself, what frees it for itself. In this sense, by resolutely projecting being-guilty, Dasein appropriates the inappropriable *as* inappropriable. *I must be the improper (inauthenticity) properly (authentically).* Ultimately, one is responsible *from* out of the facticity of existence, and *for* it. Responsibility will then manifest the essential exposure of human beings to an inappropriable that always remains "other" for them.

The "inappropriable" may be in fact the secret resource of appropriation (responsibility as properly being one's own). For Heidegger to be thrown is to be thrown into a responsibility.[38] *This immediately means that responsibility will be for this very thrownness,* that is, for the inappropriability of Dasein's being. In "Introduction to Philosophy," Heidegger thus explains that precisely that over which Dasein is not master must be "worked through" and "survived." He writes: "Also that which does not arise of one's own express decision, as most things for Dasein, must be in such or such a way retrievingly appropriated, even if only in the modes of putting up with or shirking something; that which for us is entirely not under the control of freedom in the narrow sense . . . is something that is in such or such a manner taken up or rejected in the How of Dasein" (GA, 27, 337). If thrownness does not designate some fall from a higher realm, but the very facticity from which Dasein becomes a care and a responsibility for itself, then the weight of existence is from the outset an original responsibility. The inappropriable in existence (facticity), as we see in the phenomena of moods, is primarily felt as a weight or a burden. Facticity is given to be read in the phenomena of moods. Thrownness is *felt* in the mood, a mood that manifests an ontological truth of Dasein. What is most striking in those descriptions is how Heidegger describes moods in terms of the opacity and withdrawal of our factical origins, as an expropriation of our being that seems to break and foreclose any possibility of responsible appropriation. What weighs is the inappropriable. Heidegger speaks of a "burden" (*Last*). The being of the there, Heidegger writes, "become[s] manifest as a burden" (SZ, 134). But, interestingly, the very concept of weight and burden reintroduces, as it were, the problematic of responsibility. In a marginal note added to this passage, Heidegger later clarified: "Burden: what weighs (*das Zu-tragende*); human being is charged with the responsibility (*überantwortet*) of Dasein, appropriated by it (*übereignet*). To carry: to take over one's belonging to being itself" (SZ, 134). The burden is described as "what weighs," as what has to be carried (*das Zu-tragende*). The weight of facticity, the burden, is to be carried, Heidegger indicating the taking on of facticity as the carrying of the weight. The weight is facticity; the carrying is the taking on of facticity: such is the "facticity of responsibility." The sentence continues thus: "man is charged with the responsibility (*überantwortet*) of Dasein, appropriated by it (*übereignet*)."

Being withdraws in the very "throw" that brings Dasein into existence. But it is this withdrawal itself that *calls* Dasein, summons it to be this being-thrown as its ownmost. In its very eventfulness, being withdraws, is the mystery: such a withdrawal, as Heidegger stresses in the first lecture of *What Is Called Thinking?*, *calls us*.[39] The origin of responsibility is the withdrawal of being in its givenness as this withdrawal calls us. For as Heidegger explains, this "withdrawing is not nothing. Withdrawing is an event. In fact, what withdraws may even concern and claim man more essentially than anything present that strikes and touches him" (WCT, 9). This withdrawal touches us and calls us to take it on as a weight to carry, insofar as we have to assume this withdrawal and thrownness in a "free throw." Dasein's belongingness to being, to *Ereignis*, happens from a certain expropriative motion, which Heidegger calls *Enteignis*. One notes the presence of such expropriation in all the characterizations of Heidegger's responsibility, of our being-responsible: from the "ruinance" of factical life in the early writings and lecture courses to the *Uneigentlichkeit* of existence in *Being and Time* and the being-guilty of conscience; from the thrownness felt in moods and the weight of a responsibility assigned to an inappropriable to the withdrawal of being as origin of the call (what calls to responsibility is a withdrawal) and the *Enteignis* within *Ereignis* of the later writings, one finds that responsibility in Heidegger is each time described as the exposure to and experience of an inappropriable, an inappropriable that is not opposed to appropriation, but "plays" in it and lets it be, in a motion named by Derrida, in one word, "exappropriation." Original responsibility is hence a responsibility to such withdrawal, responsibility to a secret. It is indeed around this motif of the secret that Heidegger may be closest to Levinas, if it is the case, as Derrida wrote, that "the other is secret insofar as it is other."[40]

NOTES

1. Emmanuel Levinas, *Entre Nous*, trans. Michael B. Smith and Barbara Harshav (New York: Columbia University Press, 1998), 105. Hereafter cited as *EN*.

2. Emmanuel Levinas, *Autrement qu'être ou au-delà de l'essence* (Paris: Le livre de poche, 1996, 252). Hereafter cited as *AE*. All translations mine.

3. Jacques Derrida, *The Gift of Death* (Chicago and London: Chicago University Press, 1992), 46. Hereafter cited as *GD*.

4. See Emmanuel Levinas, *Humanisme de l'autre homme* (Montpellier: Fata Morgana, 1972); rendered in an English translation as *Humanism of the Other* (Urbana: University of Illinois Press, 2005).

5. See for instance *Ethics and Infinity*, 37–38 (hereafter cited as *EI*), and *Is It Righteous to Be?*, ed. Jill Robbins (Stanford, CA: Stanford University Press, 2001), 31–37.

6. On Levinas's role in the early reception of Heidegger in France, see Dominique Janicaud, *Heidegger en France* (Paris: Albin Michel, 2000), 31–36.

7. Emmanuel Levinas, *On Escape* (Stanford, CA: Stanford University Press, 2003). Hereafter cited as *OE*.

8. Jacques Derrida, *Adieu à Emmanuel Levinas* (Paris: Galilée, 1997).

9. The French word "visage" immediately gives a human character to the face as thematized by Levinas, as visage refers exclusively to the human face, whereas the term "gueule" refers to the animal's "face." The humanism of Levinas's thought is thus already inscribed linguistically, in the French language.

10. Martin Heidegger, *Four Seminars*, trans. Andrew Mitchell and François Raffoul (Bloomington: Indiana University Press, 2002).

11. Jean-Luc Marion, "The Saturated Phenomenon," *Phenomenology and the "Theological Turn." The French Debate* (New York: Fordham University Press, 2000), 176–216.

12. In *Otherwise than Being or Beyond Essence*, Levinas undertakes an analysis of the skin, the "contact of a skin," emphasizing its thinness (*minceur*), thin surface, "almost transparent," already pointing to the face's poverty and lack of substantiality. The skin is thus thought of in terms of the exposure and poverty of the face. *AE*, 143.

13. Hans Jonas, *The Imperative of Responsibility: In Search of an Ethics for the Technological Age* (Chicago: University of Chicago Press, 1985), 26–28, 202. On the role of fear in Jonas'a account of responsibility, see Jean Greisch, "L'amour du monde et le principe responsabilité," *La responsabilité. La condition de notre humanité*, directed by Monette Vacquin (Paris: Editions Autrement, 1995), 72–93.

14. Emmanuel Levinas, *God, Death, and Time* (Stanford, CA: Stanford University Press, 2000), 172.

15. In Françoise Dastur's words: "Do we really have to choose between Lévinas, who asks us to contemplate 'otherwise than Being,' and Heidegger, who leads us to another way of thinking about Being?" in "The Call of Conscience. The Most Intimate Alterity." *Heidegger and Practical Philosophy*, ed. François Raffoul and David Pettigrew (Albany: SUNY Press, 2002), 88. Hereafter cited as *HPP*, followed by page number.

16. On this practicality of the thought of being as originary praxis, see *Heidegger and Practical Philosophy*.

17. Jean-Luc Nancy, *Being Singular Plural* (Stanford, CA: Stanford University Press, 2000), 32.

18. "The Being-with of the Being-there," *Rethinking Facticity*, ed. François Raffoul and Eric Nelson (Albany: SUNY Press, 2008), 123.

19. Martin Heidegger, *Sein und Zeit* (Tübingen: Max Niemeyer Verlag, 1953), 250. Hereafter cited as *SZ*.

20. Françoise Dastur, *Heidegger et la question anthropologique* (Louvain: Editions Peeters, 2003), 23. Hereafter cited as *HQA*, followed by page number. Note the reflexive used by Françoise Dastur: *s'émouvoir* literally would be "to move oneself" and thus implies the prior presence of a self.

21. Emmanuel Levinas, *De Dieu qui vient à l'idée* (Paris: Vrin, 2000), 135.

22. Among numerous examples, see for instance, "The I and the Totality," *EN*, 22.

23. For instance in *Autrement. Lecture d'Autrement qu'être ou au-delà de l'essence d'Emmanuel Levinas* (Paris: PUF, 1997).

24. Françoise Dastur, "The Reception and Non-Reception of Heidegger in France," *French Interpretations of Heidegger* (Albany: SUNY Press, 2008), 265–89.

25. Martin Heidegger, *The Essence of Human Freedom*, trans. Ted Sadler (London: Continuum, 2002), 10. A few pages later, Heidegger explains that the question on the totality of beings is a "going-to-the-root," which in turn "must take aim *at us*" (24) and represents a challenge to us.

26. Martin Heidegger, *The Zollikon Seminars*, trans. Franz Mayr and Richard Askay (Evanston, IL: Northwestern University Press, 2001), 161.

27. Ibid., 176.

28. On this point, I take the liberty of referring the reader to my *Heidegger and the Subject* (Amherst, NY: Prometheus Books, 1999).

29. Martin Heidegger, *Basic Writings* (New York: Harper and Row, 1977), 235. Hereafter cited as *BW*.

30. Martin Heidegger, *Beiträge zur Philosophie (Vom Ereignis). 1936–38*, GA 65 (Frankfurt aM: Klostermann, 1989). English translation by Parvis Emad and Kenneth Maly, *Contributions to Philosophy. From Enowning* (Bloomington, Indiana: Indiana University Press, 1999), 3. Hereafter cited as *Contributions*.

31. Martin Heidegger, *Introduction to Metaphysics*, trans. Gregory Fried and Richard Polt (New Haven, CT: Yale University Press, 2000), 116.

32. As Richard Polt remarks, the hyphenated *Ent-scheidung* "indicates a division (*Scheidung*) that opens up a domain of unconcealment." Richard Polt, "The Event of Enthinking the Event," in *Companion to Heidegger's Contributions to Philosophy*, ed. Charles E. Scott, Susan M. Schoenbohm, Daniela Vallega-Neu, and Alejandro Vallega (Bloomington: Indiana University Press, 2001), 91. This domain, Heidegger writes, "must originarily and inceptually be opened up in a leap (*ersprungen werden*)." *Contributions*, 323, tr. modified. The leap, precisely, is of decision. Ultimately, decision is the disclosure of being, in a leap.

33. Paul Ricoeur, *Oneself as Another*, 342.

34. Martin Heidegger, *Phenomenological Interpretations of Aristotle* (Bloomington: Indiana University Press, 2001), 100.

35. Heidegger, *Zollikon Seminars*, 159.

36. On this question, see my "Derrida and the Ethics of the Im-possible," *Research in Phenomenology* 38 (Spring 2008).

37. *Einleitung in die Philosophie* 27 (Wintersemester 1928/29), *Gesamtausgabe* (Frankfurt aM: Klostermann, 1996), 340; my emphasis. Hereafter cited as GA 27.

38. As Françoise Dastur explains (in *HPP*, 91), responsibility needs to be understood "as a constitutive structure of a being that understands *itself* only by responding for itself, assuming responsibility for itself, since its facticity, far from being assimilable to the *factum brutum* of a natural being, must on the contrary be understood as that which constrains Dasein to assume responsibility for its own Being."

39. Martin Heidegger, *What Is Called Thinking?* English trans. J. Glenn Gray (New York: Harper and Row, 1968), 7–10, 17–18. Hereafter cited as WCT.

40. Jacques Derrida, "Autrui est secret parce qu'il est autre" (*Autrui* is secret because it is another), interview by Antoine Spire, *Le Monde de l'Education* (July–August 2001), www.lemonde.fr/mde/ete2001/derrida.html.

PART IV

OTHER OTHERS

CHAPTER TEN

DISPLACED

Phenomenology and Belonging in Levinas and Heidegger

Peter E. Gordon

All of you are at home, in your language, your allusions, among the books and works you all love. But I'm on the outside.

—Paul Celan, as quoted by Yves Bonnefoy[1]

I would like to acquire more of the wisdom that lies concealed in *stabilitas loci*.

—Martin Heidegger, Letter to Karl Jaspers,
sent from Todtnauberg, 5 July, 1949[2]

Imagine something that does not belong. This can be any quotidian thing—a spoon, a shoe, a toy. But one must picture it in a location that does not seem correct. One discovers very quickly that this image has a touch of surrealism about it, and it is perhaps not without humor: The spoon may be planted in the ground like a strange flower. The shoe may be hanging from a light post as if it were ivy. And the toy? If we imagine the toy

210 PETER E. GORDON

beyond its proper bounds, we can see how quickly the surrealism becomes melancholy: a toy displaced and far from the voices of children may signify loss, abandonment, even death.

It is a commonplace of everyday speech to say that something does not "belong," that its proper place is elsewhere but not here, that its surprising occurrence in native space is a mere accident or, at most, a sign of trespass: a migration *sans-papiers*. A place, a region, a territory: all suggest sites with boundaries, the contrast between inside and outside, between geographies known and unknown. The domestic and the strange, the placed and the displaced: The terms adhere to our habitual language, and they structure much of everyday experience. But what is it for something to be where it should be? What lends that domesticity its coherence and its familiarity? Is it the very concept of the "familiar" that first generates the unfamiliar? Then by what logic is any place "proper" such that displacement has become possible?

Although I have raised these questions in an informal fashion, they point to problems of great complexity in the history of phenomenology. In what follows I want to explore these problems in greater detail, casting light on the fateful interrelation of two concepts, belonging and displacement, as theorized specifically by Heidegger and Levinas.[3] Most of this chapter concerns Heidegger and what might be called the *nativism* intrinsic to his concept of world. First, I will provide a brief review of certain standard motifs of belonging, laying special emphasis on the way Heidegger conceived of *worldhood* as the practical horizon in which everything has its *proper place*. But with this preliminary sketch accomplished, I will then indulge in a phenomenological experiment.[4] In *The Fundamental Concepts of Metaphysics* Heidegger writes that while the human being is "world-forming" (*weltbildend*) the animal is "poor in world" (*weltarm*).[5] We can accordingly let loose an animal into Heidegger's world, to study its disordering effects and to gain further insight into Heidegger's notion that what does not belong represents a threat to native space. This is admittedly an unusual experiment, and it breaks with the tone of sobriety typically associated with Heideggerian speculation. But my purposes are serious: the animal, the stranger, the other are names for the phenomenon of disruption that Heidegger calls the "deworlding of the world" (*die Entweltlichung der Welt*). As a coda to this chapter I will ask whether Levinas's concept of alterity manages to escape this logic or whether his philosophy actually depends upon, and perhaps *can never truly dismantle*, just this contrast between the familiar and the strange.

BELONGING TO HEIDEGGER

One could say that the concepts of place and displacement lie at the very core of Heideggerian phenomenology. In *Being and Time* one can read that

"Das Zeug hat seinen *Platz*" (The tool has its *place*; *Sein und Zeit*, 103). To anticipate Levinas's transformation of these claims we should also take note of the French translation by Martineau: "L'util a sa *place*."[6]

What is a *Platz*? How is it that the tool "has" its place? To have, to be rooted, to possess: immediately the concept of place appears tied to belonging and to the very "being-there" of being-in-the-world. Heidegger writes: "Der Platz ist je das bestimmte 'Dort' und 'Da' des Hingehörens eines Zeugs." The place is the distinctive "here" and "there" of the belonging of a tool. In the French translation Martineau wrote: "La place est chaque fois le "côté" et le "là" déterminé de l'*être-à-sa-place* d'un util" (*ET*, 142). But Martineau failed to render the important word, *Hingehören*, the "belonging-to," which has to be the point of departure for understanding Heidegger's notion of worldhood: What is the *Hingehören*? If something can belong, then it can also be a foreigner. But what would it be to *not belong*, to be a visitor or an interloper, a stranger amongst the familiar? Is there already something like a *politics* to the modest being of ordinary things?

It is well known that for Heidegger the world is first discovered already rich with practical significance. The thing is not first an object but a tool. And the significance of a tool would be impossible were it not already woven into a world. But this interwovenness, this 'belonging-to-the-world," is not a mere property or a subjective value superadded to the objective thing. It is constitutive of the very being of the tool: "Die jeweilige Hingehörigkeit entspricht dem Zeugcharakter des Zuhandenen, das heißt seiner bewandtnismäßigen Zugehörigkeit zu einem Zeugganzen" (Its belonging-somewhere at the time corresponds to the equipmental character of what is ready-to-hand; that is, it corresponds to the belonging-to which the ready-to-hand has towards a totality of equipment in accordance with its involvements; *SZ*, 102; *BT*, 136).

There is, apparently, a certain *double-character* to the idea of belonging. One could say that "belonging-to-a-place" *itself* "belongs to" (*gehört zu*) the tool as the very being of its usage. A difficult and apparently paradoxical argument, that this phenomenon of "belonging-to" itself *also* and *necessarily* belongs. Perhaps this is an infinite regress. But, if so, it is nonetheless evident that this notion of *Zugehörigkeit* cannot be eliminated from the Heideggerian interpretation of place: "Der platzierbaren Hingehörigkeit eines Zeugganzen liegt aber als Bedingungen ihrer Möglichkeit zugrunde das Wohin überhaupt, in das hinein einem Zeugzusammenhang die Platzganzheit angewiesen wird. Dieses im bewordenden Umgang umsichtig vorweg im Blick gehaltene Wohin des möglichen zeughaften Hingehörens nennen wir die Gegend" (*SZ*, 103). From the tool to the place. We have now learned what first constitutes a "region" (*Gegend, Ort, coin*): the "Zeugzusammenhang" (*l'ensemble d'utils*), the interconnection of practical objects. No single object when standing alone has the right to the dignity of a tool: "Taken strictly, there 'is' no such thing as *an* equipment" (BT, 97). Heidegger says on the contrary that all tools call upon other tools, and they connect to one another in a relation that is both intimate and irrevocable. There is in this *Umwelt* no atomism, no pluralism of monads each of which would exist in a condition of mutual indifference. The entire assembly of tools is instead meaningful *only as a whole*: Not alone but cleaving together they comprise a differentiated but internally affiliated totality. All objects are plunged into this society and first gain their permits of belonging in accordance with what one might call the rules of a phenomenological kinship:

> Zum Sein von Zeug gehört je immer ein Zeugganzes, darin es dieses Zeug sein kann, das es ist. Zeug ist wesenhaft "etwas, um zu . . ." Die verschiedenen Weisen des "Um-zu wie Dienlichkiet, Beiträglichkeit, Verwendbarkeit, Handlichkeit, konstituieren eine Zeugganzheit (SZ, 68).

> To the Being of any equipment there always belongs a totality of equipment, in which it can be this equipment that it is. Equipment is essentially "something in-order-to . . ." A totality of equipment is constituted by various ways of the "in-order-to," such as serviceability, conduciveness, usability, manipulability. (BT, 97)

Each thing must have its proper place within this *Zeugganzheit*. Technically, this is the first and most consequential appearance in Heidegger's philosophy of what Levinas will term a *totality* and against which Levinas will introduce the "infinity" of the other. I will return to the contrast between these two terms at the end of this chapter. But what is it that for Heidegger first permits this totality to cohere? What is it that makes possible the interconnection among its parts? Heidegger writes: "In der Struktur "Um zu" liegt eine Verweisung von etwas auf etwas" (SZ, 68). "In the 'in-order-to' as a structure there lies an *assignment* or *reference* of something to something" (BT, 97). The totality of equipment is like a fabric at whose every juncture one discovers a "*Verweisung*"—a knit, a tie, a *renvoi*, a reference, a sign—in virtue of which each moment of the totality points to and is bound by its neighbor.

An identity through a regime of differences: this theory of signs confirms the spiritual affinity between Heidegger and structuralism. But we should take care to note in passing that this is not yet the "différance" of Derrida: what Heidegger describes as a totality of differences resists the volatile movements of "deferral." The *Verweisung* has the structure of an arrow: it does not *defer* meaning; it *indicates* and in fact *fixes* the being of the world. And the system of these differences is stable, coherent, and familiar. Here, therefore, at the heart of Heidegger's phenomenology, is the technical term which refers us back to Husserl, even while it also anticipates the anthropological logic of difference-in-unity which for Lévi-Strauss will characterize as the elementary structures of kinship.

To understand this structure one must understand the idea of the sign, of indicateon, or *Verweisung*. One could of course follow Heidegger's own references to other texts: In a footnote to *Sein und Zeit*, section 17, "Reference and Signs," we are referred back to Husserl, whose theory of formal reference in the *Ideen* and signs and signification in the *Logische Untersuchungen* provided the initial inspiration for the existential analytic.[7] But these signs cannot multiply without end. Instead we can follow Heidegger's own illustration: "Vorläufig gilt es, eine Verweisungsmannigfaltigkeit phänomenal in den Blick zu bekommen. Zeug is seiner Zeughaftigkeit entsprechend immer *aus* der Zugehörigkeit zu anderem Zeug: Schreibzeug, Feder, Tinte, Papier, Unterlage, Tisch, Lampe, Möbel, Fenster, Türen, Zimmer" (SZ, 68). Later on, it will be helpful to have this same itinerary of things transposed into the French, thus:

En attendant, il importe de procurer un aperçu phénomenal sur une multiplicité de renvois. Conformément à son usualité, un util est toujours *issu* de son appartenance à un autre util: l'util pour écrire, la plume, l'encre, le papier, le sous-main, la table, la lampe, le mobilier, la fenêtre, les portres, la pièce. (*ET*, 104)

Provisionally, it is enough to take a look phenomenally at a manifold of such assignments. Equipment—in accordance with its equipmentality—always is *in terms of* its belonging to other equipment: ink-stand, pen, ink, paper, blotting pad, table, lamp, furniture, windows, doors, room. (*BT*, 97)

Here in all its domesticity is the well-ordered map of Heideggerian space. One can picture the philosopher himself as he develops his example: he casts his glance around him, and he lists each tool as it signals, points, or refers to the next tool, and on to the next, each of them latching onto its immediate neighbor until they form a totality, the familiar world of the writer who finds himself encircled by an ensemble of quotidian things. Most of us who read Heidegger (scholars, accustomed to our offices and our libraries) will feel ourselves immediately at ease with this scene: a familiar example of familiarity.

Another example is even more familiar: the hammer. If Nietzsche taught "how to philosophize with a hammer," it is Heidegger who grasps the hammer as a phenomenological illustration: "Equipment," writes Heidegger, "can genuinely show itself only in dealings cut to its own measure (hammering with a hammer, for example); but in such dealings an entity of this kind is not *grasped* thematically as an occurring Thing, nor is the equipment-structure known as such even in the using" (BT, 98). Heidegger hastens to add that the example itself must be grasped in the right fashion: "[T]he less we just stare at the hammer-Thing, and the more we seize hold of it and use it, the more primordial does our relationship to it become, and the more unveiledly it is encountered as that which it is—as equipment (BT, 98). From such illustrations Heidegger now concludes that the deepest kind of knowledge is only to be found through the intimacy of use. This knowledge lies therefore at the furthest remove from the Platonist's *theoria*: "The ready-to-hand is not grasped theoretically at all, nor is it itself the sort of thing that circumspection takes proximally as a circumspective theme" (BT, 99). The kinship of all things in this scenario is so profound that each individuality and particularity must *retract itself into the totality*: "The peculiarity of what is proximally ready-to-hand is that, in its readiness-to-hand, it must, as it were, withdraw [*zurückzuziehen*] in order to be ready-to-hand quite authentically." Each tool alone must "withdraw" into the plenitude of the work itself. More precisely, the tool simultaneously *both* effaces itself *and* gains its primordial identity *only* when it fuses into the totality of signs:

> Das, wobei der alltägliche Umgang sich zunächst aufhält, sind auch nicht die Werkzeuge selbst, sondern das Werk, das jeweilig Herzustellende, ist das primär Besorgte und daher auch Zuhandene. Das Werk trägt die Verweisungsganzheit, innherhalb derer das Zeug begegnet. (SZ, 70)

> That with which our everyday dealings proximally dwell is not the tools themselves. On the contrary, that with which we concern ourselves primarily is the work—that which is to be produced at the time; and this is accordingly ready-to-hand too. The work bears with it that referential totality within which the equipment is encountered. (BT, 99)

Here is Heidegger's bold affirmation of *totality* as transcendental condition, and as the final law of endogamy for everyday things. Nothing can be what it is if its place is not secured within the global context of use. The "work" itself is accordingly dependent upon the differential network of signs: "The work to be produced, as the '*towards-which*' of such things as the hammer, the plane, and the needle, likewise has the kind of Being that belongs to equipment. The shoe which is to be produced is for wearing (footgear);

the clock is manufactured for telling the time" (BT, 99). A shoe is to be worn; a clock is to tell time. These would be mere truisms were it not for the fact that their purpose is precisely to force our philosophical attention away from metaphysics and back to the most familiar truths. Against all philosophies of essence and accident, substance and property, here we are brought before the apparently self-evident lesson that the usability of the thing—its *mode d'emploi*—is what first constitutes its being. But because we now understand that each thing is joined to another, the work which has been "ordered" only has sense within this intimate system: "The work which we chiefly encounter in our concernful dealings—the work that is to be found when one is "at work" on something—has a usability which belongs to it essentially; in this usability it lets us encounter already the 'towards which' for which *it* is usable. A work that someone has ordered *is* only by reason of its use and the assignment-context [*Verweisungszusammenhanges*] of entities which is discovered by using it" (BT, 99). Repeatedly we find ourselves within these systems of intimate signification. There are many illustrations such as this one, not only in *Being and Time* but throughout Heidegger's writing. But most of them seem to betray the same ethic of familiarity: no object is out of place; no thing does not belong.

We should not underestimate the importance of this analysis. We know what will eventually emerge from the study of the workshop, the writer's office, all of these scenarios of familiar work: Heidegger will want to show us how philosophical "theory" is born at the moment of a *disruption*. The hammer is broken, is too heavy, or is missing. Or, here is the most instructive example, a foreign object intrudes. Something "stands in the way [*im Wege liegt*]" (SZ, §16; S 73): "That to which our concern refuses to turn, that for which it has 'no time,' is something *un*-ready-to-hand in the manner of what does not belong here [*in der Weise des Nichthergehörigen*], of what has not as yet been attended to" (BT, 103; SZ, 73–74).

What shows itself, then, will be a specific manner of being, which Heidegger characterizes as a "not-belonging-here" (*das Nichthergehörigen*). And from this intrusion the entire network of familiarity will be thrown into jeopardy. Suddenly there will be something exogenous, a trespasser, an object without reference. Here, then, are the categories, the *existentialia*, that govern Heidegger's entire phenomenology: *Zuhanden* and *Vorhanden*, the familiar and the strange, that which belongs and that which does not. And the second is always *derivative* yet also, it seems, a *threat* to the first.

DISRUPTION AND DEWORLDING: THE ANIMAL AS THE OTHER

The preceding had the purpose of revisiting certain very familiar passages from Heidegger, so as to show the extraordinary emphasis upon what one might call "the domestic." For what else are Heidegger's little catalogues of objects but voyages into the commonplace? The paper, the pen, the table, the chair: how could a world be *more* familiar for a philosopher than this? The hammer, the shoe, the clock: all of this seems to redescribe, and thereby to *reinforce*, the prose of the world. One might even risk exaggeration to say that throughout the existential analytic there is a certain *moralism of the habitual*: It is not *only* that these lists are familiar. They are in fact *exercises* in familiarity, object lessons in the quotidian character of commonplace life.

We could say also that Heidegger avails himself of a typical double-sense of the example: every example is both an *illustration* (a particular case that stands for the general of the same type) and a *model to be followed*. Every description is also a prescription. An exemplary student is not like all students since he is precisely in his excellence the student all students strive to be. Here, then, we might say that a certain *morality* is built into Heidegger's description, the requirement that every being *must* refer—*be a sign for, point toward* (in French: *renvoi*)—another being within its world. This *renvoi* is imperative since it is the network of signs that first makes possible the intelligibility of a location and the being-there of Being. And what would be a being if it were not the recipient and the messenger of the *renvoi*? It would be a kind of monster: isolated, a breach in domesticity, a being without reference would *not yet* be a being in the relevant sense of the word.

But what would be the fate of this peculiar apparition, the object that doesn't seem to belong in any obvious sense? To answer this question, I will permit myself to indulge the reader's patience with a small (and perhaps slightly humorous) lesson in phenomenological description. This will be an odd exercise, and one can be fairly certain that something so disrespectful has rarely been performed upon a Heideggerian text. Here, again, is Heidegger's description of an office. But this time, let us allow for an intrusion of a singular item at the end. Purely for poetry's sake, let me construct this passage, once again, in French: "L'util pour écrire, la plume, l'encre, le papier, le sous-main, la table, la lampe, le mobilier, la fenêtre, les portes, la piéce, le raton-laveur."

Why this example? In his late reflections on the animal, Derrida permitted his own cat to intrude upon his analysis. But, *pace* Derrida (who observes in his cat something still untamed), a cat after all is a *domesticated animal*. To activate Heidegger's reflections on the foreign and the natural, we require an animal who is clearly *wild*. I have selected this particular animal because it appears in a certain poem by Prévert, "Inventaire" (*Inventory*), a delicate catalogue of random things which belongs to a genre situated somewhere among Breton, Borges, and Edward Lear.[8] But such reasons are incidental. The perversity and obvious humor of such an exercise is meant to show that we are willing to forego anything that might resemble an internal reason. What matters is only that something outside and unforeseen should announce itself in this description, something that startles the philosopher and stares at him with alien eyes.

But Heidegger has anticipated just this kind of intrusion (even if the very definition of an intrusion is that it has not been anticipated). It even has a name: Heidegger calls it a "Störung der Verweisung," a disruption of the reference:

> Die Struktur des Seins von Zuhandenem als Zeug ist durch die Verweisungen bestimmt. Das eigentümliche und selbstverständliche "An-sich" der nächsten "Dinge" begegnet in dem sie gebrauchenden und dabei nich ausdrücklich beachtenden Besorgen, das auf Unbrachbares stoßen kann. Ein Zeug ist unverwendbar—darin liegt: die konstitutive Verweisung des Um-zu auf ein Dazu ist gestört. Die Verweisungen selbst sind nicht betrachtet, sondern "da" in dem besorgenden Sichstellen unter sie. In einer Störung der Verweisung—in der Unverwendbarkeit für . . . wird aber die Verweisung ausdrücklich. (SZ, 74)

> The structure of the Being of what is ready-to-hand as equipment is determined by references or assignments. In a peculiar and obvious manner, the "Things" which are closest to us are "themselves"; and they are encountered as "in themselves" in the concern which can come up against something unusable. When equipment cannot be used, this implies that the constitutive assignment of the "in-order-to" to a "towards-this" has been disturbed. The assignments themselves are not observed; they are rather "there" when we concernfully submit ourselves to them. But *when an assignment has been disturbed*—when something is unusable for some purpose—then the assignment becomes explicit. (BT, 105)

Thanks to our unexpected visitor, the office is disturbed. It is not simply that the philosopher is "taken by surprise" or that something has appeared at the window which perhaps "does not belong." Heidegger's claim is far stronger: The animal does not merely shock the thinker from the calm of his thoughts. The animal in fact *disturbs* the network of the references, just as a fly might send violent vibrations through a spider's web: eine Störung der Verweisung, un renvoi est dérangé. An innocent creature but a dangerous consequence. For if the world itself is nothing but the sense of "location," the "region" or indeed the "environment" (Umwelt), which is formed by these assignments, then once they are shaken, the fragile sense of *place*, or indeed of *Being itself*, threatens to come apart at its seams.

At this point one may ask: What is the *necessity* of this argument? What has compelled Heidegger to regard the unfamiliar as something so radically *other* to the familiar world? Why so radical and so *hyperbolic* a distinction? And, a related question: How is it that Heidegger can insist simultaneously upon the domesticity of Dasein's world but also, elsewhere in the same text, develop so consequential an investigation into the *uncanniness* (*Unheimlichkeit*) of Dasein's ownmost being? Is Dasein *both* at home *and yet also* not at home? And why is it that "home" is for Heidegger always so rigorous a coherence? Dasein is supposed to be without essence or foundation, an opening upon the world, but through its very manner of opening it is also a closure upon only those elements of the world with which it can establish an ontological intimacy. Its commerce with the world seems always a merely local economy and seems necessarily to establish a border. A border has two sides. Within the lines, the world is laced tightly together and shows itself in all its coherence as the *worldliness of the world* (*die Weltlichkeit der Welt; la mondéité du monde*). Beyond the lines, however, there is no reference, no *Verweisung*, no *utillage*, no *Weltlichkeit*. Kant required an "affinity" among my representations, a categorial synthesis without which my experience would be "less than a dream."[9] It seems we have voyaged this far (and notwithstanding Heidegger's characteristic antipathy for what one might call metaphysical dualisms) only to return to a quasi-Kantian universe divided in two between the ordered and the disordered, the familiar and the strange. But how strong a contrast is it? Is the contrast so-powerful between belonging and not-belonging—*Hingehören* and *Nichthergehören*—absolutely without appeal and without modification? Is it necessary or merely provisional?

Let us think again of the little animal who made his appearance at the end of our phenomenological investigation. My deeper reason for indulging his appearance was to exploit Heidegger's own claim that the animal is "poor in world" (*weltarm*). From this it seemed to follow for Heidegger that the animal is indeed an agent of disruption, an *other* that threatens to unravel the worldly bonds of human space. Granted, this contrast between animal and human being may seem a remnant of the metaphysical humanism Heidegger would famously combat several years later. But in the winter semester of 1929–30 he is still content to juxtapose the "world-forming" (*weltbildend*) capacities of the human being with the "world-poor" (*weltarm*) condition of animal life. He even proposes his own zoological illustrations. He mentions, with his own quasiscientific specificity, four animals in all: a beetle, a bee, a lizard, a dog. Concerning all four he issues the stern verdict that, unlike humans, their actions are characterized as only responsiveness or instinct: "The animal is encircled [*umringt*] . . . by the reciprocal drivenness of its drives."[10] The human being by contrast finds itself before a world that is "manifest" (*offenbar*) in the special sense that it is revealed *as an equipmen-*

tal totality, and each of its constituent items is revealed "as" such-and-such within a referential whole.[11]

Hidden in this distinction is not only an afterthought of humanist convention but also a certain philosophically consequential contrast between the wild and the domestic. The animal obeys the sovereign commands of natural instinct, while the human being, though perhaps not enjoying God's full sovereignty over nature, at least enjoys the capacity to mark out its domain with the interpretative signs of daily intention. The contrast between animal and human is, most crucially, the distinction between *world-poor* and *world-forming*. And what happens when the wild imposes itself upon the domestic? This is for Heidegger an occasion for disturbance, crisis, *die Entweltlichung der Welt*. It is as if nature were a threat to the home, an intrusion upon the fragility of the philosopher's carefully articulated world.

But what has authorized Heidegger's initial assumption that the world is a domesticity? Let us consider the animal's appearance as signifying the appearance of *any* displacement, of any item of unexpected "nature." Why is this appearance altogether *so* striking? Must one *always and necessarily* be surprised? Must the world be truly *disturbed* by things unknown? Is the *Umwelt always* and *necessarily* a *coherence*? Are there not ways of living such that one would not cling always to what is most familiar and near? Or can the unfamiliar itself be *made* familiar? Or is it merely a beginning in the adventure of knowledge? Perhaps, we might concede, one must in any case *begin* always with local knowledge. And perhaps this *beginning* is what Heidegger means to describe with all of his tender illustrations of artisanal life. And maybe it is still possible that each encounter that puts us in touch with an elsewhere might eventually widen the local horizon so that the elsewhere might be brought close: a process of learning, a Heideggerian enlightenment. But how would this be possible? How can the displaced find its place? What is required for the not-belonging (the *Nichthergehörige*) to be welcomed into the arms of the familiar? And is the familiar *itself* always familiar? Couldn't the quotidian world *itself* show itself as always already shot through with variations and displacements? With these questions in view, let me turn from the animal back to the human being.

DISPLACED PERSONS

Imagine a person who does not belong. This can be any person, of any color, class, nation, sexuality, or religion. The list of possible markings by which a person is designated as non-native to any context is of course infinite, and we should be skeptical of any attempt to confine this list to only the most familiar categorizations. But one must imagine this person as *displaced* from the place that is considered proper. There is no longer any surrealism to this experiment; it is instead deeply political, and it plays upon all the various logics of nativism and exclusion, familiarity and estrangement, nationalism and xenophobia. Consider, for example, the following historical example.

In the immediate aftermath of the Second World War, the Allies found themselves faced with a bewildering phenomenon. There were hundreds of thousands, indeed *millions* of Europeans who no longer seemed to have a home. The numbers were astronomical. According to the historian Michael Marrus, they included 7.2 million former Soviets from German prison camps, 2 million French, 1.6 million Poles, 700,000 Italians, 350,000 Czechs, 300,000 Dutch, 300,000 Belgians, and many more. It was left to the Allied armies occupying Western Europe to cope with this astonishing mass of human misery. All of them were "DPs" (displaced persons) in the generic sense of the word. And it was this term—in English but also in German, French, and throughout much of Europe—that was used to describe populations uprooted by war. "Displacement" is a trauma consequent upon a loss of proper place, though its intensity and its politics are intelligible only if the "proper" is affirmed.

There can be no doubt concerning the bureaucratic complications of repatriation: Who belonged where? Which countries were to admit whom? Which state or national group bore the responsibility for feeding and housing which refugees? In one of the earliest efforts to cope with this situation, it was proposed in some military manuals that the displaced masses be subdivided into two categories: "refugees" (citizens displaced *within* their own countries but hoping to return home) and "displaced persons" in the strict sense of the term (persons displaced *elsewhere* in Europe whose legal status and future remained uncertain).[12]

This adds up to a perverse but perhaps unavoidable logic: displaced persons with a place, and displaced persons without a place. The example may help to illustrate how difficult it is to escape the rhetoric of belonging and nonbelonging, especially when the places in question are sovereignties, regions bound by informal codes of familiarity, language, religion, and ethnicity, and by more formal rules that extend certain rights only to citizens but never to noncitizens, natives but not temporary residents, laborers with *cartes d'identité* but perhaps not laborers *sans papiers*.

But these political consequences seem to be inscribed in the very beginnings of phenomenology. The political is merely the logical issue of an aesthetic and perhaps ontotheological presuppositions. Already in the workshop, the writer's study, the field, and the forest, Heidegger wished us to recognize as an authentic place only what first showed itself as coherent. In such a place everything was neatly arranged and stowed away, and nothing revealed itself except what belonged: *das Hingehören*. Whatever did not find its place in this sphere burst upon the scene as an alien disturbance.

At the limit, what lay beyond the intimacy of the "proper" could be given no name at all save the nameless name of the "unintelligible."

Domesticity and incoherence, civilization and savage nature (including, we can suppose, the animal)—it is perhaps unsurprising that Heidegger, nourished in his earlier years by the neo-Kantian philosophy, would draw a sharp contrast between the natural and the human. In *The History of the Concept of Time*, Heidegger says: "*Nature is what is in principle explainable and to be explained* because it is in principle incomprehensible. It is *the incomprehensible pure and simple.* And it is the incomprehensible because it is the '*unworlded' world* [i.e., the universe]."[13] The expectation that life *at home* must always exhibit a fundamental coherence exerts a powerful hold on Heidegger's philosophy, so powerful in fact that the "incomprehensible" can only appear as a paradox: a world that is not a world. The world is "deworlded." Heidegger calls this "die Entweltlichung der Welt," which Martineau translated into French as *le monde démondanisé*). [14]

From these reflections one can see perhaps yet again what Derrida so often showed us concerning phenomenology, that Heidegger, despite his best philosophical intentions, was still a captive to ontotheological metaphysics with its longing for foundations. The Heideggerian sense of location with all of its semantic variations—*Gegend, Ort, Platz, Welt, Umwelt*—must always exhibit a certain *stabilitas loci*.

A place that must always fear its displacement, a ground that is always in danger of groundlessness. To emphasize this theme, Levinas on several occasions would quote Pascal's observation that to affirm "my place in the sun" is to set in motion a process that will lead to the usurpation of the entire world. But for Heidegger "world" itself presupposes this ownership and ratifies his campaign for authenticity (*Eigentlichkeit*) and "ownmost" (*eigenste*) being. Upon this primordial intuition will be founded, eventually, all of those so-infamous political-cultural categories—"heritage" (*Erbe*), "people" (*Volk*), "tradition"—that transform *Being and Time* into nothing less than a politics and a polemics: "Dasein has had its historicality so thoroughly uprooted by tradition that it confines its interest to the multiformity of possible types, directions, and standpoints of philosophical activity in the most exotic and alien of cultures; and by this very interest it seeks to veil the fact that it has no ground of its own to stand on [*in den entlegensten und fremdesten Kulturen bewegt in mit diesem Interesse die eigene Bodenlosigkeit zu verhüllen sucht*]" (BT, 43; SZ, 21). Heidegger both *wants* and *denies* this stability: we have no "ground" (*Boden*) and yet we are asked to cleave to the familiar. Only this can explain why Heidegger takes care to warn us in *Being and Time* that we should not go straying after "the most exotic and alien of cultures" even while he simultaneously declares that Dasein exhibits its very own *Unheimlichkeit*. One seeks a ground *elsewhere*, rather than a certain groundlessness that is "one's own": *die eigene Bodenlosigkeit*. But the imperative throughout is clear. Heidegger insists that what *belongs to* Dasein be retained. Even as he resists the language of grounds, Heidegger nonetheless manages to affirm an ontology of the proper, the authentic, that which is most *one's own*.

LEVINAS, OR, THE PERSISTENCE OF DEWORLDING

How would this logic be undone? How could one avoid the unhappy dualisms of strange and familiar, displacement and place? An almost-unthinkable utopia: one would have to imagine a phenomenology without stability, without the persistent moralism of the Heideggerian "authentic." The question that animates Levinas is, how does one move *beyond Being-as-familiarity*?

It has been encouraging to believe that Levinas accomplished just this utopia. But in closing this chapter I would like to suggest that if we regard his philosophy in the light of the above analysis, we may come to suspect that despite his better instincts Levinas remained captive to the Heideggerian dualism after all.

For what is the Other but a being who violates the rules of my native landscape? Alterity for Levinas is the unassimilable, the pure excess of a phenomenon that forbids description and carries its own signification from an elsewhere essentially incommensurable with the references by which I structure my native world. We are accordingly asked to believe that because alterity is what escapes immanence, it can only be the *super*natural, as if all knowledge were a domestication and alterity necessarily a transcendence patterned after divine revelation. But this is once again the drama of Heideggerian deworlding, and it is dependent upon Heidegger's own logic: my encounter with the Other is, after all, the traumatic encounter with an apparition so wild and so unfamiliar it verges on the unintelligible and only allows itself to be described as a *failure* of description. For Heidegger this is the alterity of nature; for Levinas it is the alterity of the non-natural, of the Other (or, perhaps, of God). For Heidegger it is the Störung der Verweisungen, the disruption of the references by which Dasein's world is *a world at all*. For Levinas it is, once again, a disruption and even a revelation, a piercing of the familiar by something beyond.

Every time there is an appeal to the *Other*, one must therefore ask: *Other to what?* And the answer can only be that the *Other* remains *other* only to a horizon that is presumably closed. Seen in this light alterity can only appear if one has already *accepted* the logic of Heideggerian familiarity. The very *logic* of "otherness," in other words, presupposes nativism as the very condition of a phenomenological horizon. Without that presupposition, there would be no trauma to my solipsism, no shock to the Same. This seemingly traumatic appearance of the other—whether it is an animal, a person, the stranger, *the* ethical appeal—simply would not appear *as* other. Otherness, in other words, is otherness *only* within a system that has already conceded a world structured according to the logic of domesticity. The very event of otherness remains operative only if domesticity is presumed.

It is the reputed virtue of Levinasian ethics that it wished to place Heideggerian immanence in relation to transcendence. But the terms by which this ethics is set in motion—totality and infinity—are no less hyperbolic and no more susceptible to amendment. Ethics must be a relation to an absolute, or it fails as ethics and turns into its radical opposite: the state of animal nature as *bellum omnium contra omnes*. Logically this would seem to be almost unavoidable: The Other (*l'Autrui*) can be other only in relation to a sameness that retains its self-identity. And from this it follows that alterity may depend for its own structure upon the logic it claims to disrupt. What is lost to this philosophy, in other words, is a vision of quotidian existence that does not presuppose the narcissism of native space and a prior closure of the phenomenological horizon. The Levinasian appeal to alterity denies this vision and commits instead an illicit repetition of the philosophy it was meant to overcome.

This repetition is illicit, I would suggest, because it arises from an inflationary transformation, by which what should have been purely a political and historical observation was transformed into a metaphysical event within the "logical plot of Being."[15] For it may be helpful to recall that the problem of the displaced person—the person who is treated, one could say, *as* an animal—emerges in specific circumstances in history as a political *effect*. (One might even say that there are conditions in which the animal, too, is treated *merely as an animal*, if by this we are careful to say we mean that it is reduced to the Heideggerian sense, that is, it is treated as "world-poor.") As Hannah Arendt observed, to find oneself displaced, *sans domocile*, or stateless, is to find oneself decontextualized, robbed of the world—robbed, in other words, of the artificial conditions by which human beings can enjoy the fragile experience of freedom.[16] But the terrors and displacements by which the human is "displaced" and even "deworlded" of the world, should not be construed as a metaphysics.[17] To extol such a displacement is to conceive of alterity as if it were the beginning of ethics rather than the end and consequence of ethical violation. It is tempting to think that this is precisely the confusion that continues to inspire those philosophical discourses that rely upon an extravagant contrast of the other and the same. For such discourses serve only to inflate the other into a metaphysical principle rather than dismantling the social conditions of its exclusion.

NOTES

1. Benjamin Hollander, ed., "Paul Celan," in special issue, *Translating Tradition: Paul Celan in France*, Acts 8/9 (1988): 9–14.

2. Walter Biemel and Hans Saner, eds., *Martin Heidegger und Karl Jaspers: Briefwechsel. 1920–1963*,(Frankfurt aM: Vittorio Klostermann, 1990).

3. I have explored similar themes elsewhere; see Peter E. Gordon, "Fidelity as Heresy: Levinas, Heidegger, and the Crisis of the Transcendental Ego," in *Heidegger's Jewish Followers: Essays on Hannah Arendt, Leo Strauss, Hans Jonas, and Emmanuel Levinas*, ed. Samuel Fleischacker (Pittsburgh: Duquesne, 2008).

4. My efforts build upon some of the insights from Derrida's criticism of Heidegger's residual commitments to metaphysical humanism, as well as Derrida's later reflections on the place of the animal in Levinas and Heidegger. See Jacques Derrida, *The Animal That Therefore I Am*, ed. Marie-Louise Mallet, trans. David Wills (Fordham: New York, 2008). For a general summary of the problem of the animal in twentieth-century phenomenology, see Matthew Calarco, *Zoographies: The Question of the Animal from Heidegger to Derrida* (New York: Columbia University Press, 2008).

5. Martin Heidegger, *The Fundamental Concepts of Metaphysics: World, Finitude, Solitude*, trans. William McNeill and Nicholas Walker (Bloomington: Indiana University Press, 1995), ch. 3, 184ff. And on this theme in Heidegger compare Giorgio Agamben, *The Open: Man and Animal*, trans. Kevin Attell (Stanford: Stanford University Press, 2003).

6. Martin Heidegger, *Être et Temps*, trans. Martineau (Paris: Gallimard, 1986), hereafter, *ET*; German quotations are from Heidegger, *Sein und Zeit*. 17th German edition (Tübingen: Niemeyer, 1993). Hereafter *SZ*; English translations are from *Being and Time*, trans. Macquarrie and Robinson (New York: Harper and Row, 1962). Hereafter *BT*.

7. Edmund Husserl, *Ideen zu einer reinen Phänomenologie und phänomenologischen Philosophie*, Band 1, §10 ff.; *Logische Untersuchungen*, Band 1, Kap. 11, and Band 2, 1.

8. Jacques Prévert, "Inventaire," in *Paroles*. Folio (Paris: Gallimard, 1949), 208–10.

9. Immanuel Kant, *Critique of Pure Reason*, trans. Paul Guyer and Allen Wood (Cambridge and New York: Cambridge University Press, 1999), A112.

10. Heidegger, *Fundamental Concepts of Metaphysics*, 249.

11. Ibid., 274 and *passim*.

12. Michael Marrus, *The Unwanted: European Refugees in the Twentieth Century* (Oxford and New York: Oxford University Press, 1985), 300.

13. Martin Heidegger, *The History of the Concept of Time*, trans. T. Kiesel (Bloomington: Indiana University Press, 1985), 217–88. Martin Heidegger, *Prologomènes a l'histoire du concept de temps* (Paris: Gallimard, 2006), 316.

14. On this theme in Heidegger in relation to the natural sciences, see Peter E. Gordon, "Science, Realism, and the Deworlding of the World," in *A Companion to Phenomenology and Existentialism*, trans. Mark Wrathall and Hubert Dreyfus (Oxford: Blackwell, 2006), 425–44.

15. Emmanuel Lévinas, *Totality and Infinity: An Essay on Exteriority*, trans. Alphonso Lingis (Kluwer: Dordrecht, 1991), 289. Whether Levinas escapes this repetition of Heideggerian holism in his later philosophy, specifically in *Otherwise than Being, or, Beyond Essence*, is not a question I can address here.

16. Hannah Arendt, *The Origins of Totalitarianism* (New York: Harcourt, Brace, 1951), 266–51.

17. For an account of Arendt's general turn away from metaphysical accounts of human nature as grounded upon cryptotheology, see Peter E. Gordon, "The Concept of the Apolitical: German Jewish Thought and Weimar Political Theology," in *Hannah Arendt: Verborgene Tradition—Unzeitgemäße Aktualität?* Stefanie Rosenmüller, ed. Heinrich-Böll Stiftung, hrsg. *Deutsche Zeitschrift für Philosophie.* Sonderband 16 (Berlin: Akademie Verlag, 2007), 59–74.

CHAPTER ELEVEN

WHICH OTHER, WHOSE ALTERITY?

The Human after Humanism

Krzysztof Ziarek

For some time, alterity and difference have been the central issues in philosophical, cultural, and political discussions, which have increasingly taken on an ethical tenor. The intensifying process of globalization, with the global operations of capital and the world market, the advances in communications and genetics, and the problem of difference and multicultural societies, has only added urgency to the question of rethinking the place of the human in the contemporary world and the ethics that could follow from such a reconceptualization. What complicates the situation further is the question of what kind of ethics the twenty-first century needs: one based on the centrality of the human, one that would also include animals, or perhaps a more capacious environmental ethics, with the global environment at stake.

Many philosophical discussions of these issues have been informed by Levinas's notion of radical or absolute alterity, the idea that underlies his strenuous polemic with phenomenology and Heidegger's thought in particular. Levinas's critique of Heidegger, and especially of his "understanding" of being, is motivated by the sense, pervading all of Levinas's writings, that the thinking of being is tantamount to comprehension, to understanding beings in terms of universality and totality. To put it simply, for Levinas, "being" leads to the exclusion, domination, or violent suppression of alterity.

The inequities and violence of history flow from this tendency in being toward uniformity and erasure of genuine alterity. This is the reason Levinas underscores the urgency to abandon the climate of Heidegger's philosophy and explains it as the need to leave behind the neutral, uniform, and anonymous realm of being, or of ontology, in order to develop a "radical" ethics, understood as a relation to absolute alterity beyond comprehension, that is, alterity signifying otherwise than being, as the first philosophy prior to ontological thought. In the end, the other for Levinas has to signify otherwise than being:

> Other than Being. Being excludes all alterity. It can leave nothing outside and cannot remain outside, cannot let itself be ignored. The being of beings is the light in which all things are in relationship. Its very night is a mute and concerted hammering out of all things, the obscure labor of the totality, an uninterrupted thrust of generation, growth, and corruption. But the other distinguishes himself absolutely, by absolving himself, moving off, passing, passing beyond being, to yield his place to being.[1]

Levinas clearly pitches these lines as a thinly disguised critique of Heidegger's insistence on thinking being as the key to transforming contemporary philosophy and leaving the purview of metaphysical thought. Yet when Heidegger himself writes about being, he presents his critique of metaphysics in terms of making possible alterity and letting otherness be, which is not dissimilar from Levinasian aims. Writing in *Contributions to Philosophy* about the importance of nothingness and nihilation, Heidegger remarks:

> *Holding sway in terms of the not, it [be-ing {Seyn}] makes possible and enforces otherness [Andersheit] at the same time.*
>   But whence comes the utmost confinement to the one and the other and thus to the either or?
>   The uniqueness of the not that belongs to be-ing and thereby the uniqueness of the other follows from the uniqueness of be-ing.[2]

"Being excludes all alterity"; being "makes possible and enforces otherness." This simple juxtaposition reveals how different the sense of being in Levinas is from the one at issue in Heidegger's thought. One could say that being (*l'être*) in Levinas has the same, or at least quite similar, meaning that the metaphysical concepts of being and beingness (*Seiendheit*) have in Heidegger, concepts which Heidegger's thought relentlessly critiques and destructures in order precisely to allow for an other sense of being, that is, for the sense of being as not just making possible but in fact enforcing otherness, radically opposed to the notion of being as excluding all alterity. *Sein* or *Seyn* (being) in Heidegger clearly does not correspond to what *l'être* means in Levinas. That is why those who take Levinas at his word (about the unavoidable allergy of being to alterity in Heidegger) and simply follow his critique, perpetuate a persistent erasure of the pivotal difference between Levinas's understanding of being (and the way his texts tend to present Heidegger's understanding of being) and Heidegger's own (re)thinking of being as the event (*das Ereignis*). For is not Levinas after all seeking a notion of the other that would guarantee or enforce otherness, preventing it from any attempt at assimilation, exclusion, or presentation?

My aim here is not to resuscitate this by now quite old polemic but to explore instead the stakes of the often neglected or unremarked difference between *l'être* and *Seyn* and the implications this difference has for what can be seen as the differently ethical tenor of Levinas and Heidegger. Keeping this difference between *l'être* and *Seyn* in mind, I want to point to two crucial points of proximity between Levinas and Heidegger, so far mostly ignored in the critical discussions of their work. First of all, in their different articulations of the human after humanism, in Heidegger's "Letter on Humanism" and Levinas's *Humanism of the Other Man*, they both indicate that at stake in their work is the dignity of the human. As Levinas puts it in "Humanism and Anarchy," "what is at stake is giving back to him [man] the highest dignity."[3] This means for Levinas a radical shift from the humanism of the ego, that is, humanism based on the notion of the subject as the consciousness of all being, of everything that exists, to the humanism of the other human, that is, a humanism founded upon the unpresentable, absolute alterity of the other (human) as a singular being. Levinas's writings on the humanism of the other human being can be seen as his response to Heidegger's critique of humanism in "Letter on Humanism," a response which does not, however, pay its due to the fact that Heidegger too makes his critique pivot on the notion of the dignity of the human, dignity which has not been given proper attention by metaphysics.

> "The 'substance' of man is ek-sistence" says nothing else but that the way that man in his proper essence becomes present to Being is ecstatic inherence in the truth of Being. Through this determination of the essence of man the humanistic interpretations of man as *animal rationale*, as "person," as spiritual-ensouled-bodily being, are not declared false and thrust aside. Rather, the sole implication is that the highest determinations of the essence of man in humanism still do not realize the proper dignity [*Würde*] of man. To that extent the thinking in *Being and Time* is against humanism. But this opposition does not mean that such thinking aligns itself

against the humane and advocates the inhuman, that it promotes the inhumane and deprecates the dignity of man. Humanism is opposed because it does not set the *humanitas* of man high enough.[4]

Heidegger underscores the fact that "the *humanitas* of man" is not thought "high enough" by metaphysics in order to forestall the misunderstanding of his opposition to humanism as an ethical failing of his thought, or worse, as an implicit endorsement of violence or inhumanness. As he remarks, his critique of humanism is not tantamount to "a defense of the inhuman and a glorification of barbaric brutality" (*BW*, 249), because "opposition to 'humanism' in no way implies a defense of the inhuman but rather opens other vistas" (*BW*, 250).[5] The reason *humanitas* has not been thought "high enough" is because it has become obscured by the metaphysical privilege given to reason, spirit, values, and technology. As a result, metaphysical humanist articulations of the human, whether Renaissance, Marxist, existentialist, or Christian, all fail in different ways to think the dwelling characteristic of being human. The distinctive "dignity" of the human being comes from the way humans dwell, that is, participate in the event of being. The "dignity" (*Würde*) of the human dwelling does not lie first in rationality and the technological culture it has produced, or in spirituality and the culture of values it has engendered. It is "higher" than these human values in a very specific sense: it points beyond the human to the dignity and worthiness of being.

As is evident, Levinas and Heidegger approach the question of the dignity of the human from two different perspectives. While they agree that the humanist ways of thinking the human have failed to address the dignity of the human being, they see this dignity as informed by different relations: for Levinas, it is the relation to the radical alterity of the other, and for Heidegger, it is the relation to being as a way of dwelling and maintaining the play of the fourfold. What is even more interesting is that in both cases this rethinking of the human after humanism pivots on a critique of the notion of power. Levinas remarks, "The human only lends itself to a relation that is not a power" (*BPW*, 10). In *Totality and Infinity*, Levinas explains the subject's relation to the other in terms of the disabling of the subject's power, a kind of power not to be able to exercise power over the other: "The expression the face introduces into the world does not defy the feebleness of my powers, but my ability for power [*mon pouvoir de pouvoir*]."[6] The face signifies an undoing of the very powers of the subject, the powers of representation and comprehension. In this context, the ethical comes to mean then a disabling of power and an opening of a relation that does not lend itself to power.

In *Besinnung*, recently translated into English as "Mindfulness," Heidegger makes clear that his transformation of thinking has at stake freeing or releasing being from the self-overpowering operations of power: "Be-ing: the *powerless* [*Machtlose*]—*beyond power and lack of power* [*Unmacht*]—better, what is outside power and lack of power, and fundamentally unrelated to such" (166).[7] The terms Heidegger uses—*das Machtlose, machtlos,* and *macht-frei*—point to the essential unrelatedness of being (*Seyn,* not *Seiendheit* or Levinasian *l'être*) to power: being is detached from power, released (*losgelöst*), and as such beyond power and powerlessness, conceived inevitably as lack of power: *Unmacht* or *Ohnmacht.* For Levinas, being or *l'être* is power par excellence, power of and as comprehension, totality, and universality. For Heidegger, *Seyn* as the event is a letting-be seen as a releasement, disengagement, and freedom from power, as well as from its ghostly companion, powerlessness. As the power-free, being cannot be matched by any power or superpower, simply because it does not happen in terms of power: the radical otherness of its event does not submit to power. That is why the "less" is *macht*-loss (power-less) does not indicate a deficiency or lack but rather a refusal and an otherwise than power. "Considering the ground of its unfolding, be-ing is never power and, therefore, it is also never powerlessness [*Ohnmacht*]. If nevertheless we name be-ing the power-less [*das Macht-lose*], this cannot mean that be-ing is deprived of power. Rather the name power-less [or better, power-free] should indicate that given its unfolding, be-ing continues to be detached [*losgelöst*] from power. However *this* power-less *is* mastery" (B, 170/M, 192–93). Heidegger presents the power-less, understood as the power-free, precisely as dignity: and the dignity of the human lies in the specific task of allowing being to show that power and the power formed relations are in essence (*wesentlich*) foreign to being.

Levinas's project is to release the other as a singular being, or as the face, from power. The face signifies precisely the emptying of (my) power over the other's alterity. I can kill the other, but such a killing only confirms my lack of power over the other's otherness. The other lends himself only to a relation that is not a power, which means that ethics is a relation otherwise than power. Since Levinas sees being (*l'être*) as the paramount instantiation of the relation of power, annulling all alterity ("Being excludes all alterity"), his ethics has to come "prior to" or on the hither side of being: otherwise than being. Being becomes the supreme threat to the other's unrepresentable difference or alterity, and the language of being becomes tantamount to the erasure of otherness. As such, being is capable only of comprehension and of being "said," since it disallows any saying that cannot be inscribed into what is said. That is why Saying (*le Dire*) in Levinas is reserved for the way in which alterity, the face, ruptures all ways of presenting, all figures and devices of representation. While being is the said, the other's alterity becomes the saying which ruptures the said with its signification of otherwise than being.

Heidegger's writings from 1936 through the end of World War II make clear that the "other," nonmetaphysical thinking he seeks to develop as a critique of modernity and modern operations of power (*Machenschaft* or machination) aims to release being, and thus all beings and the relations among them, from power. While this releasement from power obviously includes the relation to the other (human), it does not limit the power-free to human beings but instead extends the releasement to all kinds of others: humans, animals, things. If for Levinas the other is other precisely by virtue of not lending itself to a relation of power, for Heidegger, other beings, including things, when they are let be, are given in their otherness precisely by way of relations that are power-free (*machtlos*). The guarantee of ethics for Levinas is an otherwise to being, a sense beyond meaning, a direction toward alterity, an openness and subjection to the other: an undo-ing of the power of the subject, which becomes tantamount to the release of alterity from the power of presentation and comprehension, the power which Levinas associates in his work with being. What makes ethics pos-sible, and, in the same gesture, also inevitable, is the fact that the other does not submit to power but instead signifies otherwise than power. It is the singularity of this each time other "face" that ensures the possibility of ethics without guaranteeing "my" ethical behavior. The election signified by the other's evasion of power makes both ethical and unethical behavior possible: an ethics beyond any and all ethical prescriptions, the trace of an ethical relation beyond power.

This is the point where Levinas and Heidegger almost meet but which also signals a crucial difference between them, the difference which, as I suggested earlier, pivots on the distinction between Levinasian *l'être* and Heideggerian *Seyn*. In Levinas, the singularity of the other, manifested as face, is what frees itself, and possibly also my relation to the other, from power. In Heidegger, it is the nothingness, the nihilating force of being, which, enforcing otherness, makes the other possible as singular, and thus as other. The radical difference of *Seyn* from being understood metaphysically as beingness (*Seiendheit*) consists in the fact that while beingness assimilates and excludes alterity, *Seyn* not only makes it possible but in fact enforces it. For Levinas, the other singularly frees itself from the power of being (of *Seindheit?*) to erase its alterity and incorporate it in its universalizing and totalizing "said." For Heidegger, it is the nihilating vector or force of *Seyn* that lets each being happen as singular, enforcing its otherness against the conceptual pull of thought. It is *Seyn* that renders the other (human) sin-gular and allows for the ethical signification of otherness.

In this context, it is impossible to mistake Heidegger's *Seyn* for the significations Levinas assigns to being (*l'être*): totality, universality, anonym-ity. In fact, *Seyn* and its otherness-enforcing event is, within the horizon of

Heidegger's thought, what makes otherness and difference, and thus also the ethical relation, possible to begin with. If, from Levinas's perspective, the thought of being remains deaf to the claim of alterity and thus precludes ethics—and is, in fact, essentially unethical—for Heidegger, the thinking of being (in the sense of *Seyn*) as the event makes otherness possible and opens the possibility of ethical relations: ethical relation to the other (human) for sure, but also relations to nonhuman others, not only animals but things too. It is possible to say that this thinking of being (*Seyn*) is protoethical through and through in Heidegger, as it would precisely allow for being to unfold as power-free and in the same gesture would also make possible and enforce otherness. For Levinas, it is only the other's relation to the subject that is not a relation of power, but instead an ethical exposition free from power. By contrast, for Heidegger, relations to any and all beings can be part of *Gelassenheit* or releasement: not only the human otherness signifies as power-free but all relations to otherness can become otherwise than power in the mode of *Gelassenheit* or a releasement from power, for the very possibility of otherness hinges upon freedom from power, which means that it depends upon being happening as power-free. In this perspective, one could see Levinas's thought not in terms of its proclaimed disjunction from Heidegger's but as part of a broader power-free relationality, which includes relation to the (human) other—ethics in Levinas's sense—but opens beyond it toward animality, things, or world.

This moment of proximity with respect to freedom from power marks, however, also Levinas's critical difference from Heidegger: for Levinas, the properly ethical is only the relation to the (human) other. While Levinas does leave open the possibility that certain animals can have an animal face, that is, an ethical signification, it is clear that his thought locates the human, and its relation to the trace of illeity (the divine), as the basis and guarantor of the ethical relation. Writing about subjectivity as an inwardness turned inside out, Levinas remarks, "This inwardness is an obedience to a unique value without anti-value, which it is impossible to escape, but which, 'akin' to the subject, is neither chosen nor not-chosen . . . This value is, by an abuse of language, named. It is named God" (*CPP*, 136). The absolute alterity of the other means that the other absolves himself from any and all relations, that the height of the other's ethical signification exceeds all relations, relations which Levinas takes to be in principle thematizable. Relations cannot escape being "said": they are thematized, (re)presented, and comprehended, thus leaving no room for alterity. The only form of "relation" that is ethical is, in fact, a nonrelation: an absolving of the other's alterity from power. The other is, therefore, possible only as absolutely other: "But the other distinguishes himself absolutely, by absolving himself, moving off, passing, passing beyond being, to yield his place to being" (*BPW*, 74).

In another place, however, Levinas seems to break out of this "strict" sense of absolute otherness reserved for humans, as he indicates that the trace of alterity inscribed in the ego signifies responsibility for the whole world: "The ego, I, am a man supporting the universe, 'full of things.' This responsibility or saying, prior to being and entities, is not said in ontological categories. Modern anti-humanism is perhaps not right in not finding in man, lost in history and in order, the trace of this pre-historical and an-archical saying" (CPP, 139). For a moment here the "responsibility or saying" seems to extend to the entire universe, "full of things," and not just to the other (human). The human (subject) would claim its importance and dignity against modern antihumanism by virtue of bearing the trace of the ethical saying, with responsibility and saying no longer limited to the human other but embracing and "supporting the universe, 'full of things.'"

This unusual, even surprising, moment in Levinas, could perhaps be seen as his rare "Heideggerian" moment. For we have to remember that for Heidegger, it is precisely things that bear open and offer the world: "But how does the thing presence? The thing things. Thinging gathers. Eventuating the fourfold, it gathers the fourfold's stay, its while, into something that stays for a while: into this thing, that thing."[8] What is much more characteristic and familiar in Levinas's approach to things, however, are the following statements: "If things are only things, this is because the relation with them is established as comprehension" (BPW, 9). Or "To relate oneself to beings qua beings means, for Heidegger, to let beings be, to comprehend them as independent of the perception which discovers and grasps them" (BPW, 6). One can accept Levinas's judgment here only if one interprets letting be as comprehension, as he proposes, which certainly does not correspond to Heidegger's thinking of letting be as releasement from power, or as a power-free relating. For letting be signifies above all a sparing and a saving, and not comprehension, sparing and saving that need to be extended and offered to things, to allow them precisely not to be merely things but to gather and bear the world.

> The thing stays—gathers and unites—the fourfold. The thing things world . . .
>
> If we let the thing be present in its thinging from out of the worlding world, then we are thinking of the thing as thing . . .
>
> If we think of the thing as thing, then we spare and protect the thing's presence in the region from which it presences. Thinging is the nearing of world. Nearing is the nature of nearness. As we preserve the thing qua thing we inhabit nearness. The nearing of nearness is the true and sole dimension of the mirror-play of the world. (PLT, 178–79)

Insofar as things stay the world, letting things be things allows humans not only to take part in the play of the world, to remain in its nearness, but to maintain its play as, in essence, power-free. By contrast, for Levinas only the other proposes and offers the world by thematizing it: "The Other, the signifier . . . manifests himself by proposing the world, by *thematizing* it" (TI, 96). Thematizing the world allows the other to signify its alterity otherwise than the being which his discourse thematizes, and thus to interrupt the very process of thematization through the unpresentable trace of his or her radical alterity. The thematization of the world matters ethically in Levinas only insofar as it allows one to offer the world to the other, to thematize it so that it can be a gift. In Heidegger, the world is open in its play and maintained in its power-free being for the sake of its being power-free, and not simply for the sake of the other. In Levinas, the world cannot fail but to submit to thematization, to be re-presented and turned into a totality of the said. To prevent the assimilation of the other's radical alterity into the totality of the said, one needs the interruption of the saying, saying conceived specifically as the rupture of thematization, or as unthematizable otherness which withdraws and refuses itself to themes, comprehension, or concepts.

Heidegger offers us a different understanding of language and saying, where the very occurrence of the world as the event disallows not only the ultimate thematization of the other (human) but of any, always singular, being. "That we cannot know the essence of language—according to the traditional concept of knowledge, defined in terms of cognition as representation—is certainly not a defect; it is rather the advantage by which we advance to an exceptional realm, the realm in which we dwell as the *mortals*, those who are needed and used for the speaking of language. The saying will not allow itself to be captured in any assertion. It demands of us a telling silence as regards the propriative, way-making movement in the essence of language, without any talk *about* silence."[9] The silence which marks the withdrawal of the saying from the said ruptures thematization and comprehension and continuously relodges the unsaid, silence, and the saying in the various forms of representational discourse. These silent marks of the saying in the way-making of language cannot fail to be recognized as the traces of otherness, intrinsically dislocating and opening what can be said. The saying marks the way in which being has always already made otherness possible precisely by the way it withdraws from the said: the withdrawal (of being) is the saying of being, which is the saying of beings into their said, thematized expression. But as the saying lets beings be brought into words and thus said, this very letting also marks the silent refusal of being to what is being said. Thus the saying both makes the said possible and marks being's withdrawal from the said.

Being makes possible and enforces otherness precisely by the very way
in which it gives to be, withdrawing and refusing itself so that the time-
space is opened for beings to be: to exist and to be said or thematized in
their existence. This withdrawal and refusal is the way being "says" beings:
its saying both allows beings to be brought into words and represented,
and simultaneously ruptures this very process of thematization to maintain
otherness as possible. The saying makes the said possible but makes it possible in a way that enforces otherness, marking the said with silence and
withdrawal. Again, the difference between Heidegger's *Sagen* and Levinas's
le Dire lies not in the way in which they "signify" otherness through the
rupturing effect of its withdrawal from the said but in the scope, as it were,
or in the range, of the saying's rupture.

Though his characterizations of the saying clearly echo Heidegger's
reflections on language, Levinas consistently ascribes the capacity for the
saying exclusively to the (human) face. Only the human other signifies by
way of the saying, since only this other has the capacity to interrupt the
thematization of his/her alterity. In Heidegger, the saying brings into the
open the play of the world as the fourfold, but does so in a way that simultaneously marks the world with the trace of being's withdrawal, so that the
thematization of the world as world, of humans as others, but also of animals
and things, never becomes complete or never turns into the said without
a remainder. In other words, it is not only the other (human) whose face
constitutes a remainder over signification and thematization, or, in short,
the ethical saying. Rather, each being comes to be said in such a way that
its alterity is "spared" and protected. Heidegger says that only when beings
can be let be can the world happen as world, that is, as a world that is said
precisely in a way disallowing its thematization without a remainder. While
it appears that the world, with animals and things in it, can be totally thematized, or, more precisely, thematized as a totality in Levinas, in Heidegger,
such thematization entails a forgetting of the in essence power-free disposition of being and a forcing of beings into power relations. When being is let
be in its power-free sway, then no being comes to be thematized without a
remainder, for being's capacity to make possible and enforce otherness disallows such thematization. On this point, the difference between Levinas and
Heidegger appears to be clear: while only the other can evade the power of
thematization because being for Levinas cannot escape forcing beings to be
thematized, for Heidegger, being as the event is the power-free nihilation,
which disallows the closure of thematization and makes possible the marking
of each being with the trace of unthematizable otherness.

While in Levinas the interruption of the saying is understood as
the trace of the otherness left by a human being, Heidegger, interestingly
enough, introduces a critical distinction between the trace and the hint in

Mindfulness, where the trace signals a being's otherness, and the hint, by contrast, marks being's capacity to enforce otherness. Being, as Heidegger puts it, does not leave traces: "But be-ing never leaves a trace in beings. Be-ing is the trace-less; is never to be found among beings as a being." This is the case not because being allows for a thorough thematization which would absorb and cancel "all alterity" (*BPW*, 74), as Levinas suggests, but because it is being which, enforcing otherness, allows the other to leave a trace. Only a being can leave a trace, and in Levinas, only a human being can leave a trace. Being, however, is not even approachable through beings, or through the ontological difference, that is, through the difference of being from beings, as Heidegger argues in *Mindfulness*: "Be-ing is and will nonetheless never be a being" (*M*, 175). Since it can never be a being, being does not leave traces: it remains trace-less or trace-free (*spur-los*), unencumbered by the way in which a being signifies its alterity. Instead, as Heidegger remarks, being gives a hint (*Wink*), and its hint is precisely the hint of its having made possible and enforced otherness. "Event (*Ereignis*) lets being as such arise in that it refuses itself without a trace, and so simply *is*" (*M*, 178). Heidegger indicates that beingness (*Seindheit*, possibly corresponding to what Levinas calls "being") is the trace of an uninterpretable, traceless trace. This "traceless trace" is in fact not a trace strictly speaking, since only beings leave traces, but instead a hint, which only being can give: while beings leave traces, being gives a hint. When Heidegger indicates that being (*Seyn*) happens as traceless, he makes this tracelessness parallel to being's capacity to be power-free: insofar as being happens as power-free, that is, as unrelated to power, it is also traceless, which means that it gives a hint of the power-free. "What raises no claim, is trace-less and power-less, is hardly credible to the representation that knows only beings. And when such representation concedes that 'the claim-,' 'the trace-,' and the 'power-less' *is*, representation must assess it right away as what is feeble and nothing and thus lacks what distinguishes beings as the actual (the effective)" (*M*, 178). The suffix *–los*, used three times in this quotation, indicates that being's event happens as principally disengaged from and free of traces, claims, and power.

While at the first glance this distinction between a "trace" and a "hint" might seem like splitting hairs, it is a consequence of Heidegger's drastic and far-reaching rethinking of the notion of difference, carried out in *Contributions to Philosophy* and *Mindfulness*. The distinction between "trace" and "hint" suggests that being cannot be thought in terms that pertain to beings, that is, terms such as "difference," "trace," "claim," "power," perhaps even "otherness." This is the case because only a being can make a claim and exercise power and thus perhaps can leave a trace (of its alterity). By contrast, being happens as a traceless and powerless letting be. Unlike beings, it lacks, therefore, "actuality," seems "feeble" (ineffective), and appears as "nothing": as the anonymity of the absence of beings. Heidegger consistently reverses these "negative" connotations, taking them away from the grasp of binary thinking: powerless is not the absence of power but otherwise than power, that is, the power-free; tracelessness is not ineffectiveness or being so weak and powerless as not to be able to leave a trace but instead indicates the nobility of letting be without making any claims. In short, the suggestion that being is trace-free and claimless comes from Heidegger's insistence that thinking needs to leave behind the ontological difference (between being and beings), as being (*Seyn*) cannot be approached in terms of difference (or identity).

It would take a different study to show how this rethinking takes place over many years in Heidegger's work and explain the pressure that his demand for the other beginning, that is, for thinking to begin "again," and this time not through differentiation and identification but otherwise, that is, in terms of the nearness marked by the hyphen in Da-sein, finds its reflection in the difficult and often misunderstood idiom of nearness, time-play-space, giving, and nihilation in his later texts. It will have to suffice here to indicate that the most significant implication of this other beginning is that being's refusal happens "without trace" and, therefore, requires a thinking that would step back from the thought of difference and otherness, and invent a new idiom, the idiom of giving and event, of *es gibt*, "prior" to the notion of identity (the subject) and difference (its other). When Heidegger writes that beingness (*Seiendheit*) is the trace of a trace-free trace, he seems to suggest that beingness constitutes the trace of the way in which the event of being happens, the way it gives time and being. In short, beingness is the trace of the hint of being, the trace of the hint of the way *es gibt*, it gives/there is. Only within the time-play-space given with the hint of the way *es gibt*, can there be traces of otherness. In this context, it appears that Heidegger wants to think the hint of *es gibt* apart from the manner in which one can think the way that otherness "traces."

For Levinas, the trace is always (and already) the trace of the other, that is, of the other human. For Heidegger, traces of otherness and difference are thought apart from the hint of being's event, of *es gibt*. It remains a question for another occasion as to whether and how the Levinasian *trace* is related, or not, to Heidegger's double discourse of *Spur* and *Wink*, or whether we possibly have here three distinguishable, though interlaced, ways of tracing and hinting: namely, the trace of the "absolute other," the trace of (any) other being, and the hint of *es gibt*. These distinctions would be merely "academic" was it not for the fact that they do lead to quite different senses of the dignity of the human (after humanism) mentioned at the beginning of this essay. Levinas's response to what he sees as the displacement of the (human) subject from its central position in being reestablishes the dignity of the human through its election to be responsible for the other. "Modern antihumanism, which denies the primacy that the human person, a free end in itself, has for the signification of being, is true over and above the reasons it gives itself. It makes a place for subjectivity positing itself in abnegation, in sacrifice, and in substitution. Its great intuition is to have abandoned the idea of person as an end in itself. The Other (*Autrui*) is the end, and me, I am a hostage" (*BPW*, 94). The relinquishing of the idea of the human being as an end in itself makes room for conceiving the human in terms of an anarchic responsibility for the other. The displacement of the humanism of the subject by the humanism of the other (human) radically exposits and reverses the relation subject/other: the subject becomes turned inside out, so that its primary "signification" is not consciousness or identity, but the sign, or the face, of the other. It is clearly an inversion of anthropocentrism, if by anthropocentrism one means the (human) subject-oriented thematization of being and experience. In Levinas we have instead the other-oriented (de)thematization of being, the said interrupted by the saying of alterity, such that the subject can come into being only as always already called to responsibility, claimed by the other, even taken hostage by him/her. Before coming to (be) itself, the subject is nothing other than the trace of this claim of alterity, the claim which opens up ethics and envelops all being in an an-archic ethical signification. It seems, therefore, appropriate to see Levinas's ethics as a kind of "other" anthropocentrism: both an other version of the preeminence of the human, though this time of the other human and not of the I/subject, and the anthropocentrism of the other. For what becomes radically dislocated in Levinas's thought is obviously the priority of the subject but not the priority of the human, as many commentators have remarked. In fact, the displacement of the human subject from its central position allows for the long overdue recognition of the "proper" direction and orientation, of *le sens* or the "sense," of being: the other. The dignity of the human in Levinas is really the dignity of the other, or, more exactly, an election or elevation to dignity by way of the other. "My" dignity is my election to responsibility for the other demanded by the other's excessive "height," marking the other's alterity. The dignity of the human being flows from bearing this trace of the other's alterity.

If in Levinas the dignity of the human is owed to the alterity of the other human, in Heidegger, that dignity comes from the capacity of the human to be Da-sein, specifically to be-there as the site for being to give there to be (beings) in a way which would remain free from power. In its relation to Da-sein, in its being-there, the human is not considered primarily for itself, for its own sake, or for the sake of the other (human), but instead for the sake of being. And what takes priority here is in a way not the human in relation to the Da, but the Da itself, and specifically insofar as the Da opens up in relation to the human. Heidegger's critical point is that what unfolds essentially (*Wesen*) in humans is not human to begin with, because it is the Da, the clearing of being, to which humans belong and in relation to which they come to be "human" in the first place. Speaking about "the clearing of being," Heidegger remarks: "But this domain is through and through not human, i.e., not determinable and not sustainable by *animal rationale* and even less by the *subjectum*. The domain is not at all a being but rather belongs to the essential unfolding of be-ing . . . The priority of Da-sein is not only the opposite of any manner of humanizing [*Vermenschung*] of man; this priority grounds a totally other essential history of man, one that is never graspable in terms of metaphysics and thus also not in terms of 'anthropology'" (*CP*, 345, modified).

This priority of Da-sein does not mean, however, that relations to others, human or otherwise, are not important. Rather, it suggests that the relation to other humans, animals, or things, need to be thought from within the Da, understood as the site where the hint of being's refusal, of *es gibt*, is heeded. The shift from Dasein as the human manner of being to Da-sein as the site (*Ort*) of *es gibt*, begins explicitly with *Contributions to Philosophy*, where the Da in Da-sein both is and is not "human" strictly speaking. The Da is the site of being's always already beginning as the event, but this event can take place only with the human participation in the Da, and, more precisely, with the human having been displaced into and as the "there" of being, as Da-sein. It is important to remember here that, although not human, the Da does not open up without the humans, or more properly, the mortals, being "there."

Heidegger's consideration of the human after humanism is concerned less with the human "as such" than with exploring the relation to being, that is, with understanding the extent to which the access to the question of being happens always through Da-sein, and thus through the human participation in the Da. What interests Heidegger is being's unfolding as the event, for the event and its beginning pivot precisely on the transformation of the human being into the Da of Da-sein, that is, into the site of the hint of the event. For this reason the "strange" humanism which Heidegger proposes in "Letter on Humanism" is less explicitly about thinking the human or the interhuman than about nearness to being: "It is a humanism that thinks the humanity of man from nearness to Being. But at the same time it is a humanism in which not man but man's historical essence is at stake in its provenance from the truth of Being" (*BW*, 245). Since it is being that "makes possible and enforces otherness," any thinking of relations to others, whether human or not, needs to open up from within nearness to being. Not from the subject or from the other human but from within nearness to being, that is, nearness to the hint of *es gibt*. It may not be farfetched to say here that for Heidegger, the trace of the other (human) would be possible only within the hint of being's event, that is, within the site (*Ort*) of the traceless and power-free *es gibt*.

To restore the "proper" dignity to the human, the human must be (dis)placed in relation to being, and so it becomes necessary—however paradoxical it might seem at first—to abandon the humanistic, and metaphysical, conceptualization of the human being, and of its others, and to reclaim instead the dignity, the worth (*Würde*), of being. The worthiness of being lies in its specific temporal-historical force of nihilation, which enables possibilities and opens being as the futurally unfolding nexus of relations, to human others, things, and animals, and thus to the ceaselessly reenacted world. In short, the "dignity" of being is the event, its *es gibt*, whereby the metaphysical determinations and thematizations of being, as well as beings, are called into question so that the event can be let be with its nihilating force, which makes possible and enforces otherness. The dignity of being is the each time singular possibility of the freedom of its event, its release from the historically determining metaphysical frameworks, that is, its "freedom" from power.

What Heidegger calls the worthiness of being, taken as its force of nihilation, provides the perspective in which it is possible to recognize the dignity of the human. To the extent to which the humans can enter into the Da and be as Da-sein, their dignity lies in the specific capacity to be attentive and heed the originative force of nihilation unfolding as the Da, that is, to give its due to the all pervading dignity of being.[10] This dignity of being, being which happens by way of enforcing otherness, makes it possible for the other to "be" other: namely, for things to be other as things, which gather and stay the world, for animals to be other in their specific ways of being, and for the human other to trace his or her alterity. To say that the dignity of the human is the nonhuman Da-sein means to give heed to the worthiness of being, that is, to the worthiness of that which enables and enforces otherness. If for Levinas the dignity of the human after humanism lies in the other, that is, in the humanism of the other human, for Heidegger, it comes from the recognition of the hint that *es gibt* (it gives) and, one could say, therefore, also the hint of "it gives otherness."

Levinas repeatedly affirms that the other is absolute in his or her alterity, absolved of all relations. Yet relations from which Levinas wants the other to be absolved, that is, to be beyond and otherwise than them, are relations of power: the other does not lend himself to a relation that is a power, as he puts it. For Heidegger, the hint of *es gibt* points precisely to the possibility of being as power-free, and thus to the event, in which "there is" otherness and there are "others" as originarily power-free, disengaged from power relations. It seems to me that one could trace here

KRZYSZTOF ZIAREK

a genuine proximity between Levinas and Heidegger, a proximity that rests in their attempt to think a (non)relation free from power. The difference that really matters here lies in the fact that Levinas gives the absolution from power only to the other (human), to the force of the nakedness of the other's face. Heidegger sees the event, the *es gibt*, as unrelated to power, as disengaged from violence, mastery, and dominion, or, in short, as power-free. This difference in the scope of power-free (non)relations leads to the difference between Levinasian ethics of the other as apparently pertaining to interhuman relations and Heideggerian poetic thinking of the power-free relationality, in which being is granted as power-free to all beings. It lets them be as what they are: things, humans, animals; in short, it lets the world "world," as Heidegger remarks.

I have tried to open here to questioning a commonly held idea that Levinas's thought has to be opposed to Heidegger's, because, as Levinas himself claims, the thought of being is inimical to ethics. I prefer instead to see Levinasian ethics as running parallel to Heidegger's understanding of being as unfolding power-free, granted, of course, Levinas's much more intense investment in making the ethics of the human other into the first philosophy. For would a fleshed out ethics of the power-free relationality be that much different from ethics conceived as a relation that does not lend itself to a power? It would be different in so far as Heidegger's *Seyn* makes possible otherness in its various significations and thus also makes possible ethical relation to all beings, human and nonhuman alike. But this difference would clearly not only not mean that Heidegger's approach to being somehow precludes ethics, or is intrinsically nonethical or simply indifferent to ethics, but rather that Levinas's thought, in the context of Heidegger's power-free event, remains limited to the human or ambiguous at best about the scope of ethics, especially about the relation between ethics and animality, not to mention the question of ethical comportment to things, objects, or environment. Without forgetting the very different tenor of Levinas's and Heidegger's writings, their quite distinct circumstances, and the cultural and political context of their thought, which certainly makes Levinas's apparent lack of engagement with Heidegger's thought beyond *Being and Time* understandable, would not Levinas's thinking be able to lay a claim to its radical (ethical) difference from Heidegger's only at the price of replacing the preeminence of the subject with the *absolute* alterity of the other (human), in fact, of the "more" *human* other, whose height always already exceeds the subject? Would it not further necessitate placing the other as the transcendent ethical "reference point" of all relations and thus marking the other's alterity with what Levinas calls the trace of illeity, that is, with the sense/direction (*le sens*) of transcendence, inescapably pointing to the unique value (mis)named "God," if only by an abuse of language, according to Levinas's own formulation? "This inwardness is an obedience to a unique value without anti-value . . . This value is, by an abuse of language, named. It is named God" (CPP, 136). If there were to be a radical differend between Heidegger's and Levinas's discourses, with their distinct senses of being (Seyn and être) and Saying (Sagen and le Dire), would it not end up being a version of the differend between "Greek," and therefore "pagan," poietic thinking and monotheistic, "Judeo-Christian" theo-logy, where theology would be the saying or naming (logos), by an abuse of language, of the trace of alterity as "God"?

NOTES

1. Emmanuel Levinas, "Enigma and Phenomenon," *Basic Philosophical Writings*, ed. Adrian Peperzak, Simon Critchely, and Robert Bernasconi (Bloomington and Indianapolis: Indiana University Press, 1996), 74. Hereafter BPW.

2. Martin Heidegger, *Contributions to Philosophy (From Enowning)*, trans. Parvis Emad and Kenneth Maly (Bloomington and Indianapolis: Indiana University Press, 1999), 188. Hereafter CP.

3. Emannuel Levinas, *Collected Philosophical Papers*, trans. Alphonso Lingis (The Hague: Martinus Nijhoff, 1987), 130. Hereafter CPP.

4. Martin Heidegger, "Letter on Humanism," *Basic Writings*, ed. David Farrell Krell (New York: HarperCollins), 1993, 233–34. Subsequently abbreviated as BW; "Brief über den Humanismus," *Wegmarken* (Frankfurt am Main: Vittorio Klostermann, 1978), 327.

5. For an excellent and extended discussion of Heidegger's rethinking of *humanitas* in "Letter on Humanism," see Françoise Dastur, *Heidegger et la question anthropologique* (Leuven: Peeters, 2003), 65–82.

6. Emmanuel Levinas, *Totality and Infinity: An Essay on Exteriority*, trans. Alphonso Lingis (Pittsburgh: Duquesne University Press, 1969), 198.

7. Martin Heidegger, *Mindfulness*, trans. Parvis Emad and Thomas Kalary (London and New York: Continuum, 2006), 10. Hereafter M. The German text was published as *Besinnung, Gesamtausgabe*, 66 (Frankfurt am Main: Vittorio Klostermann, 1997). Hereafter B.

8. Martin Heidegger, "The Thing," *Poetry, Language, Thought*, trans. Albert Hofstadter (New York: HaperCollins, 1971), 171–72; translation slightly modified. Hereafter PLT.

9. Martin Heidegger, "The Way to Language," *Basic Writings*, ed. David Farrell Krell (New York: HarperCollins, 1993), 423–24.

10. For an extended discussion of nihilation and its relation to thinking politics, see my essay "The Other Politics: Anthropocentrism, Power, Nihilation," *Letting Be: Fred Dallmayr's Cosmopolitical Vision*, ed. Stephen F. Schneck (Notre Dame: University of Notre Dame Press, 2006).

CHAPTER TWELVE

ELSEWHERE OF HOME

John E. Drabinski

> There can be no question of getting out of this *uniqueness without unity*. It is not to be opposed to the other, not even distinguished from the other. It is the monolanguage *of* the other. The *of* signifies not so much property as provenance: language is for the other, coming from the other, *the* coming of the other.
>
> —Derrida, *Monolingualism of the Other*

What does it mean to begin thinking elsewhere of home? What does it mean to come to language—and so to thinking and being—as an elsewhere that both is and is not one's home? That language places us elsewhere of home, that our home becomes both carved out by and relocated to an elsewhere in the experience of language—this is a peculiar and decisive point at which Heidegger and Levinas come to a common philosophical space. But it is also where a certain break with Heidegger and Levinas might be necessary, a break that, however necessary, is only possible after the *crossing* of both thinkers. In the reflections that follow, I want to explore the problem of monolingualism raised by Édouard Glissant and Jacques Derrida as a crucial intervention in the crossing point between Heidegger and Levinas. That crossing point, in being relocated to an elsewhere from within the here of language, has the pretension of exiting the totalizing and totalitarian sense of the Western tradition. Perhaps Heidegger and Levinas, even just as they meet in this crossing point, are still bound to that tradition in ways only the postcolonial elsewhere can make clear.

For Heidegger and Levinas, the experience of language is neither trans-parent nor even particularly local. Language moves us—or reveals us as having already been moved, depending on the temporality of the particular analysis—to the space between articulation and what prompts, then lies beyond, that articulation. Crossing happens in two senses. Both of these senses guide the critical analysis that follows. To begin, this liminal experi-ence of language, which lies at the heart of both Heidegger's and Levinas's work, gets us to the point where words unravel. *A first, chiasmic sense of crossing.* As well, that liminal point-which-is-not-one exposes how mono-lingualism sets a limit to that liminality and its transcendence. *A second sense of crossing as canceling, negation.* Crossing therefore raises a fundamental question, and it is Heidegger's and Levinas's question already: between Hei-degger and Levinas, and then after, what is the meaning of transcendence?

I want to begin my reflections here with an explicit sense of an ulti-mate destination. And to elevate the stakes. I mean the destination of this chapter, to be sure, but more emphatically a destination of thinking *after Europe*—elevating the stakes away from Eurocentric meditations on language and toward questions of global entanglement. This thinking "after Europe" is absolutely crucial for philosophy's twenty-first-century moment, and I here begin with a simple question: what does it mean to think between Europe and the Americas? "Between" is of course the decisive term here, as it marks the insurgent character of each side of the conjunction. One colonial, the other diasporic—neither persists without passing through the other. This conjunction, like all thought-ful distinctions, is separated and intersected by historical experience. Historical experience between Europe and the Americas largely generates a language of perpetrator and victim. But there is also continuity and fracture: Europe's centuries-long self-reflection is both distinct from and intersected with the experience of conquest, trans-port, enslavement, and exploitation in the Americas. For all the talk about breaks in the intra-European narrative, especially after the experiences of the two world wars, Europe has always been able to tell a story about rup-tures and breaks in its own language, and so always about interruptions of home. Ruins and ashes—those figures that dominate European consideration of catastrophe—describe a collapse of home and a language in which one has made that home. Ruination, of course, presupposes that structure torn asunder by the violence of history.

Alongside this sense of collapse, and because of a historical experience intimately connected to the European sense of itself, the Americas sit in a peculiar relation to home and language. In terms of that destination toward which I will work, my concern here is with the Caribbean in particular—in part because of what is posed *against* monolingualism in the Caribbean, and in part because the Caribbean raises a most intimate series of questions for

European philosophy. The Americas, the very name in fact, are unthinkable without both the European experience of language and the experience of European language. Those are not reversible phrasings. To "experience" language is to always say something about how and where one makes a home. Heidegger was right to say that language is the house of Being—with particular emphasis on the being of the being who speaks and is spoken by language. Levinas surely could not object to this location of language and subjectivity in one and the same home, even as his work tracks the denucleation of subjectivity by ethical Saying. And therein lies the greatest enigma of thinking about home as language, language as home, and how the experience of both places us elsewhere of any locale. The character of that locale and location, and so what it means to be placed elsewhere by language, is both the beginning and end of my reflections.

THE MONOLINGUAL HOUSE OF BEING

My ultimate question, which threads together a reading of Heidegger and Levinas, is quite straightforward. What does it mean to think geographically? That is, what does it mean to locate thinking in a place, which is at once space and time, rather than outside our location? Historical experience *ought* to be our first leading clue. The question of geographic thinking is not mine, but native, as it were, to the question of language and home. No matter the shattering effect of transcendence, we all come from somewhere in our words, the words of the Other, and the dismantling effect enacted in the encounter between those words. The encounter is always already historical. Heidegger's work has long insisted on this very sense of a beginning to thinking, where every beginning begins again in the encounter with what has preceded. That insight seems to me indisputable, and the seriousness of such an insistence has produced the twentieth century's most profound meditations on subjectivity, language, and meaning.

The folds in history and into the present condense the problem of beginning (again). That condensation is the enigma of home and language, a peculiar extension into breaks and ruptures, but also a sense of what persists across the rifts of historical experience. Consider Derrida's introductory words in *Monolingualism of the Other*, which bring Heidegger's identification of language and the home into contact with the *ethical* moment of deconstruction. Derrida writes:

> I am monolingual. My monolingualism dwells, and I call it my dwelling; it feels like one to me, and I remain in it and inhabit it. It inhabits me. The monolingualism in which I draw my very breath is, for me, my element. Not a natural element, not the

transparency of the ether, but an absolute habitat. It is impass-able, *indisputable*: I cannot challenge it except by testifying to its omnipresence in me. It would always have preceded me. It is me. For me, this monolingualism is me.[1]

Language is an *absolute* habitat. With that qualification, Derrida marks out a sense of language as home in which my negotiation of anything called the undecidable comes from a location, a substantiality, an absolute site in which my subjectivity—maybe even *our* subjectivity—is caught sight of and put in question, a transcendence, then, that begins or remains anchored in an immanence *of sorts*. The "mono" of monolingualism marks the persistence of the same, a tradition or a place (viz., Europe), and "lingualism" names the vicissitudes of history—the breaking apart, the sedimentation, and so all of the delimitations of memory, forgetting, and retrieval.

If monolingualism locates the subject in a home, a home of language, and from that home a certain kind of responsibility is possible, then we can surely see in Derrida's short reflection a crossing of Heidegger and Levinas. To wit: if language is the house of Being, and we take up our very subjectivity in that home, then that subject, caught in the vicissitudes of diachrony in language, is vulnerable to the Other who speaks. The Other speaks as the one hosted by the home in all those complex senses of the host we find in Levinas and Derrida. And so my reflections here interrogate this movement of language and home, opening upon a difficult articulation of ethics and the ethical, in order to arrive again where I have just begun: the fragility of the home, of finding oneself in language, and so the possibility of an articulation of an outside the home from beyond. To cross Heidegger and Levinas, to think between home and dispossession, is at once to glimpse responsibility and to see how profoundly indebted our sense of responsibility, even as it departs from all modes of totality and closure, is to a sense of continuity across fracture, the mono- of monolingualism, which nevertheless re- or dislocates to the elsewhere of language.

How to begin with Heidegger?

In *Being and Time*, perhaps the most explicit account of our being-at-home is found in Heidegger's articulation of what at least initially appears to be the contrary of home: the uncanny. Of course the decisive and quirky twist to Heidegger's account of the uncanny is the notion that our home *is* the un-at-home-ed-ness that defines the uncanny as uncanny. The existen-tial analytic, which of course proves to be an important site of contestation and transformation for Levinas, stretches Dasein out across space, time, and history in such a manner that Dasein's location as to be fundamentally rethought or perhaps not thought at all, except as another name for the delocation of location in transcendence. To transcend is to be always ahead of oneself, whether that ahead is the temporality of anticipation or, as with the recasting of transcendence in Heidegger's later work, the excessive character of the language in which we find ourselves and *become* as speakers, thinkers. The linking of anxiety and uncanniness in *Being and Time* links the relation between mood and disclosure with the care-structure of subjectivity. The result is a fully developed sense of worldhood in which the facticity of Dasein becomes visible as finite and historical. To be at home is to be not-at-home, for the world is our home. And so too are language and history.

Setting language in history opens up Heidegger's shift of emphasis—or maybe complete overturning—from fundamental ontology to the history of Being. Language functions again as home in the history of Being, even more prominently so. The companion problematic of history and loss, however, only deepens the sense of un-at-homeness we find in *Being and Time*. Anxiety discloses so much for the early Heidegger, but as his attention turns from the existential analytic as the site of the disclosure of the meaning of Being to the problem of Being's retreat and retrieval, uncanniness is pushed further into the open between-space or threshold. Even as the experience of history and the withdrawal of Being exacerbate the anxiety—maybe even melancholy—of our encounter with language, the question of home remains always prominent as both a mood and a figure of thinking. Indeed, Heidegger will claim in *The Fundamental Concepts of Metaphysics*, lectures delivered near the very moment of the famous *Kehre*, that the problem of home lies at the heart of what it means to do philosophy. To be *in relation* to home as a primordial ground—lost and as a constitutive mood—makes philosophy move from abstraction to disclosure. In the context of a brief discussion of Novalis, Heidegger writes: "Philosophy can only be such an urge if we who philosophize are *not* at home everywhere . . . Not merely here or there, nor even simply in every place, in all places taken together one after the other. Rather, to be at home everywhere means to be at once and all times within the whole."[2] Yet, this whole is not conceived by Heidegger to be totalized or even totalizing—since *Being and Time*, the transcendence of the Heideggerian subject, whatever the variations, is crucial. In the *Fundamental Concepts of Metaphysics* lectures, Heidegger thinks home and the uncanny in terms of what *drives* thinking toward Being as such. This drive is indicated in the mood and experience in which we undergo the experience of thinking Being. Heidegger writes: "This is where we are driven in our homesickness: to being as a whole. Our very being is this restlessness. We have somehow always already departed toward this whole, or better, we are always already on the way to it."[3] This trajectory underpins much of Heidegger's work, even as it takes on an at times tragic register. The experience of language in the middle and later work is often figured as a gathering place or threshold—the Greek temple, borders and boundaries in George's poetry—and yet it is exactly this sense of homesickness that saturates the moment of Being's withdrawal with mournfulness and even melancholy.

The Heideggerian trope of "on the way" is well known and perhaps even well worn. With that turn of phrase, Heidegger is able to name the simultaneity of presencing and withdrawal of Being in language. Language is therefore a site of the interval, both home and the uncanny; what is most intimate is most foreign. "Our relation to language," Heidegger writes in "The Way to Language," "is defined by the mode according to which we belong to propriation, we who are needed and used by it."[4] In the figure of the threshold, the intertwining of monolingualism and home-as-homesickness comes into a bit of relief. If by the monolingual we mean, at least in part, that a thread pulls together even the fragmentation, loss, or devastation of language, then the importance of a nuanced sense of home, almost to the point of being a *pharmakon*, is clear. Language is the house of Being, as the *Letter on Humanism* famously puts it, which here means that our being, subjected to Being and Language, is at home where the boundaries of home cannot obtain. To be is to be at home, subject to and of a transcendence across the intersections of historical experience. The word crosses thresholds, carrying with it all the dismantling effects of historicality. Heidegger's monolingualism is not simple Germanic prejudice or privilege (though it is also that), but the location of the foreign in the familiar, exceeding the meaning of the word with history and possibility, loss and renewal.

The condensation of meaning in the word entwines the question of loss and renewal. Heidegger's exploration of the problem of retrieval shows the purchase of home and language so conceived. Across historical loss and epochal shift, there is the persistence of the word that makes *tradition* possible and therefore also a *conversation* with tradition. The monolingual tracks loss and withdrawal, but the thread of continuity in the word transforms that loss and withdrawal into an abundance, a gift to thinking and of thinking in language. On retrieval and the characteristic of continuity in difference, Heidegger writes: "For us, the criterion for the conversation with historical tradition is the same, insofar as it is a question of entering into the force of earlier thinking. We, however, do not seek that force in what has already been thought: we seek it in something that has not been thought, and from which what has been thought receives its essential space. But only what has already been thought prepares what has not yet been thought, which enters ever anew into its abundance."[5] This passage underscores the continuity of the monolingual in Heidegger's conception of history, language, and thinking as, to borrow the older term from *Fundamental Concepts*, homesickness— the transcendence of what is given in and to the word, coupled to the drive of retrieval of what's been lost to history. Monolingualism makes the word pregnant with the unthinkable as the future of thinking. That is, the word is exceeded by the force of the unthought in what has been thought. Both the unthought and the thought are preserved in the passing of language in history. The passing of language in history bears always presence. Indeed, one could object here (rightly) that Heidegger hardly conceives language on such a model of presence, thinking instead of how the word at once functions in reactivation and fails to bring the originary thought (and so unthought) into presence. Consider this well-known passage from "The Origin of the Work of Art," where Heidegger considers the presencing in the abandoned Greek temple. He writes, "The temple, in its standing there, first gives to things their look and to men their outlook on themselves. This remains open as long as the work is a work, as long as the god has not fled from it."[6]

But of course the god has fled, and we cannot retrieve the presence of the god. The god will not return; epochal change is not reversible, and loss is real, transformative. At the same time, this is configured as a *loss* and not just irreconcilable difference because of the continuity of language and home—what we could just call *tradition*—operative in the relation of the thinker to the temple. No matter the break, fracture, and falling apart, there is the force of monolingualism: a home, even in the elsewhere of thinking.

LEVINAS, HOME, IMMANENCE

Heidegger's account of language and home shows an important intimacy between the two, even as both are figured as fracture, loss, and difference. In an obviously different register, we find very much the same logic in Levinas's work. How are we to think this "between Heidegger and Levinas"? What is the meaning of home and language for Levinas, and how does that meaning bring his thought in contact with his long-standing foil, Heidegger?

We can start with Levinas in two sites. That is, Levinas's work itself begins twice in *Totality and Infinity*, first in the preface, then again in the opening chapter on metaphysics and transcendence. The preface elevates the stakes of the text, famously situating the destiny of philosophy between two possibilities of war and at least a glimpse of peace. War, "fixed in the concept of totality, which dominates Western philosophy,"[7] is opposed only by a morality or moral consciousness that interrupts and makes a demand; the victory of peace over war *in history*, after all, is only accomplished in the coming of "the eschatology of messianic peace."[8] The demand is what haunts totality, disrupting the pretensions of totality to, well, being total. The very little, which is not nothing, for which Levinas can hope is the insurgent movement of the singular. That movement is an interruption of totality initiated by what is most remote, most separate, most small in our world: the other outside or beyond those categories under which war has placed him. The Other therefore carries the promise of peace against war, which, in the end, is really about finding the trace of something counter to the persistence of what is totalizing.

But we can also begin reading Levinas after the preface. The opening chapter of *Totality and Infinity* does not commence with such elevated stakes, but instead outlines the ultimate aim of Levinas's explorations of the (counter-) economy of exteriority. Just at the first page, we do not yet have the fully developed account of how the Other comes to put me in question, how subjectivity is rendered separated to the point of unredeemable debt, so any sense of the One-for-the-Other is still to come. The opening chapter describes instead Desire's metaphysical movement—the movement toward the absolute, the Abrahamic sense of journey. Metaphysical Desire names a subjectivity to come, but the description is important in its own right, if only because Desire puts the matter of home under the rubric of ethical critique. This is only a provisional, even indecisive, moment in Levinas's account of home, as it later becomes clear that we cannot have a sense of the ethical without the substantiality of the home. The deconstructive function of home—something Derrida helps us to see—emerges out of the ruins of this initial characterization of home as dwelling, maintenance of self, and possession of the world. But first there is the violence of making one's home in the world. Levinas writes:

> The *way* of the I against the "other" of the world consists in *sojourning*, in *identifying oneself* by existing here *at home with oneself*. In a world which is from the first other, the I is nonetheless autochthonous. It is the very reversion of this alteration. It finds in the world a site and a home [*maison*]. Dwelling is the very mode of *maintaining oneself*, not as the famous serpent grasping itself by biting onto its tail, but as the body that, on the earth exterior to it, holds *itself* up and *can*. The "at home" is not a container but a site where *I can*, where, dependent on a reality that is other, I am, despite this dependence or thanks to it, free.[9]

There is much here to consider. To begin, Levinas rehearses the destination of the thinking of interruption. Interruption *accomplishes* the critique of dwelling and the making of one's home in the world that has already come to pass. That is, the world is "from the first other," so the making of home can only displace what is first. I maintain myself against that other-from-the-first. The "I can" of subjectivity, which is really just a figure of the home as the possibility of activity, gathered to the interior of the self, is the expression of freedom that forgets its originary dependence. To dwell is to be at home, but at home only with one's own self. Home, it would seem, is intractably bound to the logic of usurpation.

Nevertheless, when Levinas turns to the problem of eros in the closing sections of *Totality and Infinity*, the home comes to be saturated not only with a call of obligation, but also with a practice of the same in *welcoming* the Other. Derrida was surely right to call the problem of welcoming the crossing of the ethical and ethics. Welcoming is the enactment, however fractured and incomplete, of ethical subjectivity. The dominant figures of the widow, the orphan, and the stranger *need* two senses of home: the home from which they are estranged (the mark of their power to provoke obligation) and at which they arrive (my capacity to say yes to obligation, to give of my self and my body). So, the consequent matters of the feminine and the child reopen the home as an ethical space and not just usurpation—or, perhaps, because of usurpation, always the violence that conditions the intrigue of the interhuman. Is the ethical thinkable, possible without a first violence?

We needn't turn to the closing section of the text, however. The problem of the welcome emerges already in the opening chapter of *Totality and Infinity* in the context of our intersection of central concern here: language and the home. Now, while Levinas has already put the home as dwelling in question with the decentering movement of metaphysical Desire, the substantiality of the subject—an important sense of home—recurs at the very moment the Other is approached in discourse. Levinas writes,

> To approach the Other in discourse is to welcome his expression, in which at each instant he overflows the idea a thought would carry away from it. It is therefore to *receive* from the Other beyond the capacity of the I, which means exactly: to have the idea of infinity. But this also means: to be taught. The relation with the Other, or Discourse, is a non-allergic relation, an ethical relation; but inasmuch as it is welcomed this discourse is a teaching. But teaching does not come down to maieutics; it comes from the exterior and brings me more than I contain.[10]

This passage initiates a sustained reflection on hospitality in Derrida's *Adieu*, as Levinas here locates the welcome of the Other as the very labor of the ethical. Teaching transforms subjectivity from the "I can" of self-generated activity to a for-the-Other capable of responsible response, and that response—the paradoxical and elliptical logic of the host—becomes the practice of ethics. What I find most interesting about this passage and the transformation it documents is how it underscores the decisive complication of the opening chapter of *Totality and Infinity*. Desire evacuates the subject of itself and of its self by glimpsing the *already having passed* of the Other's affecting our desiring. At first glance, then, it would seem that *Totality and Infinity* can only render the home an act of violence or betrayal against transcendence and exteriority. Dwelling can only be maintenance of self, dwelling as immanence *against* the transcendence of the Other and, on a certain reading of the economy of Enjoyment, even of things.

And yet Levinas will (rightly) turn immediately to the *necessity* of the home, to my substantiality in some form or another, in order for the event of the ethical to surge into (or against) the living present with interruptive force. To wit: in order for the Other to teach me, I have to be me, facing the Other and ready to find, in that facing, some sort of address to me. Language accomplishes this double need. The word of the Other sends me outside of myself, functioning not as a medium of communication or a transmission of sense, but rather as the passage of a pure singularity across our separated relation, withdrawing at the moment I hear and begin to respond to that word. So language is first transcendence. And at the very same time, it is my capacity to hear, to listen, and to *understand in the sense of being taught*—instruction presupposes at least a minimal comprehension of the word—that makes it possible for my dwelling to be put in question. That is, language must be not only the Other's intractable and irreducible word of obligation, but also an appeal to my having made my own home *in* language such that the address from the Other functions *as* an address. This is not to suggest that Levinas cannot think about heterology and language. I do not want to fully grant Derrida's objections in "Violence and Metaphysics." Rather, I would only like to suggest that language functions as a home for Levinas, just as it does for Heidegger, and that such a sense of home is the condition of my obligation, not my usurpation. The Other accuses in *discourse*. At the very same moment of that discourse, there is the grammar—however strange and anarchic—within which that discourse moves from the Other to the one, and back again in the first, responsible, and responsive word of welcome.

Language as the home—this peculiar Levinasian home-which-is-not-one—is a threshold. For Heidegger, of course, the housing of Being in language does not make me *solely* intimate with Being, but rather estranged and familiar at the same time. Responsibility works in just the same fashion for Levinas. Separation is always paramount. I am neither absorbed into the Other, nor am I in possession of that Other; both would eclipse responsibility in one blow. Separation is also intimacy, which is why the language of denucleation is such an important innovation in *Otherwise than Being*. To be denucleated is to have made one's home and to have had that home rendered the host for another who does not stay, but keeps its distance. Which is to say, I would claim, that the home of language capable of sustaining both address (from the Other) and register of responsibility (to the Other) is shoreline thinking in which subjectivity is formed at that threshold of the wave of accusation and what persists as a ruin after that crashing:

responsibility as what remains; subjectivity as a threshold between the immanence of language and the transcendence of the word(s) of obligation.

THRESHOLDS AND HYBRIDITIES

What emerges from reading the problem of language and home through Heidegger and Levinas is a movement *of* and *in* language. Or, perhaps more precisely, we glimpse a double location.

Language is that in which we make our home, in so far as language sustains and brings *to us* what defines subjectivity as subjectivity. For Heidegger, of course, this is a question of thinking Being in the double presencing of withdrawal and revealing. The effect is the beginning of the task of thinking transcendence at the end of philosophy. For Levinas, the Other who comes to teach me, thereby enacting a creation of the Me (*Moi*), speaks to my home, even while interrupting and even dismantling that space. The effect is both the transcendence of the exterior and the intrigue of the interhuman. In both cases, it is the exceeding of the home we make for ourselves in language that marks another kind of beginning in philosophy. For both Heidegger and Levinas, home and language are located at a sense of the *threshold*. Nothing is given at the door, except the evacuation of what might *pretend*—and so cannot promise—to be interior. A thinking of the threshold, that is, that site of passage from what is most interior (my speaking, what is familiar, my home as dwelling and immanence) to what transcends (what is spoken to me, the alterity that makes me another kind of subject, the relation to the outside that marks the *other border* of the home). Derrida's remark in his introductory essay to Husserl's "Origin of Geometry" becomes surprisingly instructive here: *the absolute is passage.* If thinking is tasked with Being at the end of philosophy, and if ethics is first philosophy before philosophy's gaze, then our experience of this moment of transformation is always an experience of the threshold.

Threshold might be just another word for difference, which is to say, a word that does not gather and lock difference into an identity, transcendence into immanence. And that is why it is hardly controversial to say that Heidegger and Levinas are our two most provocative thinkers of difference and transcendence.

Yet, as I noted by way of a promise in the opening pages, this sense of difference is underwritten by a certain kind of uniformity and familiarity. To be sure, the experience of Europe is riddled with revolutionary overturnings and uprootings of tradition; it is too much to say that the West has been one and the same story. At the very same time, the thread of such a series of revolutions is strong in the sense that it is always a rift in *our* history. History is sustained by language, just as language sustains history, so it surely makes sense to call history our home. We make our lives here, in this place, with this language, drawn together even in difference by a historical movement that is our own.

What if history were to disappear and beginning were no longer a beginning again, but instead and authentically—with all the seriousness of such a disastrous collapse of what makes us able to live and speak—*a beginning with nothing*? An abyssal beginning? This is of course not a hypothetical. Rather, it describes the rupture in home and language constitutive of the experience of the Americas, in particular the Caribbean. I note the particularly emphatic case of the Caribbean because it is in the Antilles that appeals to indigenous roots are eliminated, so the language of beginning is, in a certain sense, *pure*. It is also the site in which Derrida's meditations on monolingualism begin—the polylingualism, born from the abyss, of language and home after the Middle Passage. Having gained significant distance from Negritude and Caribbean surrealism, for Glissant there is no nostalgia, nor is there any promise of reactivation of a long distant, yet still present, past. In his *Caribbean Discourse*, Glissant writes:

> The past, to which we were subjected, which has not yet emerged as history for us, is, however, obsessively present. The duty of the writer is to explore this obsession, to show its relevance in a continuous fashion to the immediate present. This exploration is therefore related neither to a schematic chronology nor to a nostalgic lament. It leads to the identification of a painful notion of time and its full projection forward into the future, without the help of those plateaus in time from which the West has benefited, without the help of that collective density that is the primary value of an ancestral cultural heartland. That is what I call a prophetic vision of the past.[11]

What I find so interesting in and important about this passage from Glissant is the intimacy of this fracture in home and language to the Heideggerian and Levinasian problematics of the same. For both Heidegger and Levinas, there is loss in the experience of transcendence; we cannot gather footing or any hold, for what withdraws from our grasp is the very condition of the possibility of such footing or hold. But that loss is simultaneously a gift; history withdraws, yet produces abundance, and the Other gives subjectivity after denucleation. Being and the Other are given in the exit of and return to home enacted in the address of language. I would venture the claim here that the pleasures of the fracture of home in and through language's capacity to interrupt and bear transcendence presuppose the ancestral cultural heartland. Heidegger and Levinas both turn, differently yet fairly uncritically, to the idea of Europe. Glissant is provocative here and, it seems to me, reveals the presupposition—for better or worse—of any metadiscourse of home and language. Anxiety saturates the Heideggerian and Levinasian subjects *after* and *astride* the threshold, but the passage is absolute. That is, this was my home, and this is the task—of thinking or of the ethical—given over to me by transcendence. It is my and our history that is transformed or put in question by the address of language, so there is a certain kind of comfort in that interruption. Loss becomes anxiety becomes gift. How else are we to think about the gift of interruption?

Glissant's obsessively present not-yet-history overturns this sense of difference and transcendence by withdrawing the very condition of withdrawal. Glissant articulates this sense of a primordial fracture without the fecund profundity of the unthought in the thought, without the space of a broken home that becomes a space of hospitality. Rather, where one might expect a ruin, there is only the abyss. What does it mean to think home and language in this primordial fracture? What does it mean to begin with the abyss?

This is of course too much of a question for my reflections here. But I want to raise it because any problematic of home and language—which, for me, is the problematic of any serious human endeavor—places the human outside of itself, at home and speaking from an elsewhere, whether that be the ek-sistent or hospitable subject. Between Heidegger and Levinas, there is much about philosophy's address to the pain of history and the encounter and about a future without recourse to simple identities. Difference thereby constitutes the very meaning of our thinking and being, but without resolving itself in either the immanence of a *here* (the content of thought) or the transcendence of a *there* (divine knowing). The elsewhere locates us elsewhere of the here and there, a location we experience in the threshold between addressing from and the address of language. Yet, this thinking is (largely uncritically) geographic. I have long objected to the term "Continental" philosophy; Europe is of course not a continent at all, but rather, in being given a name, is always a cultural fantasy. The term is important in this case, however, because the sense of Europe, even as it is broken up and interrupted, functions exactly in the sense of a continent. No matter how uneven or ambiguous, there are borders to the historical experience. And at the same time the Americas are a continent and so call for their own kind of continental thinking—which, in the case of Glissant's Caribbean, is an archipelago.

In his Nobel Prize acceptance lecture, entitled "The Antilles: Fragments of Epic Memory,"[12] Derek Walcott makes archipelagic consciousness a poetic principle, and this suggestion is important as a way of concluding here. Walcott takes up the problem of fragmentation in the Caribbean—the foundations of composite cultural form—without the center or ground of an original. Fragments do not carry the unthought, yet wholly thinkable (in the sense Heidegger sees in the ruin) with them. There is, rather, only the fragment—fragmentation as originary. This original fragmentation is the loss of the conditions for certain kinds of history—which is tantamount to a loss of the rights to the sort of loss Heidegger and Levinas articulate—and that loss displaces the sense of home as a sense of continuity. That very same fragmentation figures the experience of language, as, for the Caribbean, the experience is not the European experience of language, but the experience of the European language. This is an enormously important reversal. The experience of European language after the Middle Passage makes a fragmented home out of the first utterances that draw the speaker into history. Frantz Fanon, to cite only one example, is at his most precise and incisive when he shows in *Black Skin, White Masks* how black consciousness can never be itself in either the French of Paris or the pidgin of Martinique.

Perhaps, then, before there is home and language, there is the geography to which both must answer, a geography in which both take root from the beginning. And geography always has its own peculiar history, which generates very particular senses of threshold. The thresholds that dominate Glissant's poetry, for example, do not send one into the vicissitudes of history, where the word breaks in giving too much to thinking or responsibility. Rather, the threshold is the ruin of the corridor that passed the slave into the abyss: Glissant offers sustained meditations on the Gold Coast, Gorée, a threshold in which the two founding events of language are initiated. The first was the death of Africa. No longer sustained by *that* grammar, there can be nothing other than fantasied memory for nostalgic longing. Second was the birth of the Americas. After there is making one's home in a language that was never one's own, and so cannot but evoke the threshold of catastrophe and abyss, never a gift. It is in that threshold and in those fragments that an anxious-without-repair relation to language as a home, that *other* geography, takes up another problem of knowing and being. What is the difference of that difference? How does difference function in an archipelagic, rather than continental, thinking? Put in larger terms, how does the question of nation and culture—that home of homes—take root in something broken and structured by an irreparable *lack* before it starts? Fanon's astonishing fourth chapter of *The Wretched of the Earth* takes up this very problematic, exposing the political struggle that underlies (and even remains invisible in) the movement of language and home, not for a humanism of inclusion, not for a weakening of hegemony, but for a *creolization* that revises, decisively, even as it appropriates.

The shift in the meaning of language and home is therefore a shift in the meaning of thinking from elsewhere. Heidegger and Levinas stage an important debate (if there is much disagreement) about the meaning and significance of the elsewhere. But the problem of monolingualism and how language and home remain rooted, despite the fractures, rifts, and denucleations, in a sense of old *place* compromises the scope of their claims about thinking elsewhere of home. Yet, those very same places have centuries-old entanglements with the elsewhere of their elsewhere, and the history of European violence has produced a companion discourse, ever subversive of continental thinking, of difference, home, and language. Lack or what I above call (following Glissant) the abyss becomes productive of an elsewhere defined by its distance from problems of fracture and original, threshold and home. Rather than welcoming, there is composition out of irreducible fragments. Let me close, then, with the epigraph from Glissant that begins, and maybe even undoes, Derrida's *Monolingualism of the Other*. In *Caribbean Discourse*, Glissant writes:

> "Lack" does not reside in the misrecognition of a language (the French language), but in the non-mastery (be it in Creole or French) of an appropriated language. The authoritarian and prestigious intervention of the French language only strengthens the processes of lack.
>
> The demand of this appropriated language is therefore mediated by a critical revision of the French language . . .
>
> To the extent that French linguistic hegemony (*le domesticage*) is exercised through a mechanism of "humanism," this revision could partake in what might be called an "anti-humanism."

This antihumanism, this process of lack that begins another history out of the abyss, reminds us that thinking the elsewhere of home and the home of language as already elsewhere is always the story of a place, relocated or dislocated. The task of thinking is perhaps better conceived here as the difference of elsewheres, of homes and histories, and how that difference illuminates the quiet functioning of philosophy as a memory project—abyssal and otherwise.

NOTES

1. Jacques Derrida, *Monolingualism of the Other*, trans. Patrick Mensah (Stanford: Stanford University Press, 1998), 1.
2. Martin Heidegger, *The Fundamental Concepts of Metaphysics*, trans. William McNeil and Nicholas Walker (Bloomington: Indiana University Press, 1995), 5.
3. Ibid., 5–6.
4. Martin Heidegger, "The Way to Language," in *Basic Writings*, trans. David Farrell Krell (New York: Harper Perennial, 2008), 425.

5. Martin Heidegger, "The Principle of Identity," trans. Joan Stambaugh (Chicago: University of Chicago Press, 2002), 48.

6. Martin Heidegger, "The Origin of the Work of Art," trans. Alfred Hofstaedter (New York: Harper and Row, 1976), 168.

7. Emmanuel Levinas, *Totality and Infinity*, trans. Alphonso Lingis (Pittsburgh: Duquesne University Press), 21.

8. Ibid., 22.

9. Ibid., 37.

10. Ibid., 51. See Derrida's exploration of this passage in *Adieu to Emmanuel Levinas*, trans. Michael Naas (Stanford: Stanford University Press, 1998), 18ff.

11. Édouard Glissant, *Caribbean Discourse*, trs. J. Michael Dash (Charlottesville: University of Virginia Press, 1989), 64.

12. Derek Walcott, "The Antilles: Fragments of Epic Memory," in *What the Twilight Says* (New York: Farrar, Straus and Giroux, 1990).

CONTRIBUTORS

Emilia Angelova is Associate Professor of Philosophy at Concordia University, Montreal, Canada. Her research is in nineteenth and twentieth century continental philosophy, and Kant. Recent work has been directed to study of themes raised by Kant and transformed by Heidegger, e.g., selfhood, temporality, freedom and the imagination. She has published mainly on Heidegger and Kant; other articles are on Hegel, Deleuze, and Nancy. She is completing a book on Heidegger's reading of Kant from *Kant and the Problem of Metaphysics*; and is the editor of an anthology *Hegel, Freedom, and History*.

Robert Bernasconi is Edwin Erle Sparks Professor of Philosophy and African American Studies at Penn State University. He is the author of two books on Heidegger: *The Question of Language in Heidegger's History of Being* and *Heidegger in Question*. He is the author of over thirty articles on Levinas and is the co-editor of *Levinas: Basic Writings*, *The Provocation of Levinas*, and *The Cambridge Companion to Levinas*. He also works in the Critical Philosophy of Race and is co-editor of a new journal under that title.

Simon Critchley is Hans Jonas Professor at the New School for Social Research. He also teaches at the European Graduate School. His books include *Very Little...Almost Nothing*, *Infinitely Demanding*, *The Book of Dead Philosophers*, *The Faith of the Faithless*, and, with Tom McCarthy, *The Mattering of Matter: Documents from the Archive of the International Necronautical Society*. A book on *Hamlet* called *Stay, Illusion!*, co-authored with Jamieson Webster, was published in 2013. An experimental new work, *Memory Theatre*, and a book on David Bowie called *Ha Ha Ha Ha*, are forthcoming. He writes for *The Guardian* and is moderator of "The Stone," a philosophy column in *The New York Times*, to which he is a frequent contributor.

Françoise Dastur is Honorary Professor of Philosophy and attached to the Husserl Archives of Paris (ENS Ulm), a research unit affiliated to the French National Center for Research (CNRS). She has been teaching in the University of Paris I, Sorbonne, from 1969 to 1995, in the University of Paris XII, Créteil, from 1995 to 1999 and in the University of Nice-Sophia Antipolis from 1999 to 2003. She is the honorary President of the Ecole

Française of Daseinsanalyse of which she was one of the founders in 1993. She is the author of several books, the most recent of which include *How Are We to Confront Death? An Introduction to Philosophy* and *Hölderlin, Le retournement natal*.

John E. Drabinski is Professor of Black Studies in the Department of Black Studies at Amherst College. In addition to authoring three books, *Sensibility and Singularity* (also published by SUNY Press) and most recently *Levinas and the Postcolonial: Race, Nation, Other* (winner of the 2013 Frantz Fanon Book Prize), he has written over three dozen articles on French philosophy and Africana theory, and has edited book and journal issues on Fanon, Godard, Levinas, Glissant, and the question of political reconciliation. He has just completed a book-length study of Glissant's poetics entitled *Abyssal Beginnings* and is currently drafting a book entitled *Fragments of Home: Baldwin and the Black Atlantic*.

Didier Franck is Professor of Philosophy at University of Nanterre, Paris X, and a member of the Institut Universitaire de France. His teaching and research focus on German philosophy and phenomenology. He has published numerous books and articles on Nietzsche, Husserl, Heidegger, and Levinas, including *Chair et corps, Heidegger et le problème de l'espace, Dramatique des phénomènes*, and most recently *L'un-pour-l'autre: Levinas et la signification*.

Peter E. Gordon is Amabel B. James Professor of History at Harvard University and Faculty Affiliate at the Minda de Gunzburg Center for European Studies. Trained in both philosophy and history, he works chiefly on topics related to phenomenology, existentialism, and critical theory. His books include *Rosenzweig and Heidegger: Between Judaism and German Philosophy*, a recipient of three international awards, and *Continental Divide: Heidegger, Cassirer, Davos*, which received the Barzun Prize from the American Philosophical Society. Co-edited volumes include *The Cambridge Companion to Modern Jewish Philosophy*, *The Modernist Imagination: Essays in Intellectual History and Critical Theory*, *Weimar Thought: A Contested Legacy*, and *The Trace of God: Derrida and Religion*.

Philip J. (Max) Maloney is Associate Professor in the Department of Religion and Philosophy at Christian Brothers University in Memphis, Tennessee. In addition to his work on Levinas, he is currently writing on the New Realist criticism of phenomenology.

Ann V. Murphy is assistant professor of philosophy at The University of New Mexico in Albuquerque. She is the author of *Violence and the*

Philosophical Imaginary (also published by SUNY Press). Her interests are in the philosophy of gender, twentieth-century French philosophy, phenomenology, and political philosophy. Her essays have been published in journals such as *Continental Philosophy Review*, *Hypatia*, *Philosophy Today*, and *philoSOPHIA: a journal of continental feminism*.

Eric S. Nelson is Associate Professor of Philosophy at the University of Massachusetts, Lowell. His research areas include hermeneutics, ethics, and the philosophy of history. He has published over sixty articles and book chapters on German, Jewish, and Chinese philosophy. He is the co-editor with François Raffoul of the *Bloomsbury Companion to Heidegger* and *Rethinking Facticity* (also published by SUNY Press). He has also co-edited with G. D'Anna and H. Johach, *Anthropologie und Geschichte. Studien zu Wilhelm Dilthey aus Anlass seines 100. Todestages* and with A. Kapust and K. Still *Addressing Levinas*. He has edited special topic issues for the journals *SACP Forum*, the *Journal of Chinese Philosophy*, and *Frontiers of Philosophy in China*.

François Raffoul is Professor of Philosophy and French Studies at Louisiana State University. He has authored dozens of articles on key figures in European philosophy, translated numerous books and essays from the French, and has authored and edited eight books, including most recently *The Origins of Responsibility* and (edited with Eric S. Nelson) *The Bloomsbury Companion to Heidegger*.

Krzysztof Ziarek is Professor and Chair of Comparative Literature at the State University of New York at Buffalo. He is the author of *Inflected Language: Toward a Hermeneutics of Nearness* (also published by SUNY Press), *The Historicity of Experience: Modernity, the Avant-Garde, and the Event*, *The Force of Art*, and *Language After Heidegger*. He has published essays on Clark Coolidge, Susan Howe, Myung Mi Kim, Stein, Stevens, Heidegger, Benjamin, Irigaray, and Levinas, and co-edited two collection of essays, *Future Crossings: Literature Between Philosophy and Cultural Studies* and *Adorno and Heidegger: Philosophical Questions*. He is also the author of two books of poetry in Polish, *Zaimejlowane z Polski* and *Sąd dostateczny*.

INDEX